the superman syndrome

Why the Information Age Threatens Your Future and What You Can Do About It

Why the Information Age
Threatens
Your Future
and What You Can Do
About It

by

Robert H. Kamm

Copyright © 1998, 2000 by Robert H. Kamm

ISBN: 1-58721-704-X

PO Box 4860, San Luis Obispo, CA 93404
(805) 544-9726, fax (805) 544-0525

1stBooks – rev. 9/7/00

About the Book

In his unique book, *The Superman Syndrome*, consultant Robert H. Kamm looks beneath the obvious advances of the shimmering new technology-centered economy. He finds increasing evidence of substantial emotional and spiritual pain across America, not just among those who have benefited least, *but also among those who have benefited most.* In a realm of blurred boundaries and vanished time, business people and their spouses are negotiating away central elements of their existence, most notably the sweet enterprise of parenting. Parenting calls us to live at depth, but we cannot live at depth when we live at speed.

Why are we so easily caught up in the flash and rush of The Information Age? Why don't we hold our ground against its momentum? Why do we seem to lack the vision, strength and determination to truly structure our lives around what we espouse as our most deeply cherished values—God, family, friendship, community—rather than around work? American parents are spending dramatically less quality time with their children than was the case thirty years ago. Why have we allowed this? Why have we gone so far off track? What are the dangers? How do we master this new world and put speed in the service of depth?

Drawing on extensive experience in the front lines of business, Robert H. Kamm asks and answers all of these questions in a highly readable exploration of myth, the human psyche and workplace practices. His profound insight and unusual consulting style have already touched thousands of individuals and numerous companies. Bottom lines have thickened. Market share has increased. Customer satisfaction ratings have been catapulted. The long-term prospects of businesses have been girded *while simultaneously honoring and supporting,* as never before, the personal and family needs of the individuals that comprise them.

The superman syndrome is bound to become a household phrase and touchstone for those fighting to bend the new technology to help them become real and present parents without sacrificing the joy of creative work.

For

My grandson, Shannon

Acknowledgments

My beloved wife, Della, deserves the lion's share of acknowledgment for without her insistence, encouragement, patience and unparalleled heart this book would never have moved out of conversation into realization. My parents, Herb and Phyllis Kamm, my son, Ben, and daughter, Chelsea have also been steadfast in supporting me through this emotional expedition which unfolded, of necessity, while I was building a consulting business and working to avoid falling into the *syndrome* that is the subject of this work.

Innumerable friends, colleagues and clients have been my cheerleaders including Dr. Norm Jackson, John Scherer, Kathy Davis, Menka MacLeod, Mark Yeoell, Dr. Barry Bernfeld, Dr. Michael Brown, John Nance, Ned Tookman, Steve Nickelsen, Dr. John Mlinarcik, Bob Bartholomew, Rich Bokan, Bill Dodds, Don McKenzie, Jeff Buchholz, Steve Bruns, Pamela Murray, Phil McGowan, Ralph Ebersole, Michael Holdener, Tom Fisher, Mark Rikess, James A. Autry, Carol St. John, Phil Smart, Jr. and Phil Smart, Sr., Bea Swanson, John Shepard, Dave Schuelke, Brian Pugh, Mike Hamm, John Bovee, Michael Croxon, David Britton, Sheilagh Croxon, Steve Smythe, Rick Rogers, Bill Lawton, Mike Kelley, Greg Greenwood, Randy Kimble, Kathy Foltner, Ed Eskridge, Art King, the entire Bannister Family of Vernon, British Columbia, Miles Brandon, Rick Flores, Bill and Mary Krouse, Tracy and George Jones, Jim and Maelene Brunelli, Bill and Janelle Brunelli, Steve Dicochea, Ken Becker, Bill Theuringer, Jim Smith, Joe Whalen...all the wonderful folks at their respective organizations who have been willing to risk with me in order to push the envelope in democratizing and balancing the workplace through profound self-exploration.

A particularly full, round chord of gratitude must be sounded for all the graduates of our *LeaderOne Workshop*—each of whom has demonstrated great courage in the service of feeling and in so doing, taught me more than I knew there was to learn.

Special thanks to Kathi Brown and Anna Arnone at the National Automobile Dealers Associaton for giving me the opportunity to hone my message over the last several years by speaking at numerous national conventions.

Much appreciation is due Don and Diane Valley, Mike Carija, Randy Aispuro, Jim McConaghy, Rusty Jones, Greg Hargis, Krissy Bunte, Janet Olson, Tom Devany and all the folks who worked with me at Valley Mazda during our time of greatest innovation in the early Nineties. I'm forever grateful for the joyous workplace community we engendered and continue to be instructed by its magic.

Finally I wish to state unequivocally that I have absolutely no affiliation with either DC Comics, Inc. or Warner Bros., Inc. Superman as a comic book character and all related characters and indicia are trademarks of DC Comics, Inc. The four Superman films/videos referred to in this work are the property of Warner Bros., Inc. This is a non-fiction book of interpretation, analysis and comment. The phrase, *the superman syndrome*, refers to a phenomenon long-present in human life, for which the DC Comics character of Superman is one of the latest and most familiar cultural markers.

Table of Contents

"Myth is frustrating to the literal mind and inhospitable to the inhibited. Much of it stimulates and disturbs. All of it shades back into hearsay. There's no strictly 'accurate' version of any legend. So one should enter the myth dimension as one embarks upon a love affair. Daringly, that is, in the midst of uncertainty, and yet with a kind of reverence—prepared to face whatever may unfold."

--Alexander Eliot, *The Global Myths*

Introduction

America came roaring out of the recession of the early 1990's with unprecedented force. As I write this early in the spring of 2000, the country enjoys the most vital economy and lowest unemployment rate in thirty years. We have a federal budget surplus—something no one believed we'd achieve this quickly. A new economy has emerged, borne on the shimmering wings of information and communication technology. Yet, there's a great deal of emotional and spiritual pain across our land, not just among those who have benefited least, *but also among those who have benefited most.*

In a recent workshop at a national business convention, I asked the successful entrepreneurs and managers in my audience to raise their hands if they felt their lives were generally moving faster than they had been just three years ago. Upwards of ninety-five per cent did so. Next, I asked for a show of hands if they commonly had a hard time shifting mental gears after work "to really be present, really listen, really be connected" to spouses, significant others or children. Again, upwards of ninety-five percent indicated the affirmative.

The technology revolution, the rise of the global economy and exponential consumer demand have combined to create a world of blurred boundaries and vanished time, a world no one has ever experienced before. But for all its flash and rush, many of us are discovering it requires we negotiate away central elements of our existence, most notably the sweet enterprise of parenting. Parenting calls us to live at depth, but we cannot live at depth when we live at speed.

In the aftermath of numerous school shootings, particularly the one at Columbine High in Littleton, Colorado, we've heard some passionate rhetoric about responsibility. Rarely addressed with clarity or insistence is the core truth that superb parenting is not possible when businesses place unlimited demands on their workers and when workers are unconsciously complicit in their own subjugation to those demands by dint of their fear of job loss—amplified by the last recession—and their unbridled hunger for the latest material trappings of the American Dream. Yes, individual parents hold responsibility for the speed of their lives, but not exclusively so. Each of us functions within a system of powerfully interdependent relationships. Businesses are not exclusively responsible either, but they do comprise a significant part of the larger cultural system. Though many business leaders have been reluctant to acknowledge it, they have a broad impact on the current and future states of society. Given the pace of change, the expanding population of the planet, the degradation of the physical environment and the impact of all these on our children, it's now more critical than ever that we discuss our personal and business lives in the same breath.

Even as we blast forward on a shock wave of powerful assumptions concerning what the future *will* be, we need to understand with a new and broader vision how we arrived at our current state, what our future state *should* be and how we can create it. In the Information Age, every day, every single one of us is a pioneer in a new land, so great is the pace of change. We are facing the critical challenge of learning to balance speed and depth as no people before us in the history of man on earth. This is to say that accountability to self, family and society are not optional for *anyone*, certainly not business leaders.

It's one thing to make this statement and quite another to find a way to help good people free themselves from a system whose tendrils are entwined both within and between them. The work of Dr. W. Edwards Deming has been an extremely valuable guide in helping me find a way. Like many of his students, I wasn't particularly enamored of his technical teachings. Working in a service industry surely has something to do with my bias. Of course, measurements matter and I do use them.

But it's my conviction that the powerful insights and philosophy expressed through The Fourteen Points, Seven Deadly Diseases and Obstacles embody much of what can legitimately be called The Wisdom of the Ages. They hold all the guidance necessary to transform any organization—business or otherwise—if we're only willing to dig deeply enough.

Though Deming gave Psychology its due importance, making it one of the four pillars of his Theory of Profound Knowledge, it was not his forte. Consequently, as I moved forward working to implement those Points that had the strongest psychological implications, I found myself asking a lot of questions Deming did not answer in detail. Point Eight, "Drive out fear" was the most riveting for me. In my experience, business environments are commonly designed by the hands of fear, sometimes subtly and sometimes quite visibly. In fact, there has long been a willingness in business cultures to ignore a host of psychologically abusive behaviors in the pursuit of financial performance. It struck me that anyone committed to driving out fear would have to develop highly dynamic experiences for its principle perpetrators in order to awaken them to its damage and lead them to manage from a significantly different internal stance. By the same token, those who have a vested interest in being victimized by fear would have to be helped to find their way to greater self-assertiveness and responsibility. This would be a major undertaking for which there was no handbook.

Point Twelve, "Remove the barriers to pride of workmanship," caused me to journey further down the same line of thought. If fear and mistrust constitute the principle barriers to pride of workmanship, is conventional empowerment sufficient to bring them down? Can structural changes really reach to the depths where these dispositions lurk? What are the limits of conventional business practices? What new approaches are called for? All at once, I found myself setting aside the usual consulting agenda to devote my energies to these questions. I soon came to understand each business, and sometimes each department, as having its own special mythology, its own struggle with Destiny involving villains, heroes, bit players and chorus chants of woe and celebration. I saw individuals with their frail magic moving on and off stage in search of treasure, power, recognition, satisfaction and, above all, a depth of meaning that would unite their emotional life with their life of obligation and action. A new reverence emerged, a richer respect for each business as a complex living organism. It became obvious to me that exceptional expressive and interpersonal skills were necessary to stimulate sustainable humanistic transformation. Without them, how would it be possible to help people peer over the walls of their current paradigms to fully imagine the marvelous tribe they might become? This spirit of inquiry compelled me to assemble a more diverse tool kit than the traditional one provided through my management and consulting training. I knew I was going to have to bring broader learning and more of myself as a total human being to the undertaking. I was drawn into studying areas that are normally considered off-limits or irrelevant to business consultants—anthropology, physiology, neurology, psychology and the broad realm of counseling, child development, sociology, religion, mythology, literary and film criticism and the art of autobiographical story-telling. Gradually, I was able to develop potent personal and group change processes, processes that yielded implications and insights far beyond the normal scope of business consulting. These were learning experiences that were effectively reaching individuals below the cognitive mind where most traditional education occurs, down where the soil and root hairs of character share their subtle chemistry. It's trite but true—change is very difficult. The limited impact of many of the efforts applied to helping organizations grow is a direct result of too much reliance on dry language and depersonalized concepts. These approaches don't engage enough of the total humanity of each member of the work community because they don't engage enough of the total humanity of the change agent.

In my search for methods to create an appropriate ambiance for serious personal inquiry, I began sharing ancient myths. The technique of creating safety through story-telling has probably been around for thousands of years, but it's not one I was professionally taught. Like a lot of folks, I relish good metaphors and tales. It seemed natural to introduce them in a variety of situations to lend context, support and insight. When we share a myth of deep resonance, we can speak through its characters and metaphors to express our own feelings. Gradually, we venture out from behind the shield of the story and become increasingly relaxed and honest. It's from this rejuvenated honesty and deeper knowledge of each other's true needs that we identify the causes of fear and diminished pride in the workplace.

The more this approach succeeded, the more consciously I crafted discovery opportunities around a few specific narratives. Wanting to be sure the material was broadly accessible, I turned to the world of contemporary movies. Film is our culture's most potent form of myth creation and dissemination and is more likely to fully captivate people than any of the ancient Greek or Roman stories we heard as school kids. The figure of Superman, in particular, inspired extraordinary recognition and enthusiasm, no doubt in large part due to his long life in comic books, cartoons and TV as well as live action film. The tragedies that befell the two most notable actors to portray him, George Reeves and Christopher Reeve, only made him more real and poignant. But in addition to familiarity and poignancy, he just seemed to embody the perfect symbolism for our time—a combination of speed, power and isolation. The well-known details of his character and exploits quickly became a catalyst for hard-edged managers across the spectrum of business to surprise themselves with the breadth and depth of their own revelations. They talked avidly and even wept over how their efforts to be supermen and superwomen made them emotionally absent from themselves, their spouses and, most painfully, their children.

As much of a stretch as it might seem at first glance, working together with this very American yet universal yarn we've come to understand a great deal about the psychological and historical causes of our current social dilemma of speed over depth. We've found highly instructive meanings beneath the surface details of the myth. They've helped us to begin developing a real, practical and, yes, difficult exit strategy. This strategy provides a map for unifying the inner journey each of us must ultimately make alone and the outer journey all of us must ultimately make together. Such guidance has long been absent in a world that has generally bought into the illusion of separateness between our personal and professional lives. The challenges before us call for final rejection of such either/or thinking. They demand a comprehensive understanding of the nature of being human, at home and at work. My commitment to that perspective mandated a book that would necessarily be different from most business books. It would have to bring together diverse streams of thought and language many of which rarely if ever find their way into business discussions. Like my consulting practice, it would have to honor the total humanity of the reader. This is what I've sought to do. I have my clients themselves to thank for encouraging me to take the risk. Their lives and those of their organizations have already been touched as much by examining themselves through the Superman myth as by the strategic insights that naturally surfaced downstream as a result of this very personal inquiry. Bottom lines have thickened. Market share has increased. Customer satisfaction ratings have been catapulted. The long-term prospects of businesses have been girded as never before and the capacity for authentic intimacy in the workplace and at home has been expanded.

It's my hope that you, too, my reader will gain solace, support, insight and guidance in walking and working the daunting terrain of our time.

Robert H. Kamm, San Luis Obispo, California, Spring, 2000

Part One:

The Way In

"Myths are public dreams. Dreams are private myths."

--Joseph Campbell

Chapter One

Syndrome

"The economic interpretation of history is for the birds."

--Joseph Campbell

The concept of a superman is certainly not exclusive to our era. In fact, we could probably argue that the desire to transcend the powers of mere flesh and blood had its origins in the first hominid ancestor to observe his buddy falling prey to some horrific beast or circumstance.

Closer to home, many if not most of us were captivated as school kids by tales of ancient Greek gods and heroes who looked like us but possessed superhuman powers. A quick survey reveals this was hardly the exclusive preoccupation of the Greeks. Buddha sat under his Bo Tree and turned legions of attacking warriors into a shower of lotus blossoms. Much later, Mohammed ascended straight into the sky on his horse. Consider also the wondrous exploits of Arthur and Lancelot and the wizardry of Merlin in England, the extra-human courage of Beowulf as he vanquished the demons Grendel and Grendel's mother in Denmark. Then there's the illuminating adventures of Odin in Northern Europe and the odd but compelling belief embraced by his devoted warriors, the berserkers, that paradise—Valhalla—was a place where they could fight all day, feast every night and awaken each dawn fully healed from their wounds so they could fight on day after day, eternal warriors.

Among the many possibilities in North America, we need only look at the Haida who could transform themselves from man to beast and back again at whim. In South America, think

3

of the legendary abilities attributed to the Inca, Pachacutec, whose name meant "earthshaker." After commanding the very stones to rise up to turn the battle against the Chancas, he went on to build the enormous Inca Empire.

Fast-forwarding in time, we find that the German philosopher Friedrich Wilhelm Nietzsche and the great Irish dramatist George Bernard Shaw both publicly took up the topic of superness each in his own way, Nietzsche in the second half of the Nineteenth Century and Shaw early in the Twentieth.

Clearly, as we approach an examination of the most recent and, for us in this day, the most culturally potent incarnation of a superbeing, we should keep in mind that he has quite a pedigree in a very old, broadly-held, much-storied yearning to escape the bounds of human frailty.

Syndrome is a word appropriately derived from the Greek, *syn*, meaning "with" and *dramein*, meaning "to run". Thus, "a running with." As we use it here, always respectfully keeping its lineage in mind, we are referring immediately to the American Superman myth born in 1938 out of the minds of two teen-age boys, Jerry Siegel and Joe Shuster, and popularized over more than six decades through comic books and films—the fellow most of us think of with a capital S when we hear the word superman—Kal-El alias Clark Kent alias Superman.

For our purposes, *syndrome* specifically indicates a widespread parallel between the commonly known surface details of this contemporary myth and current socially admired behavior—*a running with* the appearance of the myth. We can go further and say that *the superman syndrome* represents the glorification and imitation of these surface details. Here are a few quick examples: Superman moves fast. Our culture glorifies and imitates such speed, more now than ever. Superman has extraordinary endurance. We admire stamina and call top performers in a variety of fields "superstars," "supermoms," "superheroes" and, sometimes explicitly, "supermen" and "superwomen." Superman feels no pain. We glorify "toughing

4

it out," "stiff upper lip," "never let 'em see ya sweat," "big boys don't cry," "don't cry over spilt milk," "swim with the sharks," "mind over matter," "it's all in your head," "suck it up," "gut it out," "no pain, no gain," and so on. All of these carry the same basic message that silently enduring pain is a mark of maturity. Originally, this referred to male maturity, but now we see it increasingly applied to women who wish to "compete" in the male world. We also see it pervasively presented to our children as the model of adult power.

In sum, *the superman syndrome* is an active glorification of speed and invulnerability with an accompanying denigration of depth and tenderness of spirit.

Our serious literature and popular media, both print and electronic, herald an endless procession of features on star athletes, political, social and military leaders who are said to achieve superhuman feats. These provide us with ample opportunities to examine *the superman syndrome* in detail. However, nowhere is it more prevalent than in the business world. The Cold War is over but our worship of the warrior plays on in the boardroom. From Bill Gates to Steve Case, from Andrew Grove to Steve Jobs, from Wayne Huizenga to Al Dunlap, CEO's, high performance managers and entrepreneurs have actively donned the cape in order to satiate our hunger for soaring heroes and compelling drama.

Of course, work-obsessed businessmen are not new to us. What *is* new is the degree to which their values are impacting the rest of our culture. Never has there been such adulation for the image of an individual who ostensibly can rise early after only five hours of sleep, get in an hour work-out, tear through the morning news, conduct the 8 AM meeting with perfect focus and control, then skip, dance and hop through the obstacle course and mine field of the day's e-mails, voice mails, live phone calls, decisions and deadlines. On he flies through power lunches and dinners—with a little help from caffeine, megavitamins, ginseng, "smart" drugs and stress hormones—ultimately arriving home to

5

put in an intense fifteen minutes or half hour of "quality time" with the kids before they go to bed. Then, ostensibly, he listens dutifully to all the spouse's tales of woe and joy, makes meaningful love, catches another five hours of ZZZ's, gets up and starts all over again.

The unrepentant, unconflicted high-flying priests of *the superman syndrome* embody a unique synthesis of intense personality traits—above all, a single-minded willingness to sacrifice all else in pursuit of "success." We might all be a lot happier if their attitude were simply, "Hey, I love working fourteen hours a day but the rest of you, whadya say you put in six? How's that sound?" Fatuous, of course. Three hundred business leaders responded negatively to a 1989 letter urging a shorter workweek. Not a single one, not one out of three hundred embraced the idea![1] Consequently, the fact that these *pure* supermen represent a relatively small percentage of the total adult population is a moot point. They wield enormous power and influence. The rest of us feel helplessly swept up by a kind of Momentum Function. We'd like to strangle and mangle The Energizer Bunny—a superman in a warm, fuzzy pink costume—because we know we can't keep going and going and going. Yet, the other side of the story is that we do. Willing or not, a huge proportion of Americans are giving themselves over to the credo that spending long hours at work, moving fast, taking on extra duty, thinking about work, talking about work, and stoically acting as if there's no cost or pain to it, working hard at our investments, hard at parenting, hard at playing, hard at dieting, hard at getting in shape, even working hard at relaxing—all these confer a badge of honor, a confirmation of worthiness, a validation stamp on our driver's license in a world that worships drive.

Under the sway of *the syndrome*, our work week has grown longer than it was forty years ago. We've added approximately an entire additional month a year![2] It's also grown far more intense. Yet no studies of average work time account for The

6

Distraction Factor—the hours we spend physically present but mentally and emotionally absent to our families. We the consumers are being consumed by our jobs, yet no one measures this phenomenon. If men have long tended to allow their obsession with work to interfere with their personal development and family relationships, that tendency has been multiplied by the shift from an industrial to a high-tech information-saturated market place. Stephen S. Roach, an economist for Morgan Stanley: "Laptops, cellular phones, wireless modems and fax machines...help to extend the working day; in effect, they have created a portable assembly line for the 1990s that 'allows' white-collar workers to remain on-line in planes, trains, cars, and at home. So much for the liberating technologies of the Information Age."[3]

From observations on the streets of large and small towns across the nation, it's fair to broaden Roach's comments to apply not only to white-collar workers but nearly every category of worker, including elementary, junior high, high school and college students. The cell phone has become pervasive in the last three years alone, greatly increasing the frequency of short-burst interruptions in our days. Voice mail and email for both professional and personal use has brought a quantum leap in the raw volume of communications we must process. Computers have substantially changed the nature of work, cramming an overload of additional "to do's" into the same or fewer minutes, multiplying the sheer volume of attention shifts, the intensity of focus on small details, the frequency of small motor tasks and the raw quantity of small magnitude decision-making[4] in workers' minds in the course of a day. The ability to walk upright is one of our vaunted advantages over the great apes, yet we prefer to sit. The supreme irony here is that if we take the normal stooped, four-footed posture of a chimpanzee or gorilla and rotate it up ninety degrees, we have a near perfect replica of the posture of a man or woman seated at a computer, hands on the keyboard. So much for evolutionary gain!

Stanley Roach is right. By and large, it's not an expansion of freedom we're experiencing. It's the illusion of freedom. Call it "freeness." It carries the possibility of freedom, yes, but the probability of enslavement, even addiction. Beyond a certain threshold, freedom has very little to do with material things. It has very little to do with how many people we need to call, who need to call us. Yet, anyone not wishing to be part of this hyperactive-interactive world is in danger of being labeled an outcast, slow, irrelevant or depressed. It takes a great deal of inner strength to put effective boundaries around the use of the new power toys and tools and there is *no* evidence we're doing a better job of raising such strong individuals, individuals who can really just say, "No," to *anything* that might satisfy the quest for instant gratification. Consider the influence the TV remote control has on young children. Its illusion of power is positively entrancing. It is arguably the single most alluring technological enabler of the impulsiveness in early childhood. With the flick of a thumb, a one year-old child can blow through walls in seconds, just like the Man of Steel.

The very structure and velocity of our humanness are being transformed.

Stuffy Dreams

For twenty years, American incomes were flat while the costs of houses, cars, quality health care, college education—the major Dream Commodities—clearly were not. Real income has just recently started moving up again after that long drought. Americans never stopped wanting stuff, though. Wanting stuff is one of our most enduring quirks. We're determined to get it whether we can pay for it now or not. Larger percentages of women have come into the formal workplace (as opposed to the considerable work they do at home) than at any time in the history of industrial or post-industrial society, with the possible exception of the World War II years. The generally increased independence of women notwithstanding, their influx into the workforce is substantially a result of the *necessity to invest more hours per household* in income-generating activity in order to get the stuff Americans crave—not only the Dream Commodities, but all the high-tech communication and entertainment products whose price per unit may consistently trend downward but whose total share of the family budget has risen steadily.

The apostles of growth tell us this craving is good. It keeps the economy spinning, creates millions of jobs, boosts productivity. Jobs, yes. Productivity, questionable. No less than Lester Thurow, one of the most highly regarded economists in the country, has noted that we do not seem to know how to measure productivity accurately. He states, "Partly we don't make the efforts necessary to get better statistics because there is a possibility that we will find a lot of negative productivity growth in the service sector and end up with even lower productivity growth rates."[5] Isn't it interesting to hear an economist questioning the quality of our economic data on psychological grounds? At the very least, we are limited by an adherence to old methods that arose out of manufacturing. Only about twelve percent of our workforce is currently involved in manufacturing. How do we measure services? What is truly productive and what is "negative productivity" or what we could call "antivalue"? Does it make sense to call *any* unit of work produced by any human being, regardless of its ethical, moral or operational quality, productive? Isn't that merely a perpetuation of the absurd idea that business is amoral and therefore not accountable to society? If a large software company, valuing sales over customer happiness, rushes a product out before it's really ready and, consequently, has dozens, even hundreds of people working in "tech-support" because the software frequently burps or crashes, how should we account for the work of those tech-support people? If we count it as productive, aren't we just supporting business practice that is wasteful and abusive to the public? Aren't we just deluding ourselves pouring these work units into our national economic self-esteem? This is band aid activity compensating for the lack of quality in the product. What of the thousands of stress-filled hours of down-time experienced by every day computer users? What of the distraction and the thousands and thousands of outbursts of anger resulting from such stress? What of the accidents and mistakes it generates? Antivalues compounded. Is that factored into our productivity figures? If computer users must spend millions of dollars on various forms of so-called virus killers, are those dollars and services productive or are they antivalues? If millions of dollars are spent on technology and effective utilization of it falls far short of potential, should we factor that loss into our figures? A 1996 survey of 360 companies by Standish Group International Inc. of Dennis, Massachusetts found that "42% of corporate information-technology projects were abandoned before completion" primarily because so often "cutting-edge computer systems fail to live up to expectations—or fail altogether." U.S. companies spend $250 billion annually on computer technology.[6] Obviously, many of those billions are being tossed down a rat hole. No less than Bill Gates himself in his book *Business @ the Speed of Thought* states that many businesses are only using about twenty percent of the capacity of their technology.

If, as a result of the "success" of the Information Age, more commuters are spending more time stuck in traffic jams—700,000 hours a year by one estimate—while their cars waste more gas and pump out more pollutants, shouldn't that be factored into how we measure productivity?[7]

If we need more security systems and guards at businesses and schools, more expensive X-ray machinery at airports, more high-tech police surveillance equipment and weapons—all because of a failure to build more quality into our people from their earliest moments of life, common sense demands we ask whether or not the dollars invested in these things are productive or antivalues? If we need more child care and elder care workers because so many Americans are too busy to be either attentive parents or children, if we spend huge sums on the damage done by smokers and drinkers to themselves and each other, should we consider all the jobs created by these behaviors productive? Antivalues definitely create jobs. Imagine the work involved in fixing the Y2K problem! An April 1997 study by Capers Jones estimated the USA would have spent nearly 75 billion dollars by the time it was fixed. Then the Commerce Department, in a sleight of hand worthy of the best con artists on the planet, trumpeted in November of 1999 that the number actually came in at only 100 billion, "less than half what most experts had predicted."[8] We don't know which experts they consulted, but certainly not Capers Jones, whose estimate they over-shot by 33%! (Capers Jones' estimate for worldwide spending was about 1.3 Trillion. We can only hope they didn't under-predict that one by 33%!)

Another uncomfortable question.   If the increasing domination of technology in our culture is contributing to a widening gap between rich and poor—which it is—shouldn't we factor in an offset to productivity gains with the increased costs and losses springing from the impoverishment of millions?[9]

Finally, consider that The Bureau of Labor Statistics on which we rely for accurate numbers uses hours reported by employers for salaried employees and commonly accepts hours scheduled rather than actual hours worked. It does *not* survey employees to check the accuracy of these reports. There are also millions of individuals in a host of different fields—law, administrating, programming, medical research and general management and supervisory positions who are expected to put in many hours of over-time, hours that are neither measured, nor compensated. There are tens of thousands of executives and consultants who travel frequently, subjugating the entire twenty-four hours of any given day to the job. It could be argued that if you can't look into the eyes of your spouse and children in the evening and sleep in your own bed, if you can't get up and have breakfast with family, your day is completely defined by work and should be considered as such—all twenty-four hours.

There is a massive theft occurring—millions of uncompensated work hours conveniently ignored in order to perpetuate our illusion of productivity and progress. When we find a reasonably accurate way to account for this extra effort, as well as the antivalues rife throughout the system, our vaunted numbers will look far more humble than the zealots of the new economy would like.

Inquiry

Why are we so willing to lie to ourselves about the quality and yield of our culture? Why are we so willing to devote ourselves to the high risk of becoming a nation in which we are connected to everyone and intimate with no one? Why have we come to submit ourselves so willingly to the pervasive and invasive antivalues of *the superman syndrome*?

Certainly, the transformation from industrial to information-based enterprise is one causal factor. It seems self-evident that, all other things being equal, knowledge-workers are less likely to have literal peace of mind than those who vigorously engage their bodies in daily work. When the body stops working, it can rest. The mind, like a Timex watch, takes a licking and keeps on ticking. The more stimulated our brains, the more difficult it is to shut them off. The proliferation of in-home technology has only exacerbated the situation. We are thinking and talking more than at any time in the history of mankind and this undoubtedly would not be happening without the essential shift in the nature of our economy.

But we must question more insistently what it is that drives such a shift and sustains it even in the face of substantial evidence that millions of us are stretched nearly to the breaking point and our society is rapidly becoming unrecognizable as the nation we dreamed for ourselves. Can we largely attribute it to the uniquely chaotic unfolding of American entrepreneurial energy? Doubtful. In the end, the irreducible unit of change in any society is the individual. Economics and standard business theory as methods of inquiry are both out of their depth when it comes to grasping what moves human beings. They leave important questions unanswered, such as, "Why don't we hold our ground against the momentum of the Information Age for what we know is sweetest and dearest? Why do we seem to lack the clarity, strength and determination to genuinely structure our lives around what we say are our most deeply cherished values— God, family, friendship, community—rather than around work? Why have we gone so far off track?"

More comprehensive, more psychologically dynamic insights are called for than those managed through the usual economic and business questions, insights that illuminate root cause, meaning and probable consequences, insights that will galvanize our courage to undertake what may well emerge as the most difficult and critical transformation in the history of our species. In pursuit of such understanding, the process of elimination directs us back down into mythic caverns, where human souls whisper, chant and sing their truths. If we undertake such a venture with the daring and reverence urged by Alexander Eliot, we may illuminate dilemmas that seem unique to our time but are actually just new versions of the age-old struggle to transcend mere survival to enjoy the fullness of our humanity. In contemporary terms, it is the quest to create balance between action and relationship, speed and depth, success and soul. It's my view that the Superman myth offers us rich opportunities to better comprehend our times and find timeless guidance for navigating them.

Chapter Two

Myth

"...all myths...are psychic metaphors revelatory of universal axioms..."

--Robert Walter

Far more than a mere comic strip character or pop icon, Superman is our special blend of the Greek gods Mercury, Apollo, Hercules, Prometheus and Icarus. He's our Fountain of Youth, our Phoenix of hope rising above the flaming malevolence of modern life. He's endured all these decades and will continue to because his qualities and story have found a home deep in the American psyche. This is to say he has achieved authentic mythic proportions.

Myths are powerful stories told and retold across generations, great golden yarns vibrating with a mysterious, irresistible music as they wind themselves from soul to soul on the loom of the spoken word. Their potency derives from a twine of universal meanings whose individual strands are so tightly bound each to the other, they readily by-pass our normal critical faculties. In fact, their meanings often transcend the conscious intention of their authors, who may contribute across a broad span of years without ever knowing each other, enriching the weave while intuitively remaining true to the original theme.

In contemporary terms, we might say that long before we created compression technology, myths were the original "zipped" files. Their density of meaning and its accompanying knack for sliding around the analytic mind restrain us from dismissing apparently outlandish fabrications, such as the thought of a man flying around in tights saving the world.

What do we intend by "universal meanings"? All myths arise in specific times and places. Consequently, to one degree or another, they comment on their era and may even appear to be defined by a visible, limited landscape. However, beneath that crust, there are magnificent caverns which, in the great myths, are unbounded by history or geography. Their walls resound with an endless chanting inquiry about our origins and essence as individuals, children, parents, members of a community, a country and a race, about Mother Nature and Father Time, about romantic and platonic love, friendship, betrayal and hatred, about God, good and evil, forgiveness and revenge, about heart and mind, wisdom and deception, about how we should live as opposed to how we can or do live, about what charges the fuel cells of our souls, about dreams, work, destiny, birth and death.

No, myths do not lack for meaning. Rather, they can be cluttered with messages, some of which seem baldly contradictory or, at the very least, open to diverse interpretations. This only makes an expedition into the myth dimension all the richer in possibilities. The physical earth having been largely explored and charted by satellites, if not by men on foot, the one terrain whose shifting features still elude us is the submerged continent of the human soul.

Joseph Campbell, arguably the Twentieth Century's most ardent student and teacher of myth, lamented the absence of such central guiding stories in current American culture. He warned that our world had become "demythologized," leading to the loss of social cohesion. He was correct that, as a people, we have become increasingly fragmented and no longer ritualistically embrace a few authentically unifying myths. On the other hand, there is an argument to be made that great myths *are* present in our culture but rapidly become indistinguishable from each other in the face of the withering, incessant gattling of the Information Age which almost instantaneously mows everything down to the same size. Well…almost everything. Superman still hovers in the air above us after sixty years, enduring as a kind of national emblem.

He could not have come into being without the original DC Comics, the Fifties TV series, the animated cartoons, and especially the Warner Brothers full-length feature films (given Hollywood's ability to reach millions with such high impact)— Superman, the Movie in 1978, Superman II in 1980, Superman III in 1983 and Superman IV in 1987.[10] *However, his mythic existence is no longer dependent on these "establishing materials."* It has a life of its own in the pantheon of American imagination. (The reader will undoubtedly find it especially useful and entertaining to view the first two films at some point during the reading of this book, since I'll refer to them frequently. All four are still available for rental in video stores.) As I've indicated above, millions of people who have never read or seen any of the establishing pieces, no less been aficionados or devotees, have, nonetheless, absorbed critical aspects of the Superman story. The idea of a figure with extraordinary powers and a noble mission draws on themes thousands of years old and continues to fascinate young and old alike—the reasonable proof of which has been the success of the Nineties TV series, the popular heart-stomping ride at Magic Mountain amusement park that bears his name, the recently released postage stamp, a new Masterpiece Edition of the original comic now available in bookstores nationwide and glowing reports of how his new creators are reinventing him in the March, 2000 issue of *Wizard: The Comics Magazine*. Today, though not number one, Superman comic books still sell consistently in spite of the proliferation of an extraordinary array of other superhero comics...for which he paved the way.

Chapter Three

The Work of Human Nature

"...posterity does not concern itself with his trauma but only with his achievement."

--Alice Miller, *The Untouched Key*

Before we can make sense of the Superman myth, or any other myth as I've defined it, we have to agree that there definitely is such a thing as human nature. Without it, we could not credibly discuss the idea of universal meanings. We also have to agree that part of that nature resides in what has been called "the collective unconscious." This is a potent force operating under cover, influencing our behavior and our internal experience. It's capable of stimulating dreams as well as waking stories inhabited by characters and images with similar resonance in people across time and cultures.

When we look at it, this is actually a pretty clean idea. It proposes that, just as there is a law of gravity, there is a primary Law of Human Nature. The essence of this law can be expressed in three parts.

First, *humans have a grand capacity for physical and emotional sensitivity.* We have this capacity from birth and quite possibly prior to birth.[11] The evolutionary function of this sensitivity is to direct us to the satisfaction of our needs and inform us when we're wandering from that intention or in danger of its violation. All humans share the same fundamental needs for safety, nurturance and love. These needs are so tightly connected to each other, it's often difficult to discuss one

19

without discussing all. Their meanings may be obvious but, for the sake of clarity, let's take a moment with each.

By *safety* we mean sheltering from any forces that can violate us, causing a significant disturbance of our homeostasis. This includes all of Nature's minor and major tantrums from floods, droughts, tornadoes and blizzards to earthquakes and volcanic eruptions, from famines, pestilence and plagues to snake bites. It also includes man-made assaults—every possible physical, psychological and verbal abuse as well as the deprivations of poverty, bigotry and war. The fact is we're fairly delicate creatures. Beyond a certain threshold, we can't tolerate too much stimulation without going into a state of distress or even shock. We need to live in an environment that is respectful of our senses and their limitations.

By *nurturance* we mean the provision of an environment that supports physical, emotional and mental growth at a natural pace. This definitely includes but is not limited to the giving of adequate amounts of good quality food when hunger actually arises, not according to someone's idea of when we ought to be hungry. It also encompasses the offering of an explorable world, opportunities to discover, learn, try, do, assimilate in a manner that makes sense for the specific developmental stage of the individual. This means any and every form of the chance to do "good work." When my son, Ben, began crawling, we removed all dangers from his reach—poisons, plugs, sharp edges, breakable objects. We wanted the environment to say yes, rather than no. This was a safety issue. But then, we made sure there were plenty of interesting things around to engage his curiosity—not only toys, but also pots, pans and plastic food containers. He had free reign to pull all of these out of their low storage areas and learn about them. When it was time to put them away, we made that part of the fun. This was nurturance.

By *love* we mean, above all, a heart connection so strong with another that we can see their needs and their gifts as they are emerging and that we are consistently moved to help satisfy them. This begins from the moment of inception in the womb. It includes a pregnant woman's caring for her fetus by caring for herself, as well as the father's contribution to that whole process. Later, it means a great deal of touching, holding, gazing into the eyes. Later still, it means the gradual giving of freedoms and responsibilities the child can handle with a sense of accomplishment, rather than overwhelming her with too much...or holding her back with too little. Overlapping with nurturance, love means establishing clear boundaries based on our vision of what will best support the unfolding selfhood of another. At any age or stage, whether in a parent-child or adult love relationship, love involves a powerful sense of appropriate proximity, knowing when to stand in and when to stand back, when to hold and when to release, when to protect and when to accept risk.

Safety. Nurturance. Love.

The specific manifestations of these needs change as our lives unfold, but their essences do not. Not only do all humans share them, but we also share some powerful experiences, no matter what historical time or place we inhabit. We are all born. We will all die. Most of us will live long enough to gain an understanding of the fact that we will die—an insight unique to our species as far as we can tell. The overwhelming majority of us will also live long enough to mature physically and face responsibility. Few of us will get through to old age without experiencing moments of joy and contentment, but also physical pain and profound fear, anger, grief, shame, hopelessness, helplessness and the hurt of being violated in some way. The fact that fear, anger, sadness, disgust, happiness and surprise trigger the same facial expressions across cultures, genders and ages is just one more indicator of the universality of the range of possible human experience.

There are times when we might ask, "What's the point of having so many feelings? Why can't we just have joy, happiness, contentment?" Well, it's a package deal. Our emotional virtuosity makes us unique among all creatures and is at least part of the very substance of a survival strategy Nature/God has been playing with for millions of years. It makes us capable of loving our children, parents, siblings, friends, town, basketball team, and country, art, literature, science, engineering, architecture and so on, all in the interest of creating bonds and sculpting the world to protect and sustain us. It makes sexual love potentially a great servant of the species, its joy and intimacy tightly holding two people to each other and to the shared devotion of rearing their young. It mobilizes fear and anger so we can fight or flee threats.

But here's the second part of the primary Law of Human Nature: *there is a limit to our ability to consciously process at any given moment the full range of sensations and feelings of which we're capable.* Is this an imperfection in our adaptive repertoire? Well, it has both advantages and disadvantages, as we shall see soon enough. Not all evolutionary adaptations are perfect. They are works in progress. That's why species continue to adapt. That's also why they become extinct. (If you're looking for perfection in adaptation, don't look to humans. Look to the coelacanth…a fish that's been around for eighty million years.) Nature/God has had its own Continuous Improvement program under way long before Dr. W. Edwards Deming defined his Fourteen Points. So the truth is that *sometimes our capacity to feel is greater than our capacity to consciously process those feelings.* An experience can overwhelm us—too much grief, for example. If you've ever lost a loved one, you know you couldn't possibly have felt the full depth of sadness in one fell swoop. It takes months, even years. The same goes for a broad array of other possible experiences. If you're lucky enough to be on this planet for a while, the chances are, you're going to endure an episode that is too intense to readily process.

So, what do we do with these intense feelings when, for whatever reason, we can't fully assimilate them as they arise?

This brings us to the third part of our Law of Human Nature: *we tuck away unprocessed feelings and much of their attendant sensory information, images and potential adaptive insights.* Where? The back pocket of the mind—the unconscious.[12] In fact, these unprocessed experiences constitute the actual content of the unconscious.

This might seem totally absurd as a component of the primary Law of Human Nature if it weren't for the fact that we all have our own undeniable experiences with something other than consciousness.[13] We don't need Freud or Jung to make the case that our brains tuck away feelings for future consumption, like chipmunks stashing nuts. We all dream. What's more, sometimes, in a conscious state, we retrieve long-forgotten memories with all their attendant emotions. Where were they all this time?

To sum up: every human is capable of feeling sad, frightened, enraged, surprised, disgusted and happy. Yes, there are many subtle variations possible but these are the core emotional themes. It seems wholly logical that, to the degree that we become so deeply stirred by an experience that we are incapable of processing it into consciousness, it goes "underground" to await resolution. This energetic repository can drive all sorts of magnificently interesting behavioral patterns but it can also limit our potential for personal freedom. Freedom is dependent on consciousness and these behaviors are stimulated by forces of which we are *un*aware. It's impossible for us to grasp the degree to which we're motivated from these buried command centers, precisely because they are out of sight and out of our conscious minds. The good news is that the same subterranean system sends out signals—among them myths, dreams, stories, art, curious behavior—whose very purpose is to keep alive the opportunity we might one day become fully aware and finish the unfinished business within us and restore the sensitivity that serves our survival best in the long run. A pretty clever design, when you think about it.

While we may be capable of a nearly endless variety of fine surface details in these manifestations of the unconscious, their essence is bounded by the common treasure trove of universal human experience and feelings. After all, we are a species, which means we essentially share the same physiology. Consequently, while a familiarity with the historical and cultural matrix of a myth might facilitate and expand our appreciation, we mustn't allow ourselves to be constrained by it. Understanding contemporary contexts won't *necessarily* help us penetrate to the inner workings. In this sense, familiarity can breed contempt. We are so close to Superman, it would be easy to dismiss him as nothing more than a cartoon fantasy. Well, let's see.

Chapter Four

The Meanings of Superman

"There are more things in heaven and earth...than are dreamt of in your philosophy."

--Shakespeare's *Hamlet*

"...traces left by our childhood...manifest themselves in the very fabric of human society..."

--Alice Miller, *Paths of Life*

For the sake of our inquiry, it's important to remember we're examining the Superman myth as widely known on the broad scale, above the myriad twists and turns the story has taken in sixty years of DC Comics or in the Lois and Clark TV series.

When we discuss specific story material, we'll be referring *to Superman, the Movie*, from 1978 and its first sequel, *Superman II* from 1980, unless otherwise noted. There's good reason for this approach. First, these films were viewed by tens of millions of people of all ages in our country, as well as around the world—many of whom either never read a Superman comic book or hadn't read one in years. The breadth of the impact of these films is confirmed by the fact that they are still among current inventory at Blockbuster Video, our largest single purveyor of video rentals. In fact, the complete series of four is still actively being rented at this writing more than a dozen years after the release of IV. Second, film is the most powerful vehicle of our time for delivering mythic material into the public consciousness. The very size of the images on the screen puts us in the highly receptive state of mind characteristic of childhood. Third, the first two films represent a synthesis of the Superman biography, persona and adventures true to the spirit of the first few decades of his life in DC Comics. Raving fans certainly have the right to quibble but I doubt they will as they read more. In any case, that's the basis on which we're going to proceed.

Origins

The civilization of planet Krypton is dominated by elaborate crystal architecture—not a Silicon Valley, but an entire silicon world.[14] For all its obvious ingenuity, it feels about as sterile as a hospital delivery room, an apparent metaphor for the ice-cold brilliance of the fact-and-figure minds that populate its culture.

Though the darkest moment in the history of Krypton approaches, the Council of Five (appropriately reminiscent of the Council of Five of Ancient Greek Sparta) is busy with another matter in the Hall of Wisdom. The leaders of Krypton, despite their apparent genius,[15] have been unable to create a society free of villainous individuals. The treacherous General Zod has barely been thwarted in his attempt to establish a new world order. He and his evil lieutenants are prosecuted by the highly respected citizen scientist, Jor-El. They are convicted and compressed into a kind of giant mirror or sheet of glass and cast out into space, prisoners of what is referred to as "The Phantom Zone."

We soon learn of another shortcoming of Krypton's elders. Jor-El has determined the planet is about to suffer a catastrophic series of earthquakes resulting in its complete destruction. He urges the Council to evacuate the entire population to another location in space. The Five, in a display of intellectual arrogance surpassing even that of the builders of the Titanic, reject his conclusions and forbid him to leave the planet himself or publish his opinion for fear of spreading panic.

So, here we are only passing the threshold of our tale and we encounter some interesting messages concerning the deficiencies in the Kryptonian version of a techno-utopian Information Age. We might call its people raging materialists in the sense that they are quite brilliant at mastering the visible, empirical world but not at perceiving and responding to trouble that is out of immediate sight, at the core of the planet, or at the core of their society or, even more to the point, "at the heart of the matter," as the often used phrase goes. They have the scientific knowledge to save their population by moving it to another planet, but not the vision. They also clearly cannot stop engendering evil-doers such as General Zod. Later, we'll also learn (in *Superman II*) they don't build very effective prisons, since Zod and his henchmen eventually escape from The Phantom Zone. What's more, having put their stock in intellect, the Kryptonians are unable to acknowledge its limitations. Their superiority complex blinds them to impending disaster and the possibility of saving their population of brainy billions.[16] They seem exceptional in nearly all sciences save the science of the human soul. Sounds a lot like our world today.

Fortunately, Jor-El has been savvy enough to avoid making any promises to the Five concerning his only child, Kal-El. The boy is a mere babe in his mother Lara's arms, but his parents will save him by sending him in a small rocket across the vastness of space to planet Earth. As they prepare him for the journey, Lara expresses her concerns to Jor-El. Their son is going to a planet whose inhabitants are "thousands of years" behind Krypton. He will stand out dangerously by dint of his ability to defy gravity. He'll be an oddity, isolated and alone. Jor-El assures her that Kal-El will have the advantage of looking like humans but possessing powers far beyond theirs. Ironically, and somewhat poignantly, Jor-El is not referring to his son's intellectual superiority—a quality that at the moment seems to be the very cause of his people's impending demise. No, Kal-El will not manifest on Earth as a great scientist or political leader. He will be "virtually invulnerable" on the physical level. What's more, he will not be alone, at least not in his father's mind. Turning to his baby boy, Jor-El sighs and tells him, "...we will never leave you, even in the face of our deaths. The richness of our lives shall be yours...you will carry me inside you all the days of your life. You will make my strength your own, see my life through your eyes as your life will be seen through mine. The son becomes the father and the father the son."[17]

If we had any lingering reserve of doubt, the dialogue between Jor-El and Lara fully affirms we are, indeed, being told a *human* story, though surface details may continue to indicate the contrary. Among other things, we see that long before a book was written about it, men were from Mars and women from Venus...even if they both happened to be living on Krypton. Like so many millions of mothers, Lara speaks from the heart, fearing her son will be a freak, an oddity who will never know the joy of belonging. Jor-El, like so many millions of fathers, places his faith in material powers—physical strength and prowess. He also speaks from the head, showing far too much willingness to believe that the holographic version of himself he has built into the space ship's communication crystals will be an adequate replacement for his son's need for a real father. We can forgive him his own hubris and high-tech romantic delusion, given the gravity of the situation. But we shouldn't fail to notice that a lot of Information Age fathers in our country today who do not face such dire circumstances seem all too willing to substitute TV monitors and other ingenious gizmos for their actual presence. But, then, the Sony Play Station has three hundred games. What father can play *three hundred* games?

Back to the story.

Baby Kal-El's rocket emerges from the exploding homeland. What is the meaning of this explosion? Is it a giant metaphor for the trauma of birth? Quite possibly. If this seems a stretch, remember the hospital-like sterility of the physical environment. Consider also the enormous imperious faces of the Council of Five gazing down at us in the opening scene from great high-slung screens. They are evocative of god-doctors hovering over us, stimulating the feeling of being small and at the mercy of great forces—perhaps *the* seminal sensation of nearly every newborn child in our society.

If the idea of the birth trauma is a bit much for you, you'd be harder pressed to avoid the general conclusion that we're examining a myth about those individuals whose early life experience is in some way characterized by cataclysm. Kal-El endures not only the loss of his obviously devoted parents. His culture and entire planet are utterly annihilated. This level of trauma is clearly sufficient in itself to engender a personality given to toughing it out by suppressing the capacity to feel. By the same token, a person emerging from such origins might well have aspirations to immortality and invulnerability. Why be human if it means experiencing so much loss at such a tender age?

Since no one on our planet has literally experienced the deprivation presented in the myth—the exploding planet part, specifically—what is the meaning here? The magnitude of the portrayal is designed to put the issue of our early vulnerability in our faces. It commands us, "Don't turn away. Don't deny. Look long and hard." This forceful insistence is necessary for most of us. Our earliest wounds are exactly those we're most likely to deny out of hand, and quite understandably. When we are still in a kind of pre-operational system—pre-conceptual, pre-verbal, even pre-mobile—we have no way to "make sense" of what's happening to us because we have no "senses" in the adult meaning of the word—no ideas or explanations or contexting for what's occurring. The very big rub is that in this pristine state, we *do* have extraordinary physical and feeling senses. There is no distinction between the two. As infants, anything that negatively impacts our physical needs will simultaneously produce an experience of fear, frustration, helplessness, isolation or a variation on these "pre-emotional" themes. Our inherent fragility functions as a highly responsive early warning system to our caregivers whenever our needs for safety, nurturance and love are not being met. Why "highly responsive?" Remember, Nature/God has tried to err on the side of making sure we get what we need. A pretty clever design, given our total dependence during this time. With one exception. There is a very real possibility that our caregivers, for whatever reason, will not act in a timely manner. An infant has few options. Its extraordinary vulnerability greatly raises the odds of its being easily overwhelmed by unanswered need to the point where consciousness, such as it exists in these first weeks and months of life, fragments and tucks away the agony in that back pocket of the brain, the unconscious. And so begins the accumulation of the nightmare within us, for along with many potential delights, life offers us an astounding catalogue of possible raw deals during the tender years from conception to seven. Here's a quick take on the most obvious, any one of which could happen today and readily qualify as the kind of experience symbolically referred to by the story of Kal-El's explosive escape from Krypton.

Life's Raw Deals: The Early Years

1. An inhospitable womb. That is to say, a mother who is undernourished, or not very physically fit, who smokes, drinks, does coke, crack, caffeine, is abused or neglected or under-supported or is just plain immature…in other words, a person experiencing some form of violation of her own need for safety, nurturance and love.

2. A difficult birth—too long, too hard, too rough,

too swift, too soon, too loud, too bright, too hot, too cold, weeks in an incubator with tubes in the nose.

3. Inattentive parents.
4. Ill-equipped parents.
5. Two stressed-out parents.
6. *One* stressed-out parent.
7. *No* stressed-out parents.
8. Over-anxious, uncertain, permissive parent(s).
9. Overly controlling parent(s)—the subtle, incessant Chinese water torture directing us into this or that endeavor at the expense of our hearts.
10. Downright abusive parent(s) who mishandle, hit, yell or molest.
11. Great parents going through a terribly rough time.
12. The full range of deprivations due to poverty.
13. The horrors of political, religious or ethnic upheaval, terror and war.
14. The suffering wrought by natural disasters — everything from earthquakes to hurricanes, from famines to floods.
15. Trauma due to a serious accident or disease.
16. Add whatever I've left out, your version of Shakespeare's "thousand natural shocks that flesh is heir to."

It's in the catastrophic origins of Kal-El's life that we discover why kryptonite will be the one substance to haunt his adult years. Kryptonite is a radioactive chunk of the home planet hurled through space to eventually enter Earth's atmosphere as a meteorite. It is the dark *totem of early destruction*, an unwelcome reminder of the holocaust of his origins—Freud's return of the repressed. It is the embodiment of a memory of staggering emotional force. No wonder it renders him helpless.

Unfortunately, baby Kal-El's travail does not end with the launch of his space ship. We must remember he is completely alone in this capsule for the next few years, crossing the universe towards his new home. Again, a stark symbol of seemingly endless solitude. Of course, he has a nifty entertainment center complete with a holographic representation of his father—a highly advanced Gameboy. But babies need to be touched, cuddled, bussed on the belly, nursed at the breast, tossed in the air, carried on the hips and shoulders. They need to gaze into the live adoring eyes of their parents, crawl and toddle their way to ever-wider explorations under their loving protection. Safety, nurturance, love. What they certainly do *not* need is a major data dump, but that's exactly what Kal-El gets. As he travels towards Earth, Holographic Dad tells him, "Embedded in the crystals before you is the total accumulation of all literature and scientific fact of dozens of other worlds spanning the twenty-eight known galaxies."

Oh, what fun, daddy! More data! More data! Please, more data!

It shouldn't surprise us that Jor-El has loaded the capsule's communication module with such a plethora of facts. Being a scientist, information is his book and trade. What is the meaning of this? Is it a presaging of the full intensity to come as the Information Age rises into dominance? Is that what Kryptonian life symbolizes? Seems credible enough. The American faith in inventive and scientific skills has been with us since the inception of the nation. Thomas Jefferson's ingenuity across a spectrum of activities is an excellent example of this. We are also being served up a metaphor for one of our most popular strategies of denial and detachment. We popularly call this "escaping into your head." It entails an intense engagement of the ideational areas of the brain for the purpose of avoiding difficult feelings—in this case, the overwhelming emotional and physical deprivation of isolation.

Jor-El's intergalactic schooling of his son invites us to view the Superman myth from an even higher altitude. It not only urges us to look at our early personal history, but the darkest episodes of mankind's history. It suggests that, as a race, we are carrying around the curse of age-old cataclysms. These have brought us to the point of longing to be something stronger, smarter and tougher than our humanity can provide.

Let's take a closer look. As baby Kal-El trundles through space, the holographic Jor-El makes a very disturbing comment to him: "The early history of our universe was a bloody mosaic of interplanetary war." This is not exactly an age-appropriate lesson, Dad! But then, the whole scenario of the father educating the infant in this particular way may simply be suggesting that babies are much brighter than we've tended to think...which they are, of course. If you're one of those parents who believes your kid should be the next Einstein or Michelangelo, maybe you'll find validation here for showing him flash cards as he slips out of the womb.

The thought of this kind of dark information being given to an innocent child offends logic. It doesn't seem to make enough sense to be in the story. It would be easy to dismiss it, consoling ourselves with the thought that, after all, myths are probably rarely perfect. Like the people who create them, they can exhibit inner contradictions, obfuscations or just plain old loose threads that can dangle us in a cold wind trying to figure out the unfigurable. But a closer look reveals something thoroughly cogent. Jor-El's statement establishes the fact of cataclysms *behind* the immediate cataclysm in the history of the universe and it does so in a riveting manner. The juxtaposition of the innocence of this child and the brutality of the information he's given *is meant to disturb.* It demands we stand still, stop fidgeting, resist the urge to dash into clever intellectual rationales. It compels us to gaze through the clarity of a child's pure vision at the saddest and scariest truth about our country and our race. With minimal modification, the statement becomes, "The early history of our country and our race comprise a bloody mosaic of wars." In fact, "bloody mosaic" is a fitting description for our own century. A short list of the violence would have to include World War I, Prohibition, The Great Depression, World War II and the Holocaust, The Korean War, the Bay of Pigs and Cuban Missile Crisis, the shocking brutality of whites towards blacks, the murder of civil rights workers, the bombing of black churches, the assassination of our president, his brother and Martin Luther King, summers of ghetto rampage, the Viet Nam War, the rape of whatever political innocence or faith we had left by Nixon and his boys, the Iran-hostage debacle, the Gulf TV War, Jonestown, the Branch Davidian and the Heaven's Gate mass suicides, the bombing of doctors' offices, the World Trade Center and the Federal Building in Oklahoma City as well as other acts of terrorism, the campus murder of students by fellow pre-teens and teenagers, workers "going postal" and murdering bosses and colleagues, the ultimate trivialization of our justice and political systems by the O.J. Simpson trial and the Clinton/Lewinsky debacle, economic recessions about every decade that turn lives upside down regardless of tenure and credentials, and, last but not least, our relative inaction in the face of "ethnic cleansing."

We may be crossing a bridge to the Twenty-First Century but we're dragging along our own bloody mosaic as we go.

Cataclysm beyond cataclysm. Shock upon shock. As eager as we may be to indulge in recitations of the great accomplishments of our nation and race, the myth is telling us with measured firmness to look straight at our unending penchant for self-inflicted horror. Jor-El's remark directs us towards a long line of important evidence concerning why so many of us are so highly enamored of the dream of invulnerability and so easily seduced by a culture of speed. More on this later.

If some of us cannot easily identify with the disastrous level of events symbolized by the exploding Krypton and the thought of multiple catastrophes, perhaps it's easier to find reflections of ourselves in the images of baby Kal-El's astonishing solitude and the ensuing head-trip into the safety of ideas. Alienation and its grief can track us down many paths and jettison us off into mental ozone. In fact, maybe that's exactly what the Information Age really is—a mass-scale retreat from the gnawing feeling of aloneness to an illusory sanctuary behind the barricades of thought .

A final few insights before we move on to the next phase of Kal-El's life. Many today have a distaste for anything that strikes them as "Freudian". They don't see the use in digging into original causes. They just want to fix themselves, spouses, kids, parents, the company or the country right now in the present. They want an action plan or a "to do" list. Let's just "cut to the chase" or get to "the bottom line." A fair portion of the psychological and psychiatric communities have gone along with this orientation, focusing on symptoms and dismissing the value of delving into what drives them. This is classic *superman syndrome* behavior—the rush to take action, fix everything, save everybody and get it done now without having to invest the time to gain a real understanding of the systemic causes of our situation. Remember that all this zipping hither and yon has left some huge deficiencies in our world, just as the superbrilliance of the Kryptonians produced an enormous, blinding arrogance.

To seek to understand myth is to undertake a kind of archaeology of the soul. This undertaking deserves better than to be one-dimensionalized by a dismissive label such as "Freudian" or "blaming." We must whisk our finest brushes over ever deeper layers of clues, lean closely and ask the difficult questions that can ultimately yield a credible, cohesive narrative of our psychological and social origins. Such an endeavor is not only necessary to gain a comprehensive understanding of our situation. It's noble.

So, before you object to building a case for situating the causes of many of our current ills in individual childhood, as well as the childhood of the human race, please remember we're uncovering meanings in a myth which, like so much of global literature, is quite clearly drawing our attention to early events. Further, consider that during a long infancy and childhood compared to most of the animal kingdom, the young human is exceptionally dependent on its caretakers. This dependency places those caretakers at the center of its universe. They are experienced as the prime source of safety, nurturance and love...or their absence. There is no "contextual forgiveness" possible at this early age, no understanding that neglectful or abusive parents might only be doing what was done to them when they were little. There is only the direct, unmitigated experience of neglect or abuse. Our caretakers are our main reference points for both pleasure and pain. This leads us to consider the following logical questions. Is it acceptable to openly express gratitude to our parents and forbears for the positive endowments which they've bestowed upon us? If yes, then why is the converse *in*valid? Why can't we also feel that many of the hurts we carry and the limitations with which we struggle have their origins in the same people, places and time-frames and must be understood and addressed as such? Remember our discussion of the fundamentals of human nature. *This is not a matter of blame but of dependence, causality and meaning.*

Nowhere does this become clearer and yet more richly complicated than when we go back to examine numbers thirteen and fourteen of Life's Raw Deals, keeping in mind that America is a nation of immigrants. Baby Kal-El's first few years seem far less fantastical when we consider that he, too, is an immigrant. Think about it. How many of our citizens, since the beginning of our country, would fall under the following description?

1. Barely escaped upheaval in the homeland.
2. Left behind loved ones who perished.

3. Made a long, difficult, lonely journey to a new world.

Literally, millions. Wave after wave. The foundation of American society was formed, poured, fretted over and finished by folks who fit this description. Yes, we could say that the Superman myth is an immigrant's travail and, as such, supremely American. No wonder it has such durability.

The influx continues today, albeit to a lesser degree, but people still scamper up our shores away from poverty, famine, disease, natural disasters, repressive regimes, indentured slavery, "ethnic cleansing" and so on. Once here, millions have made additional journeys within our borders to escape a host of hardships. In fact, we could legitimately say that everyone of us is an immigrant from the Industrial Age to the Information Age, so tumultuous are the changes we've experienced in the last few years alone. The immigrant journey, for all its joy, is fraught with anguish. That anguish is an important ingredient of American marrow.

Imagine a frightened young Irishman, African, Italian, Hispanic, Swede, Russian, Pole or Asian who made his sojourn out of catastrophe and arrived, a stranger in a strange land, able to think about almost nothing but survival. What if he learned to shift for himself in the frontier towns, worked like a horse, mastered every skill he possibly could, put it all on the line to open a little business or search for gold or raise livestock? What is the benefit to our understanding if our principle perspective is to blame him for beating his kids, or slapping his wife around, believing it was "necessary" to teach them the right way to live? He believed himself a success. He survived everything. He thought he knew what it took and was trying to impart that to his loved ones. What is the benefit to us today of blaming his male descendants for spending most of their waking hours at work inundated with the tasks of the Information Age, being mediocre at marriage and parenting, eating too much, drinking too much, coveting their pill-chocked medicine cabinets and really believing that time is money?

No, this myth is not about blame. It wouldn't be so interesting if it were, since blame is just another unconscious distraction, a stubborn attempt to get rid of hurt and pin it on someone else's donkey. What's more, blame flies in the face of Dr. Deming's central message, which is that if we want to improve anything, we have to understand the whole ensemble of forces that yields a specific result. Before we can even begin to intelligently discuss the issue of personal responsibility, for example, we have to identify the high-leverage dynamics that establish a matrix in which the individual's capacity for responsibility is either developed or stunted. If this seems like dangerous terrain, it is, but it's where we must go if we're after the truth of what makes Kal-El and an awful lot of the rest of us so determined to leap tall buildings and outrun trains. Again, it's about early dependence, causality and meaning. You want to blame somebody or something? Blame it on the myth because the message is there—insistently directing our attention to cataclysms beyond the cataclysms, to terrible moments of isolation and despair in our personal lives, in the lives of our parents, grandparents and their grandparents, in the life of our country and in the life of the human race.

The Early Years

Our traveling baby tumbles into Earth's atmosphere arriving in the American heartland where he's discovered and adopted by an elderly farming couple, the Kents.

The myth provides a rural setting for Kal-El, then the young Clark Kent, to grow to manhood. Why not just drop him in Metropolis? Why the rural setting?

Of course, the young creators of the tale, Siegel and Shuster, spent their own youths in the 1930's in Ohio's open fields. And, yes, the alien babe's ship might have struck concrete and turned him into a manhole cover had it landed in the city. And, yes, pragmatically speaking, he is probably far more likely to be received by kind people here than in Metropolis, where, given the diversity and number of malefactors, he might have ended up in a dumpster or sold off by a black market adoption scam. While all of these ideas are valid, they're also too simple.

The story is extolling the virtues of life on the land as a recovery site. Rebirth from the loins of Mother Nature. In contrast to the big faces, huge population, and great cities of Krypton, baby Kal-El now finds himself in *Small*ville, a place where safety, nurturance and love seem to spring from the very soil. A good place for a new beginning. A place to be small, to have some semblance of childhood.

This theme—the benefits of reconnecting with natural forces—recurs across eras and civilizations as far back as we can go. The very image of Buddha sitting under his tree affirms this, as do the biblical descriptions of the Land of Milk and Honey where the suffering of the Hebrews will finally be assuaged, the imagery of the birth of Jesus in a stable surrounded by domestic animals, his childhood in the country town of Nazareth learning the honest trade of carpentry, his formative years in the desert searching for spiritual purity. We see it in the very act of baptism—the curing waters of the earth.

The universal longing for the easier rhythms and more authentic relationships of country life is very much a part of the American psyche. Attachment to the land is taken as an essential good, a blessing to immigrants who owned little or no land in the old country or had it torn from their grip. Many of our poet citizens have celebrated the land for its spiritual value—Walt Whitman, Robert Frost, Theodore Roethke and, more recently, Robert Pinsky, to name a few. The "back to nature" movement championed by Scott and Helen Nearing in the Sixties is another example. The current popularity of "natural" healing methods or "alternative" medicine is another. To be an American is to know and love our land, its fruits, its critters, its folks and their ways and to draw strength residing in the bosom of spacious skies and amber waves of grain, whether for an afternoon or a lifetime.

It's altogether fitting, then, that our bustling meteor-boy will have wide open plains to explore, the big sky above, fresh air, clean water, friendly beasts and good, honest work to allay his wrenching origins.

As Clark grows and discovers the full range of his powers, the mild country manners of his parents temper him. There is wisdom in the myth's meaning. It counsels modesty as a check against the kind of megalomania that led to the destruction of the entire Kryptonian population. No matter how great you long to become or actually do become, you must keep your feet on the ground (at least occasionally!) and remember the unpretentious customs of your family and friends. These are the values Clark carries into the creation of his "cover" persona as a reporter at the Daily Planet.

There is one more endowment the youth receives before departing Smallville: a sense of destiny. In the 1948 DC Comic episode, *The Origin of Superman*, his mother has already died while he's in his teens and old father Eben Kent tells the young man straight out from his own death bed that his destiny is to be "a powerful force for good." He continues emphatically, "There are evil men in this world...criminals and outlaws who prey on decent folk! You must fight them...in cooperation with the law! To fight those criminals best, you must hide your true identity! They must never know Clark Kent is a...Super-Man. That's what you are...a Superman." This strikes us as a directive from a father who knows best to a son who will do as he's told. The meaning for us? Duty comes with power and talent. You can't just go self-indulgently flying all over the place, outrunning trains and leaping over buildings. In a world as bad as this one, showing off and just having fun don't count for much. You've got to serve a higher calling. So, the party's over, boy. You're out of recovery. There's a war going on out there. Get to work.

In *Superman, the Movie*, we experience a fascinatingly different scenario. Father Kent dies before his wife. Clark is propelled towards his destiny by the loneliness that grips his heart as he mourns his dad. In that humbled state of grief, he is open to the mysterious. Sitting in his room alone one night, he's drawn out to the barn where he rediscovers the emerald crystal sent with him from Krypton. It speaks to him with mystical power. His mother understands, of course, and seems to tacitly bless his quest to discover how he is meant to use his powers. He heads north, unsure of his final destination, but trusting his inner compass.

It would be easy to dismiss the "discrepancies" here on the basis of the two versions having been written during different times, by different individuals. There may be some validity to that perspective. But to stop there would be to miss the meaty morsels we can extract by accepting both scenarios as important facets of the same mythic architecture.

There *is* duty and it is more often passed down from father to son than from mother to son. Standards and honorable action. Material behaviors driven by material circumstances. Comprehensible. Socially and historically logical After all, it wasn't women who set the Protestant Reformation in motion defining the stern moral code which, to this day, shifts and trembles like a massive tectonic plate beneath the soil of the Information Age.

In contrast, the unconditional love of a strong mother such as Sarah Kent (and Lara of Krypton long before her) attempts to counterbalance the potent male emphasis on the outer life in order to imbue a sense of inner safety, nurturance, love and trust in the immaterial world of the human heart.

Message? Though my father may have told me my duty (actually, both my fathers—the virtual and the real step-dad—a very heavy emphasis on male qualities), I can't just go off and do it. I need my mother's blessing. I need her faith in me to feel right for this journey and I need her consent in my separating from her.

There is a final exquisite confirmation of the play of these two forces in the film's version of this episode. As dawn breaks, Sarah Kent sees Clark standing out in the middle of a vast field of grain looking off into the distance. She wades through the sea of stalks to join him. They exchange a few words that make it clear they both know Clark is going to leave. Nothing is said about this being the end, the last goodbye from a young son to his frail widowed mother, but the sorrow is all around them. Now they embrace and this is no ordinary hug. They press together, their arms clutching each other with all their strength. In the heat of a desperate parting, they hold and hold and hold each other as if they both know there is something out of joint, something unresolved. Even as Sarah presses into Clark in order to bestow the blessing of her love we feel she is not ready for him to go. Her blessing is not complete, not freely given. It is infused with a yearning for him to stay. She needs him, badly, but subjugates herself to the energy of male destiny. This may be emblematic of our Protestant mores in this country, but such subjugation is far from limited to American culture. It is another universal experience across time and space that raises questions and delivers important meanings for us to consider.

Why does Clark leave his mother in an obvious state of grief? Her husband has just died. To shrug this off as "something people do, especially sons" would be an act of cultural blindness, if not outright spiritual numbness. For thousands of years, millions of sons have *not* abandoned aged parents to go "find themselves" and define their manhood. They've stayed among their people, cared and contributed to the sustenance of the family and tribe, passed the traditions on to their own children, grandchildren, nephews and nieces. Alienation *as a social norm* is a relatively new phenomenon in human existence. What causes a young man to turn his back on his frail widowed mother?

The answers abound if we've properly surrounded ourselves with the truths the myth has been teaching. A whole, conscious, integrated person would *not* take such action. Clark is not a whole man. He does not have the great and generous heart of a whole man. He has a lot of unfinished business within him. His heart is wounded, substantially numbed, still in shock from the soul-racking realities of his short life. As our Law of Human Nature would predict, he has recovered by burying those hurts but they are still operative in his personality. Now he faces yet another loss. Think of it. What if this immigrant saga were your story? Maybe it is. Your father and mother, gone. The entire world of your childhood, wiped out. The brutal solitary journey from your homeland. The discovery that you're odd, different, a stranger in a strange land. The period of recovery suddenly punctuated by the loss of yet another father, the one you've truly known and loved. The magnitude of hurt symbolized by these events would leave the hearts of very few of us sufficiently alive to generate the emotional courage to stay and face the loss of our last living beloved parent.

Again, remember our Law of Human Nature tells us that when a huge swirl of unprocessed feelings turns within us, cracks appear in the dam of our unconscious reservoir. Currents escape, influencing our thought and behavior in ways we do not understand, dividing our selfhood and setting us apart from those we would love. Suddenly, we experience high romantic callings and are no longer able to embrace the simple, the earthly and the obvious—stick around, take care of your mom, take over the farm, find a good woman, raise a family, make a good and peaceful life. It's supremely ironic that, instead, we go off questing for what's missing—our destiny—as if it's "out there somewhere." Well it might as well be out there in the big city, up there at the top of the corporate tower, over there atop an Olympic podium. In fact, to rise to the status of "a man of action" appears to *require* we subjugate the unconditional mother-blessing and its affinity for attending to our deeper

43

feelings. *Having detached from our inner truth in this manner, our destiny could be anywhere.*

So, Kal-El/Clark has discovered his powers, learned something about humility, experienced some recuperation from the now long-buried trauma of his origins. But recuperation or recovery are not to be confused with real healing, resolution and integration. The cataclysm is still there, cryogenically frozen in the center of his soul. It should not surprise us he's heading north.

The Fortress

The young man of eighteen traverses an icy landscape somewhere near the North Pole. Its sterility recalls the architecture of Krypton. As we soon find out, this *is* a kind of return trip. He heaves his green crystal into the field of white and watches as it artfully erects a massive structure whose glassy building blocks resemble those of the home planet and are nearly indistinguishable from the surrounding ice. Welcome to the Fortress of Solitude. It will serve as the seat of apprenticeship for the next dozen years, as well as the safe-haven to which Superman will return once he's embarked on his dual life in the city of Metropolis.

In short order, the holographic Jor-El appears once more to mentor his son. We might be tempted to compare the Kryptonian patriarch to J.R. Ewing of the *Dallas* TV series at this point. He certainly is possessive, reaching some seventeen years or so beyond his own death to make sure his kid takes over the family's superbusiness, which is apparently to know what is right and make a stand for it. Actually, at the critical hour of his people's history, Jor-El did express his opinion in the face of authoritative disagreement, *but he did not act on it*, preferring to "go down with the ship" doing his duty to the Council of Five rather than making an active last ditch effort to save his billions of countrymen. Now, here he is trying to correct his mistake and live anew by turning his son into the complete action hero. We are clearly back in the clutches of male power dynamics.

Jor-El's message to his son has its confusion. He repeats the statement made long ago in the tiny space capsule, "It is forbidden to interfere with human history," but now he adds, "rather let your leadership stir others." We are not privy to exactly what he means by this and we suspect neither is Kal-El. The issue doesn't get any clearer when he further states, "They (the humans) can be a great people, Kal-El. They only lack the light to show the way. For this reason above all—their capacity for good, I have sent them you, my only son."

This is sounding more and more like an order on the level of messianism. Megalomaniacal fathers will tend to load up their kids with their own delusions of grandeur. What's a son to do when the father force has such reach? Look around you in your own community. He'll probably try mightily to be worthy through ever greater accomplishments and acquisitions...or go off and be a ballet dancer or anything else his father really despises. Given that Kal-El has actually had two strong father figures painting "Public Servant" all over his brain, we have little doubt which way he'll go. Perhaps we're also getting some advance teaching about the meaning of the mild-mannered alter-ego to come. Maybe the reporter is not just a tactical cover to protect the Man of Steel's "real" identity. Maybe we're being told that high performance chaps really need a place to rest and even bumble without being judged by their Superego fathers. Maybe we're being told Clark Kent, an ordinary guy, is who a lot of supermen would actually prefer to be if only they had the courage.

In any case, we're not quite sure how a person is supposed to let his leadership stir others without interfering with human history. Something like being *in* but not *of* the world? ("Always hold in your heart the pride of your special heritage," his father coos.) More reverberations of the messiah concept. We'll have to wait for the Metropolis phase of Kal-El's life to unfold before we understand this one.

Father and son spend an entire year examining "the various concepts of immortality and their basis in actual fact." A year? We can't dismiss such a substantial investment in the topic. This is the myth's way of underscoring for us that its entire thrust has to do with the wish to escape mortality, which is to say, humanness, which is to say feeling, which is to say, once again, the unavoidable probability of misery beyond our conscious endurance. In fact, the myth may be giving us a hint about the origins of the very idea of immortality. Indeed, life after death is whatever existence we can manage after the psychic numbing of early catastrophe. Given the disconnected essence of this form of "reincarnation," it's no wonder we imagine it to be pain-free, even heavenly.

Jor-El also spends a year examining the human heart with his son. His key comment: "It is more fragile than your own." We're not surprised. You'd have to have a heart of stone, a crystal at least an 8 on the Mohs hardness scale, to survive what he has been through and not become a dysfunctional lump. In fact, the more we get to know him in the future, we suspect he doesn't feel *anything* to much depth. He's a good soldier boy who's only clear "feeling" is a sense of duty.

The location and substance of the Fortress only amplifies this message. Why such a cold place? Why a structure of white crystal? What does this mean?

Ice, of course, is frozen water, directing us to seek understanding as to why water is such a popular symbol in the lexicon of human imagery. In the biblical story of the Flood, we see it representing both the terror and blessing of the birth of a new world whose creation is based on destruction. We see similar symbolism as baby Moses, in an ark of bulrushes daubed with slime and pitch, is placed at the river's edge. The transformation from one life to another, from the bosom of one's people into the arms of another, no matter how short the journey, is fraught with fear. In Exodus 2:6 we read, "And when she (the maid of Pharaoh's daughter) had opened it, she saw the child: and, behold, the babe wept." Water upon water. Tears and birth. Later, the Children of Israel are born into a new life by the grown Moses, as he raises his staff and the waters part. Again, the experience is fraught with profound ambivalence. Still later, John the Baptist offers people a new life, a rebirth, by dipping them in the waters of the Jordan. Yet, this act, too is full of danger. We all know what happened to John, to Jesus and to so many who were "reborn" as Christians under the Roman rule—a time of great struggle and weeping.

If we skip ahead by millennia, we still find variations on the same theme more recently unearthed by Robert Bly, Ralph Metzner and David Whyte. Bly superbly renders the Grimm story of Iron John, in his 1990 book by that title. Iron John turns out to be a baronial King who was transformed by a spell into a Wild Man, condemned to dwell at the bottom of a pool till his relationship with a young boy freed him, birthed him into a new life.

In the title language of his 1994 exploration of the myths of Northern Europe, *The Well of Remembrance*, Professor Metzner reminds us of the importance of common expressions such a "the welling up of emotion from the depths" or "the well-spring of emotion". We think of how fountains, geysers, waterfalls and waves are all used to express powerful feelings. Metzner states explicitly, "Water is the element metaphorically associated with emotions and feelings, and hence the visions and dreams involving wells, springs, and waters always seem to have a powerful emotional resonance."[18]

In *The Heart Aroused*, Whyte gives a stirring interpretation of the Sixth Century legend of Beowulf that makes us aware of the pivotal importance of another body of water, a lake. Having dispatched the monster, Grendel, who arose from the depths to carry off the local king's most able men, Beowulf must enter the waters to face an even greater threat in the person of Grendel's mother. Whyte is straightforward in equating the lake with "the waters of the unconscious."[19] By going into our own depths and reckoning with our "disowned" demons, whatever their origins, we emerge into a new state of being, a new life.

As wonderful as are the works of these three contemporary authors, there is probably no better current example to be found of one particular mythic meaning of water than in Andrew Lloyd Webber's production of Gaston Leroux's novel *The Phantom of the Opera*. This is a theatrical work of enduring power, witness its long-running success. Through Charles Hart's exceptional lyrics, we learn that the Phantom dwells below the surface of Paris in a cavern, *beside a lake*. He is a neat embodiment of the unconscious mind, disfigured, a denizen of the shadows, full of desperate sorrow and a passionate need to express himself. But he must do so under cover of darkness for, as Christine Daae sings, "Those who have seen your face, draw back in fear. I am the mask you wear..."[20] He and Christine actually represent the unconscious and conscious minds of a single soul, a fact that's reinforced by the way the song is performed. The Phantom stands behind Christine, wrapping his arms around her as they sway to the music as a single being. What's more, Christine's lyrics explicitly tell us, "The Phantom of the Opera is there inside my mind." Day, as another symbol of consciousness, is characterized as "garish light...cold, unfeeling..." Night, the underground "kingdom" of the unconscious is the place of real emotion where defenses are abandoned, sensation is sharpened, imagination stirs and the secret to experiencing life to the fullest awaits: "And you'll live as you've never lived before," promises the Phantom. But in order to achieve that, Christine is beckoned to "surrender to your darkest dreams, purge all thoughts of the life you knew before..."[21] To possess the ultimate creative power, we are being told, calls for the welcoming of the "Music of the Night," a music full of darkness and dissonance, emanating from a deeply wounded shadow being who dwells at the edge of a subterranean lake. With such richly detailed context, we cannot doubt that this hidden body of water represents the unwept tears of immense anguish.

Considering all this, we shouldn't fail to mention again that our country was founded by huge immigrant populations who, until the development of commercial trans-oceanic flight, literally crossed an immense body of water to make a new life in a new world. These voyages, filled with their own particular tumult of emotions, could only strengthen the power of water as a symbol of birth, transformation and renewal as well as unprocessed agony, fear and despair.

What is so interesting about the Superman myth is the relative uniqueness and terrific clarity in choosing a *frozen* water world to be Kal-El's home base. Emotion in deep-freeze, terror frozen, the destruction of his home planet and his birth waters frozen, a state of suspended animation—literally, the soul (anima) in cryogenic freeze, an architecture of crystal tears—an icy museum of cataclysmic art. The cavernous meaning beneath meanings is that an individual can't ever successfully run from his inner truth. He will inevitably create its reflection around him whether he travels far from the place of his origins or stays put as he makes the journey from childhood to adulthood. To deny the truth of the unconscious is to be ruled by it, to be imprisoned within the jagged battlements of its flashy fortress, a solitary so-called man of action.

Forever Metropolis

After a dozen years of tutoring by Virtual Jor-El in the Fortress, Superman heads for Metropolis. There are three particularly interesting aspects of his life in the big city which we'll take up in the following order:

      1.   The troublesome attraction to Lois Lane.
      2.   The dual existence, half Clark, half Superman.

3. The dynamics of Superman's relationship to the people of Metropolis.

The Trouble with Lois

When we take into account that our hero has just spent more than a decade in isolation—about six times longer than his original voyage to earth—and that these have been the years during which young men are most preoccupied with a very particular kind of "steel," we shouldn't be at all startled to witness romantic confusion. This fellow is thirty years old, built like a Greek god and has never had a date! If Jor-El spent a year teaching him about immortality and a year on the human heart, he must have spent about ten seconds on sexuality, warning him about growing hair on the palms of his hands. This would be thoroughly commensurate with a psychological theme that has come and gone and come again down through the ages—the discomfort of the human species with the full force of its sexual nature.

So what is the myth teaching us here? In terms of sexual love, Clark and Superman represent two commonly conflicting impulses within literally millions of men who have been stunted by significant shortfalls in their needs for safety, nurturance and love during their developing years. There is an insecure, lonely little boy here who needs more from his mommy but is afraid he'll be rejected if he just stands up and asks for it straight out. He'll be much more comfortable with a cyber-babe in his computer screen than flesh and blood. Christopher Reeve's portrayal of Clark is a bull's eye on this point, with the stooped shoulders, sunken neck and chest. It's not at all surprising that a man with such a heavy legacy of loss and solitude on his back would be smitten by the first attractive female he encounters. Lois fits the psychological puzzle perfectly. She's definitely not the type to have long, sensitive discussions with a hurt and needy man-child. She's all impulse and action, an earthly female counterpart of the super side of Kal-El. Ironically, she's just the type to get wrapped up in her own pining for the perfect powerful daddy.

We already know that safety was the core need most lacking in Kal-El's early life. If we had to guess which of the core needs, Lois most missed, we'd have to place our chips on safety as well.

So Clark longs for Lois, the strong action mommy, and Lois longs for Superman, the strong action daddy.

What about the Superman side of this? In the wounded person, there's the opposite impulse—to reveal his or her worthiness for love by coming out of the shadows and boldly grabbing the spotlight. But again, notice the distance. Superman is not down here on earth where he's accessible to the arms of love. He has unconsciously learned the indelible lesson that love means need and need means hurt. So the simple arithmetic of experience has driven him to the safer place from which to keep love alive—on high, in the clouds, or in contemporary terms, in an electronic ethernet where authentic intimacy is not possible. From this pedestal, his behavior cries out, "See me, Mommy! See what a good boy I am! See how I survived! See what I can do! Watch me, Mommy!" This recalls the song in the rock opera, *Tommy*, whose refrain is, "See me! Touch me! Feel me!" But in the case of Superman, the damage is far too deep for him to get past "see" to "touch" and "feel". What can steel feel?

It's fitting this whole act is played out on the stage of the sky—remember all the time he spent there as an infant traveling to Earth? It's a kind of unconscious return to the scene of the original crime against his infant soul.

So Clark can chase stories with Lois and Lois can fly around chasing stories with Superman, but all three incarnations are limited to longing without real connection.

In the second Superman film, we get some explicit instruction on all of this. Clark reveals himself as Superman to

Lois, and, for a moment, we may be foolish enough to hope that the divided selves will be healed into one. We can be forgiven. A belief in the healing power of love is another universal confusion. Love does heal. We're just terribly unclear about what love is and how that healing works. More on this later.

Seeking the guidance of his heritage, Superman flies Lois to his Fortress of Solitude where his virtual mother, Lara, appears and gives him the bad news: "If you intend to live your life with a mortal, you must live as a mortal. You must become one of them. You will become an ordinary man. You will feel like an ordinary man. You can be hurt like an ordinary man." Mother Lara leaves no doubt about the consequences. She states quite clearly, "All your great powers on earth will disappear forever." But our man knows what he wants. Love clarifies all. Mmmm.

Not quite. Clark and Lois enjoy a brief bit of conjugal bliss away from the world only to discover that a) a common coffee house bully can kick Clark's ass and b) General Zod and his evil lieutenants are taking over the world. Clark returns to his lair in the North Pole and rediscovering the mother of all green crystals, rejuvenates himself as Superman. Whew!

The message is unequivocal. You can't let your guard down. You can't afford the indulgence of an ordinary life of love. You were right to leave the farm and dear old mom back in Smallville. To be vulnerable is to experience a little tiny bit of pleasure but a whole world of hurt. The dark past (here in the form of General Zod) will never stop threatening to overpower the present. You must be everywhere, see and hear everything. Never sleep. Your reward? You will be allowed to feel one set of feelings—the sense of doing your duty and the admiration that comes from others who are helped by it. There are no shirttails long enough to hold all the merit badges you'll earn for being such a good boy. At the core of this dutiful devotion, you will yearn and be yearned for, but you will never be able to experience real love. As far as the X-ray eye can see, there is responsibility, work…and solitude. In the outer journey of life, you're everyone's champion. In the inner journey, well...there is no inner journey. No wonder the more recent DC Comics and TV episodes have figured out a way for him to have both his powers and Lois. I mean, give a guy a break!

One last point. The myth also appears to be suggesting that the violins of longing we so revere as the essence of romantic love might literally be silenced if we truly got what we needed as kids. What? The end of romantic love? Yes, as we've known it. Why would that be so bad, considering that the divorce rate in the Information Age has held at a pesky fifty percent. Imagine, we might stop slinking or dashing around trying to find the pieces of ourselves that went numb or missing. What would adult love look like, then? Would it lack passion? Not likely. Sexual passion is natural. But it would be absent so much of the push and pull of personalities. It would lack these little boy and little girl games we play out with each other. It would lack posing, posturing and preening. Above all, it would be about great companionship and mutual appreciation. What would you be willing to give to see that reign across our land?

Split Personality

The surface of the story would have us believe that the entire Clark Kent persona is a put on, a cover, necessary to protect Superman. "Protect Superman." Interesting phrase. What's the meaning? Here's my internal conversation about it:

"Why does Superman need protection?"

"Well, there's a lot of evil out there. Maybe he needs the cover. The myth is acknowledging this and recommending 'better to be safe than sorry.' We might generalize this to the business realm which, after all, we've turned into another theater of survival. Maybe we're being told something like, 'Keep the competition guessing. Keep a low profile. Never let 'em see you coming.' Maybe this is just another rendering of Teddy

Roosevelt's, 'Walk softly, but carry a big stick' and a presaging of Andrew Grove's later version of the same mentality in his statement, 'Only the paranoid survive.'"

"Yeah, but that's exactly my hesitation. This guy's got the biggest stick on Earth. He's so strong and fast, why *wouldn't* he want the evildoers coming to him? (That would be a contemporary concept wholly appropriate to a modem-driven world—a crime fighter who works from home!)"

"No, better to keep the enemy guessing, off-balance."

"Maybe…but why would he need to disguise himself? The dude can fly faster than a dive-bombing eagle. Who would be able to follow him to wherever he might set up his local pad? Are we being told that there is no person strong enough to transcend the need for *prudent paranoia?"*

"Look. As a reporter on the Planet, he'll get constant updates on all the dastardly acts going down all over town. I mean, this is a place where people steal fruit off sidewalk stands, try to hold women up for the contents of their purses in broad daylight and generally scheme to take over the world. This sounds awfully familiar, doesn't it?"

"I see. The pragmatic rationale. Be where the news is breaking. But what's his super hearing and X-ray vision all about? I mean, the guy is the ultimate all-hearing and seeing-eye dog. He could just hover over Metropolis and see and hear the crimes in progress before any reporter ever got wind of them. I'm still having a hard time with the need for the alter ego."

It does seem pretty thin as story telling. Should we just dismiss it as one of those weak links we find in so many great stories—the point where we just have to suspend our normal judgment and accept it?

Before we settle on that decision, to be true to the nature of our inquiry, we have to ask again what the meaning might be from a mythic perspective. Is it that inside every humble, stoop-shouldered individual is a great spirit, struggling to break loose? Is flying simply a metaphor for personal freedom, the ultimate

54

American value? Is it a symbolic representation of what Abraham Maslow believed was at the top of our hierarchy of needs—self-actualization?[22] Maybe. But if this is true, it's fair to suspect the opposite might also be true, meaning that Clark is not covering for Superman at all. Superman is the mask, Clark Kent closer to the real person (just as the beautiful Christine Daae is the cover for the wounded Phantom of the Opera). Myth is a human creation and humans don't really have super powers, so ultimately we must again dismiss the idea that such details should be seen literally. This would tend to lead us to conclude that the Superman character is an incarnation of an act millions of us put on every day and, as such, is the material manifestation of unconscious factors.

Numerous validations of this idea have emerged in the four and a half-day leadership workshop I've been privileged to facilitate for the last four years.[23] In one of our principle exercises, we invite the members of our small group (twelve to twenty souls) to explore the layers of their selfhood. We begin by asking them who they are in the workplace when they're *selling* themselves rather than just *being* themselves. Ninety-five percent have no problem describing their "Social Mask" or "game face" with a list of cogent adjectives. When we ask them to come up with a name to describe this "character," they commonly use Superman, Batman, James Bond, the Terminator, Super Mom, Wonder Woman, Xena and other similar "super" names. They are also quick to express a sense of entrapment in this habitual behavior since it neither feels good nor really achieves the vaunted goals for which it's designed. They readily acknowledge there's a lot of support for putting on this act in our culture. Said one participant, "I've been getting this all my life, since I can remember—you've gotta be strong. You've gotta be smart. You've gotta have the answers. Don't let people get too close. Don't let 'em know what you're really thinking. Be bulletproof. Be a redwood. Go like the Energizer Bunny. Don't ever stop. Don't let 'em see you sweat and sure as hell don't ever let 'em see you cry. Be a man. Hell, I'm not sure I know what a man is."

Even in "New Age" parlance we find more code words for this behavior. We're promised "boundless" energy, "infinite" compassion, an "ageless" body, and a "giant" emerging from within. The over-use of superlatives and the penchant for extraordinary promises constitute one more Sermon on the Mount of *the superman syndrome*. Real human beings get tired and need rest. Real human beings run out of patience and compassion. Aging is not optional for real human beings. Death is not optional for real human beings. And, yes, real human beings have someone sleeping within them, but it's just more of a real human being, the part of us that's been standing in the shadows, the part we're loathe to acknowledge, the part that fears being less than brilliant, less than beautiful, less than courageous, less than charming, less than funny, less than strong, less than lovable.

Why is this "Shadow" important? Because it's a sign there's trouble down below in the unconscious mind, whether represented by the Greek's Minotaur in its subterranean labyrinth, the underworld of Hades, the lake-dwelling Grendels in Beowulf, the submerged Iron John, the Phantom beneath Paris or even the troll under the bridge in the fairy tale of Billy Goats Gruff. That trouble holds important truths which, when fully experienced and understood, can gradually heal the divisions in our identities, so we can truly be individuals, a word meaning "those who cannot be divided from themselves."

Some people say, "Well, sure, we all have insecurities and hurts from the past. Nobody had the perfect childhood. But we don't need to dwell on it...and isn't it wonderful that people succeed in spite of all those hurts?"

Consider, however, that having all these hurts doesn't mean this is the most desirable state of being in which to live. It doesn't mean we should be congratulating ourselves on not doing worse. It's simplistic to say we succeed *in spite* of them.

The truth is thornier. We succeed partly in spite of them and, to a large degree, *because* of them. The Superman myth is clearly instructing us that the hand of the unconscious is *directly involved in sculpting* our particular choice of goals, the particular way in which we pursue them, the degree of intensity of that endeavor and the manner in which we define success. It's naive to say we triumph over the unhealed wounds within us. The very need to "triumph" is set up by them. We have no idea what a success would look like if it were not based on such extensive scarring. We have no idea what the world would look like if it were populated by people who did not have to constantly "triumph" over their own inner life. To the degree that we are driven to such triumph, we are victims even when we are victors.

It should suffice here to underscore that the very successful people in our workshop are quick to discover through our exercise the same meaning projected by the Myth: underneath the public act, a lot of us are privately hiding a stoop-shouldered little kid who's been roughed up by Life's Raw Deals, a kid who needed a great deal more safety, nurturance or love than he or she got. These realizations are often accompanied by the emergence of specific memories whose emotional content had been long severed. In the safety of our workshop, the tears, anger and fear commonly resurface. They dramatically underscore the high cost of the cover-up of which the increased speed of the Information Age is a major component. It's exhausting running around spinning ten plates at a time, coming up with all the answers, tracking the trends, finding, training, motivating the right people, getting the systems in place and maintaining them, achieving financial security and trying to make everyone happy at home—all of this with a dashing smile and a "positive mental attitude". What's more, a lot of employees see the nakedness of their strutting emperors and lose respect for them. The Mask obviously is not the efficient and effective operating mode we'd like to believe it to be. It wastes a huge amount of energy. Our workshop participants regularly tell us that no matter how much money they make (there are commonly several millionaires in any given group), the feeling of security never stays long. *This yields the ironic insight that the central reason to work—to create a sphere of safety for ourselves and our families—seems to be one thing it can't provide.* Our participants readily acknowledge they're not spending anywhere near the amount and quality of time with their spouses and children they need and wish to. As you might expect, they return home to take substantial and sustainable actions to realign the relationship between work and family. Their first step is to begin exploring the possibility of living without the superhero mask.

The Success that Fails: Superman and the People of Metropolis

We can get right to the brass tacks on this one. Superman is an action junkie. He's an addict in a co-dependent relationship with the misfortunate feeble folks of Metropolis. He may appear to be utterly self-contained, needing nothing from anyone. But quite the contrary, he does have one overriding need. He desperately needs those little folks to need him. A king is not a king without a mass of people willing to be subjects in need of his wisdom and protection. Without the population of Metropolis committing to maintain only the most modest intelligence and skills, he can't demonstrate his loyal superness and receive his daily fix of love-from-afar. Without their vulnerability, he's nothing. Heaven forbid they should clean up their act! Heaven forbid their law enforcement guys should be equal to the challenge. Heaven forbid they should institute Kanbans—the Japanese idea of having many small police stations throughout the country staffed with officers who really get involved in the neighborhood. Heaven forbid the city should have excellent day-care and after school programs and midnight basketball. That might get kids off the street! Heaven forbid, even worse, they should figure out how to shorten the work week to make it easier to be real and present parents and raise sane children. Let's just go for one sane child per couple. Let's try that program for twenty years. Heaven forbid, they'd have made that kind of commitment a generation ago. The crime rate would have dropped so much, Superman would be out of a job. He'd be the worst thing of all, the one thing our workshop students tell us over and over again they're afraid of being seen as—*ordinary* and therefore unworthy of father's love.

But, not to worry. There is a very secure contract, unspoken though it may be, between the folks of the big city and the man-child in tights. Says Metropolis, "We'll agree to be weak if…" Responds Superman, "…I agree to be strong." Metropolis gets to feel protected (which it's not, it's in constant danger). Superman gets to feel grownup (which he's not—he's a glorified Peter Pan, a victim of arrested development).

This mirrors the unspoken contract with our leaders in nearly every area of our society. We agree to be little children who need experts for everything if people will come forward to be those expert mommies and daddies. We'll get to feel cared for (which we're not—our medical, social, legal and political fabrics are perilously frayed). The experts will get to feel really important (which they're not, at least not anywhere near as much as we all act…our need has just created that illusion). We all get to feel cared for or needed in some way as long as we all agree not to actually be responsible adults. The minute we say, for example, "Hey, I think I'll just live a sane, healthy life—eat right, exercise, get plenty of sleep, sex and recreation—so I won't need at least half of what you doctors offer…" we'll be able to export doctors to other countries. The minute doctors, for example, say, "You don't need me. You need to live a sane and healthy life! An ounce of prevention *is* worth a pound of cure…." we'll have to learn to take care of ourselves…and figure out what to do with the several hundred billion dollars a year we'll save.

This principle especially applies in the area of business leadership today, as some are finding out. When a manager decides to put the right people in the right positions with the right training and education and the right support in capital, manpower and technology and he entrusts those people with a crystal clear mission, everybody starts growing up. Systems, processes, relationships, the very nature of work itself—all change and very much for the better. On the other hand, if that manager has a profound psychological need to stand on the bow of the company ship with his fists on his hips, his red cape fluttering in the wind, it's only a matter of time before he torpedoes the ship himself. Talent is often its own greatest weakness in that it tends to make itself indispensable. The people around such a person will be denigrated, conflicted, consigned to work in some measure of fear, resentment, anger, cynicism, feebleness and hurt. What has really happened? The unprocessed cataclysmic dynamic has returned to make sure the new way can't succeed. Then our supermanager can say, "I tried and it just didn't work." But, surely, the builders of this nation didn't reject the monarchies of Europe, brave the oceans, the elements and an unknown world, fight a revolution, a civil war, two World Wars and countless other battles so that, in the Twentieth and Twenty-first Centuries we could submit ourselves to the tyrannies of bosses incapable of dealing with their own inner shadows.

As we further consider the consequences of this unconscious super dynamic, let's remember Jor-El's biblical-style pronouncement to Kal-El in the Fortress of Solitude: "It is forbidden to interfere with human history. Rather let your leadership stir others." This was followed by, "They can be a great people, Kal-El. They only lack the light to show the way. For this reason above all--their capacity for good, I have sent them you, my only son."

Has he refrained from interfering in human history? It's true, he didn't spin the world back in time and kill Hitler in the crib. He didn't change the outcome of the Viet Nam War. But he has saved the world many times from villainous designs of world domination. He *has* interfered and big-time. So much for Daddy's advice. With all his super hearing, the kid's no different than most teenagers. He flies off and does as he pleases.

Has he stirred others by his leadership? Well, sure, we can imagine he's had a positive influence on some young boys who want to grow up to be like him. But, uh, who can be like him? Nobody. That's a dream destined for failure, kid. He's the star and don't you forget it. No, this is not about stirring others with leadership. That's why we never see the innovative possibility that under Superman's tutelage Metropolis might actually become a better place to live, so his Steelness can move on and help another city's population grow up and take care of its own. On the contrary, it's all co-dependency. Metropolis isn't one lick better sixty years later!

I can't think of any aspect of the story that illuminates this more than the fact of Superman's X-ray vision. Yes, he can see through everything but lead. But that's exactly the point. That's the myth's underlying hint to us. There is a very important limitation to this man's ability to see, a kind of visual Achilles heel. He has a very tactical kind of "special" vision. He sees only what is happening in front of him right now. He's a blind reactionary.

The true visionary may be the only individual who is consistently capable of jumping from the self-perpetuating merry-go-round of his own talent. The solutions that Superman brings to Metropolis are superb examples of short-term fixes. Catch 'em, throw 'em in jail. He's a transactionalist, a doctor fixing symptoms to the neglect of causes, a fireman who's so busy stomping out fires, he doesn't have time to figure out how they're starting in the first place. What the heck, people stand around and cheer every time he does extinguish one.

Yes, he can see through walls, but not into social systems and certainly not into the soul of man, no less into his own soul. Alas, the boy's no visionary, not even close. So, he's let his daddy down. Jor-El wanted a savior, someone to "show them the light", someone who could stir, someone with a spiritual dimension. What he got was an utter materialist, an action addict, a compulsive counter-puncher imprisoned in the boxing ring, *a lower case savior whose entire life is negotiable to the demands of his work.*[24] How contemporary. We must feel sorry for Kal-El. He's clearly never read Dr. Covey's Seven Habits of Highly Effective People. He doesn't have a clue about the possibility of being proactive. For all his steely guts, he has to have at least a dim sense that in the final analysis, he just doesn't measure up. Kal-El, like many of us, was set up to fail in Jor-El's terms. How reasonable is it for a father to expect his son to become a source of light when his heart is a cold cinder?

And God?

There is one other important comment our myth may be expressing in its presentation of the dynamic between the people of Metropolis and Superman. It may well be teaching us about the dangers in our relationship with the force or intelligence we refer to as God. Superman makes a very good symbol for the Deity. He is nearly all-seeing, all-hearing, omnipotent and omnipresent and is quite comfortable in the heavens. God is "Our Father, who art in Heaven", which makes us his children down here on earth. He is so Big, we are so feeble, He gets a capital letter and we don't, just so we don't forget to stay small. We go to Him with our confusion, anger, hurt, fear, frustrations, imperfections, our needs for safety, nurturance and love. Like the people of Metropolis, we are rather ill-behaved children. We require commandments, rules, truths handed down from on high because we just can't seem to get it right on our own. There is something at the core of us that can't be trusted. We're sinners, even as babies. So here's our contract with the Almighty: we'll agree to be flawed little kids if He'll agree to be the big, strong daddy who will listen, forgive, protect, guide and embrace us. In short, we'll agree to be broken if he'll agree to fix us, either now or later in Heaven.

What if this line of thinking and believing is an insidious way to avoid taking full responsibility for who we are? Consider that our contract—we'll be broken, He'll fix us—can't be honored unless we and He agree not to ask an extremely dangerous line of questions:

- Why did He make "sin" an original part of us?
- What if it's not "original" or indelible?
- What if we actually have the capability within us to create something other than the "bloody mosaic" to which Jor-El refers, but in order to do it, we have to move out of the House and do it on our own?
- What if we've been set up to feel the need for the strong Hand by a psychological legacy descending from an old patriarchal tradition, symbolized by Jor-El and the Council of Five?

The minute we embark on such an inquiry, God, as we have conceived of him for about forty centuries, is at risk. If we're basically rabble, we need a strong leader. If we cease to be rabble, the leader must become human like the rest of us or go away or transform into something most of us have rarely contemplated. If the people of Metropolis really got their act together, they wouldn't need Superman. If we really got our act together, we wouldn't need God as we've conceived Him.

For most of us raised in the Judaeo-Christian tradition, including myself, these ideas are difficult, if not downright incendiary. They call into question a great deal of religious canon. But we turn away from them at our peril. If we consider them with courage and the spirit of authentic inquiry, we may well find that beyond the edge of our patriarchal religious paradigm is not sacrilege but an expanded set of possibilities for a whole new relationship with God.

The residue of the patriarchal legacy is pervasive in both secular and religious realms. We see it in abusive husbands and fathers, self-righteous politicians, self-important clergy and managers who covet power in the workplace and treat work as if it is society's most important activity. We see it in the mental and emotional posture that masses of people who "must be" disciplined, guided or saved by all these dark variations of Superman. On the other hand, when power is shared, the people "grow up," showing themselves to be far more responsible and capable than leaders had previously imagined. This is the belief at the center of Western Democracy. We are far from fully manifesting it, of course. We've been acting out this child role for a very long time. Adulthood is not to be gained over night. But, let us demonstrate the courage to consider that being human is not at all about a "sin" or original foolish act whose consequences are so deeply imprinted we can't possibly transcend our need for Big Daddy or Big Mommy. What if it's about a kind of glitch that we can ultimately work out with each other's help?

Summing Up: Black and Blue, not Red and Blue

We would do well to reconsider our glorification of the surface details of the Superman tale. The truth is, it's a big, deep, dark, desperate myth. Big, because it has extraordinary scope, connecting our present dilemmas back to the early history of humans in the universe, thereby urging us to ask important questions about our origins as a nation, as a species, even as children of our particular Western God. Deep, because it also calls us down into the fissures of our individual souls. Dark, because it compels us to face the long shadows cast by cataclysms across our race, civilization and personal lives. Desperate, because it shows us a reflection of ourselves as bruised, hapless players longing for invulnerability, trapped in a never-ending series of high-speed chases of which the vaunted Information Age is merely the latest and most souped up version.

It would be easy to find all this depressing, but because the myth addresses so many aspects of our frailty with such power and clarity, it provides us with an intriguing opportunity to extend our understanding so we might ultimately find our way back to the full promise of our humanity.

Chapter Five

Elaborations

"One does not discover new lands without consenting to lose sight of the shore for a very long time."

--Andre Gide

The Glitch

In trying to extend the understanding stimulated by our excursion into the myth dimension, there's probably nothing more worth probing than the idea that there's a glitch in our makeup which in large part drives *the superman syndrome* and its resulting assault on the felicitous family life at the core of the American Dream. As we contemplate this, certain questions arise that will build on our earlier look at the work of human nature:

- What is the earliest origin of the sub-division of human selfhood?
- Why should we even have an unconscious mind holding onto all that stuff we couldn't feel?
- Why aren't we blessed with the ability to just process the feelings we can and let the rest roll away like water off a duck's back?
- Why didn't Creation make us tougher?
- Why couldn't we have been fashioned as pure intellectual explorers without the "slings and arrows of outrageous fortune"?

Any attempt to answer these difficult questions must be worked at an uncomfortable crossroads of human inquiry where philosophy, psychology, science, anthropology, metaphysics and religion converge on their way to business theory and practice. When we stand at that juncture, an answer does emerge—not a complete one, perhaps, but something we can work with. I offer it for your consideration. It is shockingly simple and circular.

Theoretically, we *could* have been designed quite differently. Theoretically, we could be absent the entire limbic system at the center of our brain. It's the limbic system that appears to be the principle driver of strong emotion, both conscious and unconscious. But we weren't and aren't made that way. That's the fact. Our nervous system's architecture is a more brilliant and sophisticated variation on those of "lower" creatures. Creation has been developing this pattern for a long, long time. Our brain stem is essentially the same found in all vertebrates from reptiles all the way up to man. The feeling-dedicated limbic center, roughly one fifth of total brain mass, is found in basically the same form throughout the entire mammalian class. We like to think we're the only creatures who really feel, but that doesn't seem to be the case at all. Feelings are important servants of survival, particularly in primates. Their frequent grooming and holding, their long periods of breast-feeding—generally a minimum of two years—are all orchestrations of the feeling brain. We sometimes dismiss these behaviors as instinct, but the presence of instinct does not in any way preclude the probability of a significant subjective experience. It's more likely that, in this case, it assures it. Given the similarities in our central brains, we have every reason to believe that when a gorilla engages in mothering behavior, she is experiencing a form of love toward her baby just as a human mother does. What are pleasure, contentment and love if not various subjective payoffs a creature gets when it satisfies its basic needs?

The equation is pretty simple—satisfy real basic needs, feel pleasure. Have those needs deprived, feel pain. The result of either is *learning*, learning which supports not mere survival of both individual and species, but makes possible their *flourishing*, which we could see as the ultimate realization of millennia of vigorous experimentation. The central dynamic of our species could be expressed as this: *To feel in order to learn, in order to know in order to stay in balance within ourselves, between ourselves and between our species and the world, in order to survive and thrive.* What feeling would most impel this dynamic? Love. Love is not a frivolous gift tossed into our evolutionary gift bag as an afterthought. It's the key.

Creation has been replicating this same theme for a long time. It "likes" this instrumentation—feelings carrying the lessons of the ages. Maybe there were other possibilities, but this apparently is the one that has been diversifiable to the longest continuous chain of living innovation. In other creatures, the capacity to feel is accompanied by externally visible defensive capabilities. The gorilla has incredible physical strength, the chimpanzee agility, the rhino extraordinarily thick skin, the cheetah speed, even the lowly turtle a hard shell. Humans, on the other hand, have very humble endowments in terms of physical defenses. Our skin bruises and cuts very easily. We're not all that fast afoot. The musculature of the most powerful human is nothing to that of an ox or horse. Our vulnerability suggests we are supposed to be brilliant feelers, Creation's finest at experiencing, appreciating and celebrating the magic of life.

Here comes the paradox, recapitulating our Law of Human Nature. We have a rarified capacity for receiving and interpreting stimuli from the world with no obvious physical way to protect ourselves when those stimuli become too intense...and they certainly do become too intense. Tougher and stronger creatures than we are still not invulnerable to the traumatic events of a developing and changing planet. Volcanic eruptions, earthquakes, floods, droughts, hurricanes, and other meteorological powerhouses, as well as pests and plagues, have long been part of life on earth. Thousands of species have come and gone because of them, billions upon billions of individuals have been wiped out. Our ancestors, subjected to such environmental trauma, were facing life and death situations.

Imagine, for a few moments, a clan of early humans. At this point, we're not going to place them in an exact time frame. We could be talking about Lucy's group of Australopithecus afarensis three and a half to four million years ago. We could also be talking about a Neanderthal group a hundred thousand years ago, or a cluster of our own species, Homo sapiens, twenty thousand years ago. As reckless as this broad assumption might seem, its usefulness as a form of inquiry will become clear before long. Let's imagine just one individual. Let's call him Jasper the Gentle. He might not seem pretty by today's standards, but he's a good soul. His group numbers a couple of dozen individuals. Their community is largely unstructured and egalitarian. Everyone in the clan belongs. They're living in a hilly, forested environment. It provides ample food in the form of fruit, roots, berries, nuts, insects, small animals. There is shelter in the form of naturally occurring caves. There are predators, but not on a mass scale that threatens the extinction of the clan. Jasper's society is very simple. Everyone does his share. There is no hard and fast division of labor between men and women because of the ready availability of food. Even a heavily pregnant woman or a mother with babes in arms can successfully forage for at least part of her own food needs. Males and females share the joys and tasks of child-rearing. There are a few individuals who have either been born with some limiting deformity or whose abilities are diminished due to an accident, but the others help them and include them in activities. There are different personalities in the group, some more dominant than others, but nothing akin to the kind of complex leadership roles we've seen in both dark and light forms during recorded history. There is just no need for the emergence of such behavior. Life has its challenges, but it's relatively tranquil. These folks are not building pyramids or redirecting rivers. They spend their spare time playing, napping, exploring the immediate environment on some level of curiosity, or just sitting together and gazing out at the play of light on leaves, the wind-moved boughs, the comings and goings of birds, insects and animals.

Jasper is a strong young male who has recently mated for the first time and become a father. Given the presence of the mammalian brain within his skull, he has a great capacity to feel a strong attachment to his mate, his new infant and his entire clan. He is quite capable of experiencing what we today call love, delight, joy, contentment, caring. He's also quite capable of feeling physical and emotional pain, anger and fear.

Jasper has had a pretty fine life till now but his good times are about to end. The environment erupts with a natural catastrophe. Again, it could be a massive forest fire, an earthquake, volcanic eruption, flood, drought, hurricane, tornado or some form of pestilence. Over millions of years, in fact, others like Jasper have been visited by each and all of these "acts of God" and sometimes in combination or in devastating sequences over the span of a few months or years. For now, in keeping with the explosive nature of Kal-El's childhood, let's say we're dealing with a volcanic eruption which, among other things, sets off massive forest fires. Jasper and most of his clan have been out a few miles from their cave digging up roots. In a matter of moments, their tranquil world is in a terrifying blaze. Several of the group perish immediately. The survivors are stunned at this sudden loss of their loved ones and the sundering of their world. But there is literally no time for tears. They search desperately for a way out of the inferno. They've completely lost their sense of direction in the smoke and flame. Jasper suddenly sees an opening and yells to the others. Clutching his infant girl in one arm and wrapping his other around his young wife, he runs with everything he's got. His

71

sympathetic nervous system is at maximum amplitude, his adrenal glands at maximum output. His brain is pumping out the neurotransmitter dopamine to focus his entire being on any sign of which way to go to safety. His neurons are also pulsating out other neurotransmitters to keep the flood of feelings down so he isn't paralyzed by them. The full ensemble of life-preserving neuropeptides cascade into his system. He makes it to the river, which is far from safe, with fiery pyroclasts descending all around. Some of his people fall face down in the river, dead. Others have badly burned feet, legs, hands, heads. No one has escaped wounding. The luckier ones try desperately to save the less fortunate. Some live. Some die. The survivors realize the river is not safe. Jasper suddenly recognizes their location and remembers another cave he thinks they can make in a short, hard run. He yells and waves to the others. They take off with all the desperate skill and speed they can muster, dashing across the landscape. They make it to the cave. Jasper, still clutching his daughter, suddenly realizes she's not breathing. He rubs her, pats her, rocks her. His woman, burned and badly bruised over much of her body, tries nursing and rocking the child to no avail. It is dead. Jasper looks around him and sees a holocaust, his land consumed by fire, half the members of his beloved clan dead or missing, the remainder to the last man, woman and child, badly hurt. All of this has happened in a matter of an hour.

Imagine their state of mind. They're all stunned, as you or I would be. In any emergency, this is likely the case, but particularly in a primordial emergency when our ancestors' ability to understand events around them was so limited and their resources in dealing with nature's firestorms basically non-existent. Everything is gone. What can they do? They're in shock.

Though the ground still trembles periodically, the eruptions cease after a few days and the fires burn themselves out. Jasper and the other survivors sit stunned in the cave for several days, sleeping, gazing out at the blackened world, unable to comprehend, huddling together. Food sources have been dramatically impacted. Eventually, Jasper's mate pulls on his arm and leads him and a few others out of the cave. They dig through the burned brush and manage to find some edible roots undamaged by the fire. The rest of the clan gradually joins them. They find a trickling spring nearby and soothe their dehydrated bodies. For many days, they sleep, huddle together, dig roots, consume the burnt carcasses of unfortunate animals, drink and return to the cave to huddle once again. After a time, seeing the environment unchanged, they begin to wander in search of something better. Their wandering consumes days and covers many square miles of land. It's brutal, but they push on. Then one day, they see green in the distance, a broad open plain. It's a very different environment from the one they were used to. Like baby Kal-El, their world has exploded. Everything they knew and loved and trusted is lost, along with many of their family and friends. Like baby Kal-El, they've made a long difficult journey to a new world. And like him, as they arrive as immigrants in this new land, they'll require great powers—superhuman in comparison to their previous existence—new ways to protect and nurture themselves, in order to master this environment and assure their survival.

All the while, they've been in an altered state of consciousness, a kind of sustained shock, loaded up with adrenal hormones and neurotransmitters that have dampened their physical and emotional pain to keep them going. With this high internal chemical tide, their systems have been incapable of processing and integrating the full breadth and depth of the experience. Everything non-essential to survival has been shut out of consciousness. A kind of benign numbness has enabled them to push on through the dire conditions. They are our first Iron Men and Women, the original Olympians. In fact, they are our first gods, for they have survived the first hell. Their minds are now dedicated to learning everything about the tumultuous events. The extraordinary array of unassimilated feelings has been captured, tucked away. Their physical delicacy—the absence of shell, tough skin, the speed of other animals—has produced an internal solution, building on existing flexibilities within the looping mammalian brain structure and the reptilian brain stem it embraces. There, deep in a cauldron of cells smaller than a tennis ball, but large enough to hold an ocean of energy, most of the emotional content has been cryogenically frozen, an icy encyclopedia awaiting the warmth of a classroom well into the future.

For many months after this catastrophe, Jasper and his companions sometimes awaken in the middle of the night in the grip of cold fear or find themselves trembling and weeping in broad daylight remembering what has befallen them. Through this grieving, there is the beginning of some healing and recovery, and with it, at least a partial return to the sensitivity that was their original state of being. But the entire range is not regained. The magnitude of the cataclysm has been too great. Long-term damage has been done.

Now imagine the likelihood Jasper's travails aren't yet over. A *series* of natural catastrophes befalls him and his group in the course of a few years. This should not be difficult to envision since it occurs even today. A world in upheaval. More clan members perish. The survivors push on through blind numbness. Somehow, a few manage to endure. Eventually, after a long period of time, the planet calms itself and Jasper's people build some kind of "regular" life. But the original openness, the original deep capacity for emotional processing invested by evolution in the architecture of limbic cells is not to be readily reestablished. Nightmares may persist, but fewer and fewer tears come, especially to the men. By dint of their stronger musculature and freedom from pregnancy and the immediate needs of suckling babes, they have born the brunt of providing, feeding, sheltering, protecting in environments much less benign than Jasper's original habitat. All of these responsibilities have pushed them to the absolute limits of their abilities. No, there's not much weeping for quite a while. Just a lot of stunned gazing and, when there's time for it, some unemotional recall of the events. They have suffered long and learned to focus almost exclusively on the immediate task of making it through another day. There will be some recovery, of course. They will partially regain the ability to feel, to weep—some individuals more than others, women more than men. But their systems are forever imprinted with the knowledge of how frightening and unpredictable Life/God/Nature can be. If, before all this, they had a nascent awareness of the inevitability of death, they are now stunned into the most complete awareness of mortality ever possessed by any creature on earth.

Thus begins man's ambivalence towards God—the sense we were made with an inherent weakness or sin—and our war on Nature, giving rise to a much greater emphasis on the acquisition of things that provide a sense of comfort, safety, love...and on cleverness in the service of survival—tool-making, hunting skills, strategic knowledge of the movement of both predator and prey, knowledge of the dangerous vicissitudes of Nature/God. These, in turn, extend the kinds of physical and meteorological environments within which human life can be endured. Long before Andrew Grove of Intel fame is so much as a glint in his mother's eye, there is the imprinted behavioral pattern with a repetitive central message, "only the paranoid survive." This may well encompass a seemingly permanent shift among males of the species to favoring the left-brain functions over the right. We might go even further and say there's a reasonable probability that cataclysmic experience was a significant catalyst in each new enlargement of brain size in our hominid ancestors since before Lucy, gradually developing the "new brain" or neocortex as it exists in our skulls today. No less than renowned neurologist Dr. Antonio Damasio has written that he regards pain "as one of the main determinants of the course of biological and cultural evolution..."[25]

This process also makes sense of the prejudice we display

towards the older, deeper brain structures that account for emotional processing. It explains the illusion of "mind over matter." Mind *is* matter and energy, of course, but the element of truth at the heart of the falsehood is that the cataclysms upon cataclysms greatly dampen the conscious influence of the central brain. With our functioning settling more into the gray matter of the neocortex, particularly the analytic left side, our actual experience of our bodies and our feelings is reduced. There is an increasing contempt for the frailty of the body, the essence of "matter." Thought becomes far less informed by feeling.

Millennia before Adam Smith will equate time with money, the ticking is heard in every tissue. Pain gives birth to Time and Time is pain. Our very blood cries out for it to end. Our minds try to outrun it. When Jasper and his people previously existed in a state close to Eden, they had little need for anything akin to Time other than the spare, useful elegance of rising and setting moons and suns, the slow, graceful pirouettes of seasons. Even if such harmony was relatively short-lived, still, it was real, as real as the timeless experience of their distant descendants, Twenty-First Century children, who delight in a meandering exploration of the world until they are cast out of their own Eden with the latest version of the Jor-El information download stuck in their mental gullets like a force-fed apple—the most recent official update of Truth, Justice and The American Way. The alarm that first rings in Jasper's mind is amplified across the ages till today's child hears voices shouting, "Do! Do! Get! Get! Run! Run! Time is money!"

So, we see that the tendency to conceive of or long for superhuman, godlike abilities to transcend the frailties of flesh has its birth tens of thousands, even millions of years ago. Same for the illusion that mind or self or even soul is a separate entity, not bound by the physical.

Certainly, this process unfolds with differing degrees of intensity dependent on a host of variables but, by and large, with each new generation facing its own round of natural challenges, the process is furthered and consolidated. To whatever extent the capacity for feeling is permanently damaged, "overwhelmed," "shut down" or "disconnected," entire personality structures change within a group or clan. Anger becomes a vaunted male trait due to its ability to mobilize action against danger. There is an increased emphasis on the development of persistence, determination, staying busy, figuring things out. More of such individuals are raised by parents, especially fathers, who are now possessed of conviction on a cellular level that constant preparedness and hard work are the keys to survival. Entire ways of being change. Birth used to be a quick (an hour or two of labor), *tolerably* painful experience for both mother and child. Now, with the imprint of stress in the female body, it becomes longer, more painful, traumatic. A self-diminishing cycle is established. Mother and child are less profoundly bonded. For all the cooing and cuddling that still exists, a kind of bigotry sets in against babies. They are not really human yet. They don't really feel or remember. They're basically one dimensional bundles of need, without personhood, without any valid center of experience within them, without any inherent God or Nature-given developmental genius that can be trusted to evolve into upright adults. They are mere blobs requiring the powerful sculpting hands of their elders. This leads to the shortened duration and a diminishing of the quality of breast-feeding and the reduction of all its attendant bonding, which, in turn, refuels the process from the beginning by creating individuals with a reduced capacity for affection. Less bonding yields less bonding between parents and children, between mates, between members of the entire group. The downward spiral continues. It is millennia before the creation of our contemporary workplace, yet the seeds of uptightness over touching are already being sown. The entire spectrum of child-rearing, spousal relationships, general kinships and the clan's attitude towards other clans—all are changing. These shifts are most frequently subtle but from time to time, they are overt and dramatic.

In the midst of all this, the frequency, content and intensity of dreams and the very sense of self are altered. New customs, rules and rituals arise. In the male culture, softness and tears are denigrated, kryptonite to those who must be strong, who don't want to be reminded of the past. Rites of passage into manhood that involve self-wounding, extreme physical tests, proofs of worthiness to belong among the survivors—all become part of clans' attempts to practice, prepare, prove equal to the inevitable assaults on its existence. Strong, even fierce, single-minded leadership is born, further propelling the process of numbing through tyranny and war.

Many of those who survive these varied cyclones of Nature and man do not respond with the same level of adaptive disconnection. Some have slightly stronger constitutions. More of their incipient sensory gifts survive. Others are weaker. Their nervous systems are exhausted, depleted, tilted in some other way. They have less energy, less ability to figure it all out. Individuals in the clan who were good at finding plants to help heal physical wounds now search harder and farther afield for flowers, roots, bark, mushrooms, seeds that will heal the pain inside, the pain that cannot be seen. Cults develop around the mysterious inner voyages triggered by certain magical plants, imagistic journeys in which the old, unprocessed cataclysms come to life, but disguised by stories and symbols. Some individuals begin to eat compulsively. Others crave affection and protection from the stronger ones and are willing to do what they say. Followers are born.

A repetition compulsion is set in motion, championed by leaders. Focus. Learn. Work. Fight. Focus. Learn. Work. Fight. Focus. Learn. Work. Fight. The physical drive to stay a step ahead of disaster is more and more broadly imprinted into the mind. The growth and domination of the new brain is no longer in doubt. Feeling is still there, but under wraps, a shadow of its original form. The higher velocity of thought takes over—speed over depth, for in speed we have the illusion of whizzing ahead of pain. Across the span of decades, centuries, and millennia, the trajectory, the form, the very content of our humanness has changed.

We may try to imagine years free of natural disasters, but just looking at the events of the last two decades of the Twentieth Century, and limiting ourselves to the state of California, we see earthquakes, floods, droughts, fires and battles with natural pests that threaten various parts of the food supply. Even if we allow that our ancestors had occasional periods of relative natural calm, for the most part, there is an entrenchment of desensitization. Little by little. Life by life. It is not the "sins of the fathers" visited upon the sons, but rather *the wounds and numbness of the fathers visited upon the sons*. We started out as the planet's most brilliant feelers, but by now we are tough little guys in tights dreaming of powers that transcend our flesh-bound capabilities. Love, the most instructive feeling of which we are capable, love that would move us to create safety and nurturance around us, build bonds across families, tribes and nations, engender a sacred appreciation of the beauty of our world, love has been diminished.

Why do we appear to have our own special world-leading brand of this affliction in America? Remember that we're a nation of immigrants, marked deeply by that particular cataclysmic voyage—the escape from bigotry, tyranny, persecution, famine. In wave after wave, we were the Have-nots doggedly determined that if we survived, we would become the Have's. We would show those bastards. We would hack a better destiny from the wilderness. We would rip it from the arms of those who stood in our way, no matter how long they'd been here in the New World or how long they'd ruled the Old World. No matter what. We'd stand on our own, on our own land, in our own business in our own kind of freedom and scream at the heavens, "I'll take my share of life!"

The terrible irony is that the very ability to go into a form of shock, to shut feelings away beneath the rage of determination, *that trick of the mind which served our survival* way back in Jasper's time or in the Seventeenth Century or during The Great Depression or in the midst of World War II, or in the struggle of millions of middle-class Americans up the so-called ladder of success *now threatens our survival*. We've internalized the cataclysms of nature that dogged us. Across the span of history, through rising and falling empires, war, tyranny, enslavement, man-made pestilence, destruction of entire species and the degradation of the environment, we have savaged each other in ways no other species has ever been known to do. *We* have become the volcano.

Contemplating all this, we can accurately say that the degree to which we have placed ourselves in danger on this planet is in direct proportion to the degree to which we are still, just like Kal-El, children of the cataclysm, soldiers of numbness, determinedly fending off Nature and each other from our fortresses of solitude, unaware of the trauma that yields our achievements and, most notably, unaware of our original essence as brilliant feelers.

Syndrome Physiology

Continuous, high velocity functioning, even in the service of a noble cause, is dangerous precisely because of its double threat of *narrow focus and the illusion of invulnerability.* A capacity for such speed is only desirable in situations in which our survival is *genuinely* threatened, as Jasper's was. It's an appropriate and necessary response to such dire circumstances. Nature gifted us with it for that precise reason. It's a life-saver, not a life style.

Physiologically we are blessed with an extraordinarily elegant two part nervous system for a reason. The sympathetic and parasympathetic neural webs within us are meant to work in tandem and equilibrium.

The sympathetic system activates us to do, to achieve. We're in sympathetic mode when we're hard at work, processing high volumes of information, doing, doing, doing, flying around like a superman. The ultimate amped sympathetic state is fight or flight, war or escape. Don't be confused by the language. The more deeply we're in sympathetic nervous function, the less likely we are to actually be sympathetic to another human being. Heavy-weight prize fighters—not a lot of sympathy but a whole lot of sympathetic function. Forty flights on the Stairmaster, endorphins pumping through your system. You may be "high" but you're not going to easily access authentic sympathy or caring. Filling yourself full of caffeine or any other kind of stimulant, natural or man-made, so you can push through the "after lunch slows" or keep going and going into the evening to finish that project—a whole lot of sympath, not much feeling. In the sympathetic mode, our heart rate and blood pressure increase, and our muscles get active. Jaws, shoulders, neck, eye, lower back—all tighten. We also mess up the armpits of those nicely starched white shirts even when we're engaged principally in mental work because sympathetic functioning was originally designed as a physical activator so we could get the hell out of Dodge. Our feet, hands and noses may get cold. We pee a lot, talk loud, sometimes get that "cotton mouth" dryness, feel stressed, anxious, impatient, angry and driven because we *are*. Those neurotransmitters and hormones are telling us something's amiss and we need to push hard.

It's essential we keep in mind that intensive sympathetic function was designed into us by evolution to serve us in spurts of *short duration*. The adrenal hormones we referred to earlier give us a burst of energy by breaking down a form of sugar in the liver and combusting it like a turbo-charger. This explains the experience of extraordinary strength and endurance Jasper and his descendants demonstrated in their horrible crisis. If

81

however, the liver's fuel is used up but the stress is sustained, these hormones begin to metabolize vital connective tissue and protein itself. The extreme example is the threat of starvation in which, having utilized all the stored energy the liver has to offer, the glutocorticoids go on to metabolize muscle. *The body literally eats itself in a last-ditch effort to survive.*

That's the extreme case. But there is much damage done to our bodies short of that horrendous experience. Dr. Dennis Charney, head of psychiatry at the VA hospital in West Haven, Connecticut, has been studying changes in brain function in people severely traumatized decades ago, such as veterans of the Viet Nam War. He states emphatically, "Severe stress can change the way your brain functions biologically." But, he notes, lesser shocks also impact structures and processes in the brain.

The idea that some people thrive under sustained stress and perform better is wholly unsupported by science. "Nobody can thrive when the body keeps secreting cortisol and adrenaline...these hormones function to break down tissue. Extended release of them leads to disease."[26] The delusion of high performance under this level of stress results, in part, from the fact *that these hormones impede our capacity for reasoned feeling.* They support the narrowing of our mental processes down to the immediate challenges before us. They're like a cocaine high—bringing a false sense of well-being and competency. Thus the short-term thinking and analytical biases of so much of the business world, to the exclusion of long-term, big picture thinking. So, sure, we think we're cranking, turning out volumes of work, fattening up the bottom line when, in reality, we may be slowly signing our own death certificate and undermining the company's long-term vitality.[27]

Our sympathetic function is running amok when we habitually respond to situations as if they're crucial, a matter of life and death, when in fact, they're far from it. When a business leader stands up before his people and declares "war" on the competition, he has unwittingly chosen *the syndrome* and elevated a life-saver to the life style of choice.

The parasympathetic system is the counter-balance. It is the essence of relaxation and restoration. We "return to our center". We grow calm, regain perspective, open our hearts to genuine bonding. At first glance, we might think that couching it with a bag of chips in front of the TV on Superbowl Sunday is a parasympathetic state, but let's not get confused. To the degree that we get caught up in the game emotionally, we're in sympath. Our heart rate goes up. We sweat. Our guts get tight, as if *we* were in the game, as if the game *really* matters to our lives. No, the parasympathetic state is unmistakably different. No tight gut here. No kinked necks and backs. When you're sitting across the room gazing lovingly at your kids or spouse, you're in parasympathetic mode. Your heart rate and blood pressure both drop. Your extremities are warmer, as is your voice. There's no agenda directing what you should see, think or do so you're much more likely to see "the Big Picture". You're wide open, reflective, meditative, philosophical, capable of real caring and its ensemble of "grooming" behaviors. Your body literally restores and heals itself—anabolic metabolism changing nutrients into tissue. It is an energy-conserving state compared to sympathetic functioning.

With such profound truth in the very substance of our bodies, to dismiss discussions of how to lead a balanced life as "New Age psychobabble" is a triumph of cynicism over science, particularly in light of the work done by Dr. Antonio Damasio. Damasio has fairly banished any doubt that body and mind are one and feeling is essential to effective selfhood.[28] Clearly, the sympathetic and parasympathetic systems comprise a larger system, a gift from Creation designed to maintain balance within us. One is not preferable to the other as a way of life. One is only preferable to the other for a given set of circumstances. To be fundamentally stuck in one for a sustained period represents an imbalance.

One of my own personal experiences with *the superman syndrome* provides common sense proof of how the mythic message and its underlying science connect right into the mundane. When I was thirty-seven, I became a sales manager in a Ford dealership under a very talented, absolute raging bull of a sympath. I relished the opportunity to learn from him and to wield creative power to make our store a better place. If you've never worked in an environment like the sales or service departments of car dealerships but have a general impression that it's extraordinarily high-pressure and crazy-making, you're basically right. There are some good stores out there, but there is a widespread belief in the business that retail unavoidably involves long hours and a lot of pressure. As a salesperson, I largely managed to stay free of the pressure. When I stepped up into management, it was another story. The rip tide pulled me under and it took me a year and half to surface. I was successful like the rest of my colleagues—to the detriment of my health, my spirit and my relationship with my son. So, I picked up my superman credentials, but ultimately came to feel the price was way too high. The price exacted from my beloved son, Benjamin, was even higher. I found employment elsewhere. Before I assumed my new management position under a much gentler soul in a Mazda store across town, I took a month off. Every single afternoon for the first two weeks of that hiatus, I napped. But these weren't cat naps. I was shot, zonked, wupped, *gone* for two to three hours each day. During the first week, I'd wake up after an hour or so thinking I should go do something. I was stunned at my exhaustion and tried to push through it. But, for the first time in years, there really was nothing I had to do, so I just fell back into a drooling sleep. I added an extra thirty to thirty-five hours over and above my normal six or seven hours a night during those two weeks. The last two weeks, I napped every two or three days but for only five to twenty minutes.

In working so hard in that dealership—long stretches of ten, twelve, even fourteen hour days, I was so caught up in *the syndrome*, my body had turned to steel and I'd lost touch with the magnitude of the damage I was doing to myself. Oh, sure, I knew it was wearing me down. I knew it wasn't the best thing for my son and for my health. I knew just enough to leave. *But I knew without truly knowing at depth.* Not until those naps parasympathetically restored me did the full ensemble of my senses start to work again.

The rather scary truth about becoming a raging, achieving materialist sympath is that we can't feel what we can't feel and we can't truly know what we can't truly feel. *The loss of sensitivity includes the loss of the ability to feel the loss.* It may sound like a tautology, but another way to say this is *that we deny that we deny because we are in denial.* This is just more confirmation that the survival mechanism of shutting down to speed up actually threatens our survival when it becomes the glorified life style of choice. We freeze out a whole host of other possibilities, just like our hard-bodied hero who chose the North Pole for his penthouse and an endless avalanche of action for his particular American Way.

Clearly, *the syndrome* subjects our bodies and minds to demands for which they really were not designed.

Joseph Chilton Pearce, author of *The Magical Child*, provides another aspect of understanding. He states that the human mind was designed for the purpose of continuous learning. He also tells us that learning does not take place in a state of anxiety or constant stress. We need a threshold of safety and security to explore freely. We need moderate stimulation—a kind of short-term, low-level stress—followed by periods of rest during which we can integrate what we've learned and prepare for the next lesson. It's no coincidence that infants and toddlers, who are busy creating an entire world of understanding from scratch, take long naps.

In contrast, when as adults we're tyrannized by immediate crises, fixes, responsibilities and performance targets, our focus narrows to a pin-point, just as did Jasper's in his crisis. Inner voices pulsate with incessant urgings: "Perform! Hurry! Figure it out now! Go for it! Survive!" Life as a "smart" bomb. But this is not smart at all. Oh, sure, we're going to learn something in this state of mind, and we're going to come up with some innovations, but they're all likely to be bounded by the same circumference. Learning rooted in authentic wisdom is far less likely to occur under such sustained stress. Wisdom calls for a much better balance between free exploration and play on the one hand and the profound sensing and restoration typical of the parasympathetic experience on the other. Driven and deprived of an adequate sense of safety, nurturance and love, *we are condemned to endlessly relearn the same lessons without ever truly mastering their meaning.*

It's hard to avoid the conclusion that there's a socially acceptable addiction going on here. What is an addiction? A compulsion that's hazardous to your life, yes? So we can be addicted to work, power, sex, athletics, politics, eating, dieting, gambling, spending, saving, the limelight, soap operas, the news, the O.J. Simpson trial, films, mystery novels, tabloids, fan magazines or videos and video games. We can be addicted to thinking. We can be addicted to speed, travel, thrills, rock 'n roll or Bach. We can be addicted to change itself. Almost *anything* can become an addiction and does when we are driven compulsively and habitually to engage in it. The deeper we enter the addiction, the more surely we deny the feelings that impel the behavior. Addiction is exactly about the suppression of pain—the cataclysm, again. How do we know when something passes from the normal into the addictive? There's the rub. Denial being an inherent component of addiction, we often don't know or "know without knowing," as I said above in my personal example. Think of the smoker who says, "I know I should quit, but I enjoy it." We "enjoy" most of the socially acceptable addictions. That's really not the point. A man who compulsively works more than seventy hours a week—and has for a long time, neglecting his children's needs at home—looked me in the eye and told me he's not a workaholic. "I just *really* like work." Guess what? Nymphomaniacs just *really* like sex. Compulsive sex just isn't the best thing to put at the center of your life, any more than is compulsive work. This man's lower right desk drawer looked like a pharmacy—three kinds of pain killers, two kinds of antacids, a variety of diet pills and stimulants.

The neurological community has done a reasonable job of describing at least some of the brain chemistry underlying the more obvious substance abuses such as alcoholism and drug addiction. It's time they looked at the "adaptive addictions," those for which legal and social cover are readily available. Nobody ever went to jail just for working too hard, but a lot of people have gone to the hospital, the psychotherapist and the grave as a direct result and, no doubt, plenty have ended up in jail indirectly, by being the neglected or abused children of workaholics. I made a number of comments and suggestions to the gentlemen mentioned above, but when he kept slipping and sliding around them, I took a chance and said calmly but very directly, "Well, good. See if you can follow this circular thought, then. You'd better keep working hard because you're going to need a lot of dough to pay for the psychotherapy your kids are going to need because you were too busy working hard to just be with them. Oh, and don't forget about the divorce lawyer. They don't come cheap." This startled him and opened up a more genuine exchange in which he told me his dad had died when he was young and as a result, he didn't think he had "the gift" for being a good father. "I can provide for them, you know, make sure they have a really nice home and clothes and toys and the best schools, but I have a real hard time hanging out with them for more than a few minutes. I just get antsy." Fortunately, this young man's boss is an exceptional person and is working very hard to reduce the hours of even his most addicted workaholics. Of course, reduced hours alone won't change his behavior. He's going to have to get serious about doing some inner work.

Supermen are rarely good with kids. After all, how often do we see our favorite Kryptonian crawling around on the floor gurgling into the happy faces of toothless tots, or swinging three year olds around in circles, or having a catch with a bunch of Fourth Graders? No, he's far too busy saving the world to be a father figure.

Of course, there are supermen whose particular version of *the syndrome* is to be a superdad. They do a brilliant imitation of fatherhood that utterly deceives their kids. It's devastatingly subtle. The kids can't feel they're suffering from a lack of attention at all because Dad is physically present. It's the quality of that presence that's tainted. It's really about his need to prove what a great parent he is. It can take years of inner work to illuminate this pattern and step out of it.

The American Way

A little article in the November 21-23, 1997 USA Today cites a 1997 study by Kentucky Fried Chicken which found that "more than 55% of workers take 15 minutes or less for lunch…and 63% skip lunch at least once a week." Two other studies are also cited, one finding that just 12% of Americans take an hour or more to eat and 39% don't even take a lunch break.

So is this it? After ten thousand years of civilization, is this the best we can offer ourselves? No time for lunch. A nervous system stuck on, "Go, go, go! Run, run, run! Fight, team, fight!" A constant re-enactment of the struggle for survival? No wonder the language of victory and defeat are so important to us. No wonder we're so willing to pay millions of dollars for competitive athletes who "win for us." We need that victory badly because there's a part of us deep down inside that feels that we may *not* make it. Consider, then the meaning of winning. When we win, we *live*. To win is also to rest at last and to have time for love. No wonder we feel relief, tears, joy, even though we had nothing to do with the actual game. All we did was turn on the TV or buy a ticket. But we've symbolically survived a near death experience. We're alive, alive, alive! When we lose, we're in a black mood. Keep the wife and kids away. We've just experienced symbolic death. We tell little kids it's not about winning, but our whole world is set up around winning, not how you play the game. They see through our lie quickly enough. Now, this might be tolerable if we kept it in the sports arena. But it also dominates the business world. We might not mind business leaders' being caught up in this survival re-enactment scenario if they didn't suck the rest of us up into it along with them. But they do, and they're getting better and better at it. Business ought to be about providing safety and nurturance for our families, an extension of hunting, gathering and shelter-building and the pleasure experienced in carrying them out effectively. But it's become loaded with all kinds of other dynamics. There's a needle in the working arm. Far too many business leaders are direct heirs of Jasper. Cataclysms are pulsating in that little cauldron in their central brains. They don't want employees who are only after a reasonable wage in order to go home and be with their families. They don't want people who suggest the company define the boundaries beyond which it will ask no more of its employees. No, there is never enough work done, never enough productivity, never enough efficiency. They want people who are hungry, single-minded, aggressive, giving "a hundred and ten percent" every day. People who live for work, take it over family as the essence of self-definition...because the company is in a battle, a struggle for survival and only the paranoid survive, only the obsessed win. It's dog eat dog, kill or be killed. It's a jungle, a war zone, the theater of engagement. We've got to have the right strategy, the right tactics and guys who can take a bullet and keep going, guys willing to throw themselves on grenades, guys who don't take no for an answer because no is losing and losing is death.

Yes, a mind *is* a terrible thing to waste. Wouldn't a highly evolved culture be one that has managed to eliminate this obsession with survival? Wouldn't it have largely sent those adrenocorticoids back to the adrenal glands where they belong most of the time? Wouldn't it exhibit a better balance between sympathetic and parasympathetic living? Wouldn't it entail a lot more "grooming" behavior and be far more devoted to the tranquil pleasures of family life, friendship, community and personal enrichment? Wouldn't it have realized by now that the very need to win makes us victims of a very limited set of possibilities that enslave us to "the struggle." Wouldn't it, in fact, judge its success by how much *less* the average person must preoccupy himself with survival than in the past?

Dr. Deming

My dear patron saint, the father of the Quality Movement, Dr. W. Edwards Deming, must be spinning in his grave. He was such an advocate of joy in work. He often pounded his fist on the dais during his famed four-day workshop, declaring, "We've crushed the individual!" He tried to teach us to see the employee as our internal customer, a fellow stakeholder in the destiny of the organization. In the eighth of his Fourteen Points, he exhorted businesses to "Drive out fear" to liberate the creative spirit of all workers. Everything in his work tells us he would be deeply disappointed to learn that a prominent business leader such as Andrew Grove would extol the benefits of fear in maintaining competitiveness, notwithstanding the "egalitarian culture" of Intel and Grove's own poignant and compelling personal story. *Egalitarianism in the service of fear is no virtue.* Deming would likely send up a cry over our using the intensity of the global economy as an excuse to run scared. He saw many downsides to competition, thought it was over-rated as a way to create high quality products and services that would truly serve mankind's needs. Optimization of a system would do better. It would enable us to solve problems once and for all, with the best possible outcome for humanity. "Win, win. Why would we have it any other way?" Deming asked repeatedly of his students. In fact, competition and optimization are near polar opposites, the first driven by fear and rage, the second by trust and love.

It is a bitter irony, then, that many of the dynamics of the worldwide economy are, to a significant degree, a direct result of the assistance Deming gave the Japanese in the Fifties and the gradual dissemination of his methods in subsequent decades. There are bloodless taskmasters hiding today within Continuous Improvement philosophy and its bastard child, Reengineering. Their incessant underlying chant is, "Nothing is ever good enough. Satisfaction is for sissies. Confidence is for fools." We are prisoners in a delivery room where the doctors and nurses keep yelling, "Push! Push! Push!" but the baby—the good life, the true American Dream—is never born. More Raging Sympath Songs.

Another pungent irony: Deming believed in creating "jobs and more jobs" yet so many of the self-professed practitioners of his methods or their spinoffs have slashed and burned tens of thousands of jobs cutting into the very heart muscle of their companies even as they've invented new euphemisms to justify their actions. The recession of the early Nineties led to the "legitimization" of these methods and the canonization of fear as we discovered across our land that neither twenty years of loyalty nor multiple college degrees could protect us from being kicked out high windows. The operative philosophy became "the scared society is the productive society." Dr. Deming thought we could do better. At the core of his method was a faith that we can best provide for our material needs by attending first and foremost to our needs for safety, nurturance and love in a world beyond fear and conventional control concepts, a world in which individual joy and the good of the community were mutually supportive. Perhaps he believed in us more than we currently believe in ourselves. Given his great vision and contribution, I suggest we need to allow for the possibility that he knew something we have yet to know.

But before we consider what that might have been, we must make one more stop in our interpretive journey.

Chapter Six

Endangered Nation, Endangered Species

> *"Through the midnight streets of Babylon...*
> *we race by barefoot, holding tight*
> *our candles, trying to shield*
> *the shivering flames, crying,*
> *'Sleepers Awake!'"*

--Denise Levertov

It's now time for us to take a long, deep look at what may well be the darkest of all the messages emanating from Kal-El's tale. Without a full awakening to this bruising truth, our determination and ardor will not likely be sufficient to bring about the personal, professional and social transformations called for to protect and nurture the essence of the American Dream.

The catastrophe of Krypton is made inevitable by the materialist arrogance of its leaders. Once again, we intend the word "materialist" to mean that for all their brilliance about the empirical, measurable, material world, the Kryptonians are incapable of acknowledging trouble in the depths, at the core of things, at the heart of the matter where life does not yield readily to logic but must be felt, intuited in leaps of faith. This is consistent with our observation that when the adult Kal-El assumes his supermanly role in Metropolis years after the explosion of his home planet, his visionary capacities are bounded by material realities as well. He sees through most physical walls but not through the walls of the human heart to its essence—a limitation readily acknowledged by our own workshop participants as common among contemporary business leaders. Their vision is bounded by the facts and figures, the "to do's," the immediate tactical and strategic challenges. Matters of the heart are often either denigrated as "warm, fuzzy, touchy, feely soft stuff" or dismissed as just not business-appropriate.

Arrogance and its foundation of emotional numbness lead to the destruction of an entire world. The lesson here seems general and clear enough to require no further comment. Yet, there is a frighteningly explicit one folded into it. All of Krypton and its beings are incinerated, except for a single individual—a child.[29] A lone child out of billions. Honoring the tendency of mythic material toward inter-related meanings, we can interpret this on two levels simultaneously with barely a stretch of our imaginations. The raging materialist *within each of us as individuals* endangers all the other aspects of our selfhood, especially the inner child with its purity and innocence. At the same time, we can hear a warning that the raging materialists *among us in our society* are endangering everyone, yes, but most especially our children whose purity and innocence represent our best hope for survival and for realizing our ancestors' dream that we might develop into a community of genuine enlightenment. We see the threat further amplified in the fact that despite his being physically saved, something has been lost in Kal-El. The immigrant experience which is so understandably focused on material action, accomplishment and acquisition carries the tainted seeds of its own demise. He cannot avoid growing up to be the son of his original culture—a person in whom innocence and purity are both flattened and over-simplified—innocence in the buffoonery of Clark's ineptitude and purity in the absolutism of Superman's unquestioning devotion to Truth, Justice and The American Way. The combination of charade and savior keep him so busy he has no time for anything that remotely resembles an intimate relationship with anyone, especially the newest, most fragile members of Metropolis.

In sum, the troubling message at the core of the myth is this: the qualities of the child are at risk in America, within us and among us.

If such an interpretation appears to over-endow a story created in 1938 with extraordinary foresight, remember that...

a) its life has been continuously extended for sixty years by numerous contributors,

b) each of these co-authors has as rightful a claim as anyone else on the planet during any era to being the bearer of universal meanings,

c) by the time the first Superman film came out in 1978 the socio-economic stage was already well set in our country for the transition from an industry-driven to an information-driven high speed society with a host of unintended consequences and

d) warnings of the dangers of arrogant materialism are far from new, harking back to man's earliest literature of which many passages of the Bible are emblematic—not the least of which is Jesus' rage over the money lenders in the temple courtyard.

So, this is an old teaching with extraordinary pedigree resurfacing through what began as a comic book and evolved to iconic status. A society that does not raise its children well risks extinction for they grow up to be out of touch with the deep force that can continuously rejuvenate its vitality. Why does this ancient theme keep visiting us out of our own unconscious creativity? Because after ten thousand years of civilization, we have yet to master its truth. What *is* new today in our time is the specific risk factor we face—the pervasive deification of speed. We cannot rush into the world, deciding, doing, getting, leaving our offspring orphaned to the dubious value of virtual embrace in a silicon Fortress of Solitude and still survive as the nation which we have long believed ourselves to be. To ignore this is to put ourselves in extreme peril, for across the land the news speaks loudly of the danger, confirming what most of us already know on a gut level. Here are some of the bellwether facts

- A study by the Families and Work Institute revealed that seventy percent of American parents feel they don't spend enough time with their kids.[30] However, this inquiry focused on salaried and hourly workers. If it had included the millions of people who work exclusively, or in significant measure, on commission, as well as the self-employed and thirty to forty million managers and professionals in our economy, do you think the percentage would have been higher or lower? Every group to which I've posed this question has responded with near unanimity that it would clearly be higher. In fact, more than *ninety-five percent* of those who attend our four and a half-day leadership workshop (largely entrepreneurs, professionals, managers and commissioned technicians and salespeople) tell us neither they nor the people of their primary relationships—spouse or life partner and children—feel they spend enough quality time together. What's more, as far as I can tell, nobody has done a meaningful survey of our *children* on this question. The very absence of such a study demonstrates the breadth of our blindness. After all our talk about taking care of our customers, we don't seem to have realized that a society's *ultimate* customer is its newborns.

- Between 1960 and 1986, the time white parents spent with their kids fell by ten hours a week. In the case of black parents, it fell even more—twelve hours a week.[31] Multiply these out and what you have is about 43 fewer hours in white families and 51 in black families (calculated by simply multiplying 4.3 weeks in a month by the respective weekly numbers). *Forty-three to fifty-one hours a month less with the kids.* This study did *not* take into account The Distraction Factor—the amount of time parents spend with their offspring physically present but mentally and emotionally absent (those unmeasured, uncompensated extra hours of work). What's more, these statistics are well over a decade old. How much faster is *your* life moving today than it was in 1986? A more recent study by the Families and Work Institute found that between 1977 and 1997 the average workweek jumped from forty-three to forty-seven hours (again, only among salaried people working twenty hours or more a week...managers, entrepreneurs and the self-employed were not measured) *and the percentage working fifty or more hours a week jumped from twenty-four to thirty-seven.*[32] Who has time for parenting?

- A 1997 survey by Steelcase found that 73% of people in offices of one hundred or more do some weekend work—a not surprising indicator, but still not an in depth reading.[33]

- Here are two sets of numbers that give us some insight into the magnitude of The Distraction Factor. First, the mean hours of job-related work done at home has risen from 6 hours a week in 1991 to 8.9 hours a week in 1997.[34] Second, Americans are spending upwards of 160 hours a year more on the job now than forty years ago.[35] Think of it—an extra month a year at work!

- Approximately 12% of married women with children of six years or younger had paying jobs in 1950. *By 1994, this figure was pushing 62%.*[36]

- In 1980, single-parent families represented 22% of all American families. By 1998, that figure had jumped to 27% and if we add in the 4% who live with neither parent, we see 31% of our children being raised outside the traditional family model.[37]

- According to a recent study completed by the National Marriage Project at Rutgers University, 33 % of high school girls believed it worthwhile to have a child out of wedlock in 1976 compared to 53% in 1995—*an increase of 60%.* As primary causal factors, the study gives the growing economic independence of women and the increase in the number of children of divorce who have an understandably skeptical attitude towards the prospects of marriage.[38]

- Approximately fifteen million school-age children are left to fend for themselves on the streets or alone at home on any given weekday afternoon in America.[39]

- In the last year alone, the average screen time—both TV and computers—for two to seventeen year old Americans has risen from 4.1 to 4.4 hours *per day.*[40] A study of 3000 children ages 2 to 18 by the Kaiser Family Foundation found that this number rose to 5.9 hours a day when listening to music was factored in. Of course, music is wonderful, as *can be* surfing the Web or watching TV, but the study found that most of that 5.9 hours daily is spent alone, in a bedroom *without parental involvement.*[41] Compare this total of more than 41 hours a week to the 17 hours a week parents are directly involved with their kids (again, no accounting for The Distraction Factor) and you can stop reading right now and head for your kid's room![42]

- Psychologists at the National Institute of Healthcare Research found, not surprisingly, that the level of a father's involvement significantly impacts his children's cognitive growth, including perception, judgment and memory. Involved fathers create stimulation that causes faster movement through developmental stages.[43]

- The Journal of the American Medical Association tells us "the prevalence of psychotropic medication treatment for children and adolescents with emotional and behavioral disorders has significantly increased in the United States during the last few decades, particularly in the last 15 years. Specifically, the 5 through 14-year-old age group has experienced a great increase in stimulant treatment for attention-deficit/hyperactivity disorder (ADHD), and the 15 through 19-year-old age group has had sizable increases in the use of antidepressant medications." JAMA also states in the same report that "psychotropic medications prescribed for *preschoolers* increased dramatically between 1991 and 1995." What's going on here?[44]

- Even in the midst of the biggest economic expansion in our time, the same percentage of American children live in poverty today as did in 1980—one fifth, approximately *13.5 million*.[45]

- 11.3 million kids eighteen and under have *no health insurance*, the highest number ever reported by the Census Bureau...and since 1989, kids have lost private health coverage at double the rate of adults. In 1996 alone, 70% of all Americans who became uninsured were children.[46]

- While politicians celebrate the drop in the welfare rolls, the first comprehensive study of the effects of welfare reform on young children raises serious questions about the long-term effects of the vaunted "welfare to work" legislation. Researchers at UC Berkeley, Yale and Equal Rights Advocates found that children of these new working parents were generally being placed in low-quality child care settings that were frequently unclean and relied heavily on television and videos to occupy their time.[47]

- The number of people employed as child care workers dropped 36% between 1983 and 1997 (from 408,000 to 260,000) while the number of hairdressers and cosmetologists rose by 20% (from 622,000 to 748,000).[48] The most recent figures provided by the Statistical Abstract give us a pretty good indication of why there are so few child care workers. Child care workers earn an average of about $11,800 a year and largely receive no benefits. The Children's Defense Fund points out that hairdressers and manicurists are required to attend 1,500 hours of training at an accredited school in order to get a license, yet 39 states have absolutely no early childhood training requirements for people who set up child care programs in their homes.[49] In spite of this, full-time child care easily costs parents between $4,000 and $10,000 a year—the equivalent of annual tuition at a lot of colleges and universities. One out of three families with young children earns less than $25,000 a year. Nationally, only 1 in 10 low-income children who need financial help for child care are receiving it.[50] Consider the logic of this. We now know beyond a shadow of a doubt that far more learning takes place during our children's earliest years than, say, between the ages of eighteen and twenty-two. Most importantly, this is the time of great vulnerability, when the basic operating system of character is being encoded. Yet, we pay child care workers a small fraction of what we pay college professors, not that professors don't deserve to be well compensated. Also, not withstanding the admirable commitment of MicroStrategy's CEO, Michael Saylor, to invest $100 million for the launch of an Ivy League-quality Internet university that will make a free college education available to everyone on the planet, we should remember the wise old adage, "An ounce of prevention is worth a pound of cure." That same $100 million would have a far greater salutary impact on our culture if invested in the first five years of our children's lives. We ought to be lavishing on them the most talented, loving, aware and stimulating caregivers we can find in our society. These professionals should be as respected as doctors. They ought to earn an honorable wage. They ought to be caring for the nation's children in state of the art facilities. The reality, however, is as shockingly dismal as the compensation. The most recent broad study of the quality of day-care facilities conducted jointly by four universities concluded 15% were excellent, 70% were "barely adequate" and 15% were horrible. "Children in that vast middle category were physically safe but received scant or inconsistent emotional support and little intellectual stimulation."[51]

- How important is it that only 15% of these facilities are excellent? In the first study to follow children from infancy to age twenty-one, researchers conducting The Abecedarian Project at the Frank Porter Graham Child Development Center in Chapel Hill, North Carolina funded by the U.S. Department of Education and the University of North Carolina found that children in high quality daycare settings had a sustained developmental edge over those less fortunate. They were better in reading and math, had higher IQ's, were about half as likely to need "special ed," about half as likely to repeat

101

a grade, were less likely to become teenage parents and were more than twice as likely to attend a four year college than the control group.[52]

- A further deeply vexing comment comes from Lola Nash, a Yale University lecturer in education with thirty years of experience in early childhood programs who told *Child* magazine in November of 1998 she's seen a "dramatic increase" in the level of aggressive behavior by children in day-care over the past decade. "All the programs I work with are struggling to develop policies to handle it," she said.

- We can't leave the topic of day-care without addressing the extraordinary delusional impact wrought by an article which appeared on the front page of The Washington Post on March 1, 1999 claiming that a comprehensive, long-term study showed no negative developmental consequences from day-care. Various incarnations of the article appeared around the world. The argument seemed to be settled. Moms and Dads can jump into the workplace without any guilt or fear about leaving little Johnny or Janie with other folks for forty to fifty hours a week. However, as Tom Zoellner pointed out in his incisive article, Day Care!, for *Men's Health* in September of 1999, much of the emotional testing of the children was based on interviews with the mothers but the mothers were hardly a good cross-section of America's moms. The average family income in the sample was $15,000 to $24,000 a year, well below the national average. Half of the sample belonged to a minority group, further skewing the applicability. The median IQ of the mothers interviewed was in the low to mid-80's, whereas 100 is average. The mothers were younger than the national average when they gave birth to their children. What's more, the author of the study herself never talked to any of the mothers, never talked to any of the children and never visited a single day-care center in connection with the study. But none of this should surprise us, really. How could anyone make a credible argument for the dispensability of parenting? Everything we know from observing higher primates as well as ourselves, not to mention the common sense insistence of our hearts, tells us that attentive, consistent, loving parenting is one of Nature's non-negotiables for our long-term survival.

- Most of us seem to get the point, with or without reliable data. Workplace absenteeism rose 25% from 1997 to 1998, with an attendant 32% rise in costs, according to CCH, a human resources and employment law consulting company. The number one cause was family need. The cost numbers alone ought to be sufficient to get the attention of every employer in the land.

- Youth depression is on the rise, hitting kids across socioeconomic lines at younger ages than ever before and kids with depression and/or anxiety are three to four times more likely to develop drug or alcohol abuse problems in their mid-20's. Suicide rates for U.S. children and teens quadrupled between 1950 and 1995.[53]

- Johns Hopkins University pediatrician Dr. Barbara Howard reports that a quarter of her young patients are exhibiting stress-related problems and this proportion is on the rise. Georgia Witkin of Mount Sinai Medical School, based on her own surveys, adds that parents are frequently wrong about what causes stress in their children's lives. Parents tend to think friendship issues are at the heart of the matter, but in reality, kids' biggest concerns are "that the parents are going to be sick, or angry, or they're going to divorce."[54] This is one more piece of evidence of how delicate is the sense of

103

safety—a fragility born of living at speed, not at depth.

- There was an 18% increase in child abuse between 1990 and 1996 in the U.S, and a more than fourfold increase in the number of children seriously injured through abuse and neglect.[55] It also appears to be a pretty safe bet these statistics don't come close to representing the whole truth. There is a ample reason to believe, based on research done in the 1980's, that our methodology for measuring abuse by white middle-class and upper-class families is seriously flawed and consequently reinforces a social blindness to the depth and breadth of damage being done to America's children.[56]

- Another recent study tells us "baby boomers are seriously underestimating the presence of (illicit) drugs in their children's lives. Turning to legal drugs, in an October 1998 study, The Center for Disease Control reported a 73% rise in habitual daily smoking among youths between 1988 and 1996. The Center further reports childhood obesity has risen dramatically since the 1980's. Only *one percent* of our children eat a healthy diet day to day.[57]

- When we consider all this, it should not surprise us to discover that 40% of 4th Graders' reading skills are too poor to keep up with grade level[58] or that The Third International Mathematics and Science Study completed in mid-1998 showed US students rank *30th* among 40 countries.

- In an extensive survey of more than 20,000 young people by the non-profit Josephson Institute for Ethics, seventy percent of high school students admitted cheating on an exam within the last year.

We could pile on more studies and stats, but this ought to suffice to connect the basic dots. Of course, you may be able to legitimately quibble with a study here or there, just as you can offer studies that seem to offer good news. However, frankly, it's tough to find any that aren't mixed with bad news. Case in point: headlines recently trumpeted a drop in illicit drug use among youths ages 12-17—from 11.4% in 1997 to 9.9% in 1998 (the survey asked if they'd used illicit drugs during the previous thirty days). However, there was no change over ten years in the percentages of Americans age 12 or older in alcohol use, binge drinking and heavy drinking. The smoking rate among 18-25 year olds increased a full percentage point between 1997 and 1998.[59] In my own beloved town of San Luis Obispo, California, police and hospital personnel have recently noticed a significant increase in binge drinking among junior high school kids.[60] So, while a diminishing of any form of self-abuse is welcome, it's a mockery when government officials claim we're "turning the corner" with our youth, especially considering the fact that far more individuals die and far more lives are damaged every year by the socially and legally acceptable chemicals in alcohol and cigarettes.

In light of the breadth of information and common experience available to us, it is impossible to avoid the conclusion that the Superman myth is onto something. We have become a nation too fixated on material reality to see the depth and breadth of love *necessary to raise a fully-realized human being.* Such blindness would constitute cruel behavior at any time in history. Its impact is magnified today, given the unprecedented rate of change in our culture and the accompanying absence of firmly rooted, broadly practiced, consistently comforting traditions and myths that might guide children. As we create a world that has *never* existed before on this planet, they need safety, nurturance and love more than at any peaceful time in history. We ought to be expanding our understanding of what great parenting looks like. Instead, the increasing velocity of *the superman syndrome* is perpetrating a widespread felony. Our kids are being robbed of their parents and their childhood.

Producing dozens of different symptoms, the virus of child neglect is sweeping across the country, not just the headline grabbing kind in which poor kids are discovered locked up without food for days in squalid apartments or babies are left to die in dumpsters. Not even the kind that leads school kids to shoot their classmates. This tragedy is half-hidden beneath the headlines and research projects. It's far more pervasive than the grotesque stories increasingly favored by the press. We're referring to the kind of middle-class, upper-middle and upper class neglect embodied in a manager who, after stating he worked about sixty-five hours a week, actually said to me of his wife of eleven years and his two children, "They don't know me." We're talking about people such as a general manager of an establishment in the Southeast who described his relationship with his five year old son as "fast becoming another five-minute task on an endless 'to do' list." Others have tried to rationalize the deprivation they're visiting on their kids and themselves by becoming "event" or weekend moms and dads. But parenting is about much more than running kids to soccer or attending the dance recital or the open house at school, about much more than paying someone to put on a great birthday party with clowns and magicians, about much more than taking them to Disneyland or Magic Mountain on the weekend, even about much more than a few family dinners a week or asking about their day or helping them with a math problem or making it home in time to read to them for fifteen minutes and give them a kiss every night. It's about *a lot* of presence. It's about consistent mental and emotional availability. It's about moving at depth, not at speed-- capeless, maskless, human, well within reach.

One of our true sages, pediatrician Dr. T. Berry Brazelton, has vigorously waved the yellow caution flag before us recently, stating, "I just think our country is in deep, deep trouble…what our culture is lacking…is any attention to families early on so they can in turn pay attention to their kids."[61] He was one of the first to warn us of the dangers when a mother tries to be "supermom," dividing attentions between a child and a career and, in his great wisdom, pointed out that a working couple with one small child actually has five careers in its household—the relationship each has with the child, the relationship each has with his/her workplace and the relationship (if there's time!) they have with each other.[62]

Dr. Deming taught us in the third of his Fourteen Points to "build quality into the product" up front. What more precious "product" is there than our children's bodies, hearts, minds and souls during their most tender developing years? If we're not erring on the side of infusing our kids with qualitative parental companionship, we're blowing it as a society. We're jettisoning our kids off into the solitude of space.

Personal Sketch

Through my clients, I've frequently observed how quickly the pride of new parenthood and the adoration of newborns can disappear under the racing wheels of the world. I refused to let this happen with my own son. I considered it the battle of my life to wrench enough time from the world to have a joyful, deep connection with Ben. Like my colleagues, I was building a career, but unlike them, I optimized my schedule to create free time wherever possible...and it was more possible than most around me believed. To me, Benjamin was the coolest thing the universe ever produced (and still is now that he's in his twenties and a father himself.) He was my daily feast of miracles. Being with him, even in his infancy, was no chore. It was pure delight. When he became mobile, the magic multiplied a thousand fold.

Shortly after he turned three, we discovered a wonderful beach about twenty minutes from our home. It had two hundred-foot high sand dunes and miles of tide pools. For the next seven years, we commonly spent anywhere from *ten to twenty hours* a week out there hiking, exploring and learning about all aspects of the sea, the tides and the moon, the wind, the clouds and the stars…and about the free spirits of the waves—seals, dolphins, otters and whales…and about the creatures and plants in the tide pools—starfish, anemones, limpets, mussels, rock-boring clams, tube worms and jellyfish. We studied the plants of the dunes— which were edible and which not and we ate some and we did not die. We didn't even get sick! In the meadows and woods above the dunes, we encountered deer, raccoon, fox, bobcat, owls, hawks, herons and egrets, lizards, toads, gophers, rabbits, ribbon snakes and rattlers. We studied geology right there where it was real to us, found fossils, collected beautiful stones, polished them in a rock tumbler and then glued them to driftwood and shells in ways that made perfect esthetic sense to us. We regularly sat on the dunes and cliffs and watched sunsets so outrageous, photographers, poets and painters would have twisted their brains inside out to capture them, sunsets totally over the top with perfect ten-foot waves curling and crashing and pelicans diving and otters frolicking and gulls careening and colors cascading over us. The beauty was so intense, we'd have to stand up and scream…and we didn't care if anyone saw us because we were face to face with Creation.

And one night, walking back to the car, we decided that a person is just not living right if he doesn't take the time to see at least ten full sunsets a month. How does your life stack up against *that* standard?

I swear to you, we had grand adventures several times a week for years as Ben discovered the world and I rediscovered it through his eyes…but that wasn't all.

In the evenings, we did arts and crafts and adorned our house with our creations. We danced and cavorted and made up songs and talked about faraway places and the people in our lives and why Ben's mom and I were not together and what was going on in the world and who God was and what dreams meant. We decided you don't really know someone if you don't know what he dreamed last night. We read stories every single evening with few exceptions, for more than three thousand evenings.

Fighting the world for a little elbow-room was not my idea of success. I made a lot of elbow-room. We lived at depth, not at speed.

Certainly, I made mistakes. I was not the perfect father. I had my own past cataclysms to deal with, but I did not afflict my son with a poverty of my time or a deficit of my attention. I knew Ben and he knew his father. This wasn't "quality time". It was intimacy as a grand adventure.

I did not do all this with Ben out of guilt or an urge to compensate for the absence of his mom. I was driven by love. I utterly adored him. There was no better companion on earth than Ben. I also had a vision of what a lyrical childhood could be and wanted to make it real and held it as sacred above all else.

Through these years, my worldly success grew because I was clear about what was non-negotiable and what was not. I knew my mission in life was to rear this boy. There wasn't any title or trophy or trip or electronic toy I could win (yes, I won plenty of 'em) or any amount of money I could earn (I did all right) that should even be discussed in the same sentence as my fatherly enterprise.

When I share the specifics of those days with the folks who attend our leadership workshop, it's common for them to express deep regret over their lack of connection with their own kids…and with their own parents. Strong, tough, successful men from their twenties to their late sixties have broken down and wept in the full grip of these acknowledgments. One workshop participant said, "I knew I was missing out…but I deluded myself into thinking it was about the right day-care center and then, later, the right private school and music lessons and little league and clothes and computers and all that. And you know what? In his own sweet way, my kid's been trying to tell me all along he just wanted me. He just wanted me to really be with him…with no agenda, and no meeting or other obligation to run off to that would make him feel like I'd managed to squeeze him into my day." Before our workshop ended, this same individual wept in the realization that he had suffered the same deprivation of fathering he was now visiting upon his son.

This sense of deprivation is pervasive in our culture. It's simmering under the thinnest of masks. People only need a little safety and nurturance of their own to begin talking about it. Their stories have made it clear to me that, in the last analysis, we're not really suffering from time poverty in our land but a destitution of intimacy, an impoverishment of the heart.

In another workshop, I related how from the time Ben was about four and a half, we'd have great talks with him laying right on top of me, his chin in his hands, his elbows in my chest, his eyes a few inches from mine. A man in his sixties whose children are grown said, "You know what? I never did that. Not once. Dammit! I never had that kind of closeness with any of my kids. I was too busy building a business. I can't believe I missed that." After a thoughtful pause, he added, "I never even realized you could be that close to your kid…until this moment." Ironically, he was married when his children were small. I was a single dad. Far too often, married fathers allow the very presence of their wives to become the rationale for their absence. As a single father, I spent far more time with my son than my long-married father ever did with me. *In fact, I spent more active, engaged time with him than both my parents combined did with me...*and more time than parents combined spend with their kids today (remember, about 17 hours a week, according to the University of Michigan study). The general curse of single-parenthood is not in the fact of being without a spouse but in the common environment of immaturity (a huge percentage of single moms are teenagers), poverty and/or isolation. I was in a small minority. I was in my thirties. I had good learning skills, made a reasonable living and had a good support system of friends and

110

relatives. Still, throughout those years, I longed to share the joy and effort with someone who was as dedicated to Ben as I. He may have been getting a better shake than I had, but I knew there were grander possibilities. I often wondered what a human being would look like if he had *two* utterly devoted parents creating safety, nurturance and love for him right up into young adulthood.

Social Commitments

Like so many, I faced the day-care dilemma, so I know how important good caregivers are when you have no choice but to work. I was also very involved in Ben's preschool, elementary and high school experience. I saw what does and does not get provided. There's no doubt we need smaller classrooms. There's also no doubt that teachers should be paid a heck of a lot more, from preschool on up. They constitute one of our most under-appreciated and under-paid professions. Any society that's truly devoted to its kids would make both caring for them and teaching them highly honored and compensated professions. Sure, we should hook up classrooms to the Internet and, sure, guns should be harder to get and safer and, sure, our TV, film producers and video game creators should all find something much more worthwhile to depict than violence and, oh yes, we ought to have more small neighborhood police stations and, yes, we need to make quality health care available to every child in America, too. No argument. *But the absolute bottom line of any society is the quality of parenting, minute to minute, day by day.* Millions of American parents have abdicated the joy and central responsibility of being with their kids. We are losing the very capacity to imagine parenting as the richest and most noble endeavor of a lifetime—richer and more noble than being an admired athlete, scientist, businessman, artist or preacher. We rationalize new concepts of what good parenting looks like, but these are mere ghosts of the real thing. The best day-care givers, teachers, doctors and police can only put band aids on the emotional wounds of kids who are not receiving the active protection, nurturance and love they need and deserve from their parents. We're currently so caught up in *the superman syndrome*, I fear that improved day-care, smaller classrooms and better Internet will actually back-fire in the long run, providing more excuses for parents to ignore the core truth that their absence constitutes a quiet cataclysm, like the planet Krypton soundlessly exploding in space.

But in truth, we must go further. A society that genuinely serves the individual, as we boast of doing, begins long before its children are old enough for day-care. The protection, nurturing and love start before birth in the form of extraordinary prenatal care. We have made some strides in this area, but there are still millions of young mothers who lack either the awareness of its necessity or access to it.

A society dedicated to serving the individual provides the best birth possible. Yet, the birthing process is still largely controlled by men with the materialist mind of the Kryptonian elders. It's controlled as a business, bereft of its spirituality. The message to women is basically this: "You don't know how to have babies. It's a very dangerous thing. You really need us to manage the whole process. You never know what might happen." Fear. Mistrust of the natural endowments. Sure, we're God's chosen species, but our women are the only female primates that haven't a clue about birthing their young.

Consider the damage done by years of crazy practices in the delivery rooms of the nation. There's been some progress since the days of whacking upside-down babies on the butt. But more than twenty years after Frederick Leboyer published *Birth without Violence* and a decade and a half after Michel Odent published *Birth Reborn*, most babies in America are still being born in hospital-style delivery rooms. Their mothers are still delivering on their backs, a wholly unnatural position.

Astounding! The continuation of this practice, whose origins are in seventeenth century France, only underscores the domination of our life by controlling, analytical, males who may mean well but suffer from a superman-size insensitivity to the situation. If men had the babies, they'd be howling about such treatment. They'd make both Leboyer's and Odent's books mandatory reading for every health-care person and parent-to-be in America. A revolution would have already occurred. We'd have a "birthing brigade" of doctors and midwives making home births a safe and common practice. Birthing centers designed to empower women to take control of the process, such as Odent has created in France, would be available to all who preferred them.

A society genuinely committed to the flowering of individuality would make it of preeminent importance to support sustained and shameless breast-feeding of its children. What could be more natural than suckling our children? We're mammals. We're primates. Japanese Snow Monkeys breast-feed their young for two years, chimpanzees for four or five. The American Academy of Pediatrics says of breast-feeding that it is "the *ideal* method of feeding and nurturing infants"[63] promoting general health, growth, vitality of the immune system, cognitive and emotional development. According to the National Center for Health Statistics in Hyattsville, Maryland, the total percentage of American mothers who breast fed their babies "three months or more" between 1972-1974 was 62.3. By 1993-1994, the percentage had declined to 56.2—a drop of six points.[64] Interestingly, the Center only records the percentage of mothers who breast-feed for "three months or more". They have no data on how many breast-feed for up to six months, or up to a year, or beyond. The mere fact of this limited inquiry should tell us something. Given that approximately 60% of wives with children a year old or younger are in the workforce today,[65] the rise in two-earner households and the generally increased pace of American life, it's not surprising the number is declining. It *is* disturbing, however, that any period longer than three months seems to be of insufficient importance to merit the attention of our data gatherers. Humans have the longest childhood of any primate. The extended nurturing required by this would logically call for sustenance of a variety of bonding behaviors, breast-feeding being right at the top of the list. It appears that American babies are being short-changed, not only in their intake of antibodies which doctors acknowledge as superior to any formula in developing immunity to illnesses, allergies and very likely cancer. They're also being largely deprived of the fundamental lessons of intimacy that are implicit in the breast-feeding relationship—a powerful variable in the development of personalities less likely to be given to the obsessions and compulsions (legal and illegal) common to our culture.

Consider that a core element of *the superman syndrome* is an unbridled yearning for invulnerability. Consider that the Superman myth quite logically fixes the origin of this yearning in a cataclysmic experience early in life when we are most vulnerable, most endangered. Consider that a society unerringly committed to individual freedom would move mountains to assure that its newest, most fragile members would begin life free of all forms of deprivation. It would consider such an undertaking to be its highest calling, a sacred charge, the ultimate expression of its compassion for life.

There is no landmark study identifying the quality of birth, the quality and duration of breast-feeding and the quality and duration of holding as critical predictive variants in the frequency of a host of social and physical afflictions, including but not limited to learning disabilities, poor health, sleep disorders, attention and hyperactivity disorders, the full array of addictions (legal and illegal), crime, spousal and child abuse and a generally poor capacity for lasting mating relationships. Our failure to look thoroughly into this connection, is only more evidence of the power of denial and the domination of our society by *syndrome* sympaths who cannot see the forest for the trees. The failure to measure what really matters in business and in life demonstrates a perilous absence of mind.

Granted, for many of us, this is such obvious common sense, we have no need for scientific evidence. It would be a little bit like proving that the grass is growing in your front lawn in part because of April showers. But, as we've already discussed, there's a large contingency in our country with considerable influence that needs to see the numbers on everything.

It bears repeating: the society that does not raise its children well risks extinction. We are already trundling dangerously down that path.

Even if you're a coldly logical, childless CEO, you must see the devastating impact the declining quality of parenting will have on the future employment pool and, consequently, consumption. It's all connected up. Think of what it will cost you in hiring, training and turnover, not to mention lost productivity and lower capabilities for innovation. Think of how it currently impacts your taxes with increased costs in law enforcement, health care, workman's compensation, all kinds of insurance. If you want to build quality into the workforce, which is your absolute raw material, and quality into the cadres of consumers, start by raising sane, creative, responsible, whole children. The natural precursor of any form of Total Quality Management is Total Quality Parenting. *A smart businessperson would see it as a non-negotiable part of a successful business system.*

Yet, as we hear from Elizabeth Perle McKenna, career person and author of *When Work Doesn't Work Anymore*, our current working world is a place that "makes no allowance for anything to be more important than work."[66] Certainly, there are more "family-friendly" programs offered by businesses today than at any previous time in this century, but research has shown that men, in particular, tend to substantially under-utilize them, in large part because of a lack of active, visible and credible support by leadership. The unspoken message in the company culture is often, "Use at your own peril. These programs may be dangerous to your chances for advancement. Those of us who are really making it here put work above family."[67] If this is still the case in thirty years, if the whole world is moving at America's current pace, if hundreds of millions of kids around the globe are being brought into the world in far less than optimal conditions, if they're given short shrift at their mothers' breasts, if they're being hustled into day-care centers staffed by underpaid and under-qualified people, if hundreds of millions of parents are coming home too distracted and exhausted to be emotionally present to those kids, America's crisis will have become the world's crisis. We will be on the verge of a global catastrophe. We will be the latest endangered species.

The Good News

There *is* an opportunity side to this situation. As the world population expands, as more countries acquire the trappings of the American Way and get past the initial infatuation with jeans, palmtops, cell phones, the Web, cars with GPS and whatever else superworkaholics can create, the "only the paranoid survive" strategy will be revealed for what it is—the enemy of a more mature concept of business and its relationship with society. My bet is the burgeoning world population is going to become passionately concerned about one thing above all others in the coming decades. It won't be about voice-activated computers. It won't be about countries operating in the black. It won't be about the health of Social Security style programs. It won't be about the transplantation of pig organs into human bodies. It won't be about genetic engineering. It won't be about Presidential sex or who won the World Series or how the Stock Market is performing or what the average family income is. All of these concerns will have their place, of course, but not at the center of our world.

Our country, in fact, the entire world is going to be focused on one paramount thing—the day to day quality of life. Millions of people are going to be noticing the basic truth that with all the apparent progress we've made since Jasper's time, *we don't feel good.*

What sentience is left in us will cry out from our cells like a fire alarm, "We're stressed! We're moving too fast. We're depressed. We're not the fit, healthy, vital people we could and should be. Our relationships don't work. Life is tearing through us like a chain saw!" The so-called Third World may be the last to come to this realization, but it will come, nonetheless. Its people will discover one day that a hijacking has taken place, that their humanity has been ripped off by a fraudulent dream. At this moment, they're going to be looking around for guidance. They're going to start hearing whisperings from the vast open spaces in their hearts. They're going to start seeing visions of reunified families projected onto the night sky. They're going to start asking how we build societies whose people feel an untainted joy when they survey what they've created for themselves, their spouses and their beloved children.

Whoever will answer this question with the truth and a credible plan will wield enormous influence in the world.

Part Two:

The Way Out

"Imagine all the people…"

--John Lennon

Chapter Seven

The Water of Life

"And let him that is athirst come. And whosoever will, let him take the water of life freely."

--Revelations, 22:17

We're addicted to the working speed of the Information Age or caught up in enabling relationships with those who are. We're seriously under-performing as parents, having largely lost touch with the depth and breadth of the sacred endeavor of protecting, nurturing and loving our children. If we're suffering from "time poverty," our kids are suffering from "parent poverty," a destitution of intimacy and mentoring, an impoverishment of spirit in the midst of runaway prosperity. If this addiction has its roots deep in our brains and deep in our past, how are we supposed to liberate ourselves to engender a society that truly serves the individual from conception to death? What if, despite all the talk about responsibility in our culture, we've actually lost the capacity to be responsible? What if we're just too wrecked? What if the accumulated cataclysms have been too many, the glitch too big a factor, the damage too deep?

In his book, *The Craving Brain*, psychiatrist Ronald Ruden tells us that the addictive personality, with its significant imbalance of neurotransmitter secretions—high dopamine, low serotonin—literally loses its "response ability." It's not capable of responsible actions.[68] Dr. Ruden's focus in this particular work is primarily on alcohol and drug addiction. He might take a dim view of my belief that it's legitimate to use his findings to catalyze an inquiry into *the superman syndrome*. However, there has been no serious research aimed at gaining an understanding of what the play of neurotransmitters might be in the particular socially acceptable addictive behavior pattern commonly referred to as "workaholism." What accounts for the absence of responsible action to nurture and love the family? What goes on in the brain and blood of hard-driving workers across ages, genders, ethnic groups and professions and at what point does a negative impact on their life style and health become measurable? We have only a rough draft of an answer coming out of stress research. Esther Sternberg and Philip Gold at the National Institute of Mental Health have begun to understand the interplay between the stress response, the sympathetic nervous system and the immune response. Their work is fascinating, welcome and important but we need a far better picture of what physical, mental and emotional health looks like on a physiological level and how deviant from that is the state of someone possessed by *the superman syndrome*. It could be years before Science fully weighs in on this topic. We're left to ponder the question with what good sense we have.

Given Dr. Ruden's description, it's very tempting to dismiss the whole idea of free will, responsibility or accountability. In the end, history will have the last say, of course. If we continue the assault on our planet, its species and its atmosphere, we'll eventually have no choice but to conclude that we were incapable of responsible action. The glitch was an irreparable flaw in our makeup. Evolution ultimately selected us out, discarded us after a relatively brief experiment which revealed us to be ingenious and yet blind to its own obvious imperatives. At present, however, we have no choice but to resist that conclusion, for to accept it would invite anarchy. Where Science fails or fumbles, Faith must prevail as a servant of Evolution. We're not speaking of blind Faith here, not the other side of the coin from blind arrogance. This is Faith girded by the evidence among us of people who do awaken and change their lives very much for the better. Given our current state of knowledge and understanding, we may not be able to explain this without using words like "somehow" and "magic." As we shall soon see, this Faith is also supported by the Wisdom of the Ages communicated to us with clarity and power through one particular symbol in the Superman myth. But I'll state now that this is where I cast my lot—for the belief that despite all that we've had to survive and tuck away as a species, many of us are still sufficiently sentient that we feel something's amiss. The physiology of being, both conscious and unconscious, is more miraculous than we have imagined. We have an extraordinary capacity to store unprocessed pain and still maintain a necessary and sufficient ability to sense its presence and its insistent call for resolution. This doesn't assure that we can and will take responsibility, but it opens the *possibility* we might. While it's true that the less we feel, the less we feel, the converse is also true. Every time we reclaim a part of our humanity, a little more becomes available. The more we feel, the more we can feel. The mystery at the center of this dynamic is in fact essential to the entire Western idea of individuality. Without feeling—be it happiness, fear, anger, sadness, disgust or surprise—there is no real possibility of "I" and without "I" there is no authentically unique inner life and the experience of self-determined responsible action. We would be at the sole mercy of concepts such as Fate, Destiny, Karma, and whatever "appropriate" social order the powerful might attempt to impose on us as the only "right" interpretation of our place in the universe. The entire American experiment would be moot. The ultimate truth, of course, is probably neither responsibility nor determinism as an absolute but a blending of the two. Some of us are not capable of legitimately experiencing personal responsibility, but many of us still can...because of our enduring capacity to feel "I" as a viable force in our lives.

In the context of this reaffirmation of the potential for individual responsibility, it's fair to ask whether we should aim our energies towards personal restoration or action on a social, business and political level, but this, too, need not be an "either/or" proposition. It's not necessary or wise, in my view, for masses to go off to a retreat for years to "get their act together" and then return to reform the world. It makes more sense to concentrate on rejuvenating our selfhood *as* we are wrestling the working world towards sanity. Each effort tends to nourish the other, in my own experience and that of clients and friends. There is a continuous process of course-correction as we tack from the personal to the professional and back, moving slowly but surely towards optimal living.

So, we're going to look at a strategy for the inner journey in the next few chapters. In the chapters following those, we'll examine a strategy for the outer journey. However, first I want to make it absolutely clear that these should and, given the chance, do unfold simultaneously in real life. The inner and out journeys are inextricably woven together. At last, millions of us across the spectrum of the business world are being called to find the honor, honesty and courage to tear down the wall of illusion between personal and professional realms.

I also want to leave no doubt I *definitely* envision a gradual though major restructuring of society around authentic selfhood and family. Authentic selfhood is neither selfish nor selfless. It is not driven by unconscious need. It's devoid of the pretense of masks. It's characterized by a strong commitment to live with integrity, presence, realness, balance, competency, knowledge, playfulness, openness, patience, compassion, determination, courage in the service of feeling.

Certainly, a major restructuring of The American Way isn't going to be largely spearheaded by the highest level business people or elected officials. Far too many of these folks are unrepentant supermen. Some of them put on excellent representations of selfhood, but when we look closer, we see a lot of disconnection, an extraordinary lack of awareness of the wounds that drive their lives. If you're looking anywhere other than the mirror for leadership, you've missed the point. This is not to say people won't come forward to articulate and fight for this transformation. Some already are doing so. It's also not to say that there isn't a very important part to be played by others in your life, especially in the form of support groups. There definitely is. But crunch time is upon us. Every citizen in this country is challenged to take responsibility for the quality of his or her own life and the lives of his or her children. Courage in the service of the heart is being called forth. Many business owners, CEO's and mid-level managers, as well as the overwhelming majority of politicians on all levels, will have to be engaged firmly in order to shift their paradigms of what is best for them, the nation and the planet. There is no magic bullet. If this were easy, we'd have fixed it by now. The quest for such quick fixes is part of the *syndrome*. Ground will be gained little by little, person by person, day by day. Some die-hard supermen will plant themselves in the doorway or in our faces. Clarity, finesse, conviction, commitment and strength will be required to confront them effectively. One of the trickier challenges will be to avoid getting so swept up in the idea of a revolution that you remain a superman in opposition to other supermen. If you want to go at the problem on a public level, you're going to have to do it while not just maintaining but actually increasing the balance in your personal life. Without that balance, you'll lose perspective. Without perspective, you're more likely to be part of the problem than the solution.

Ice Water

We have many capacities as humans which serve us well when used in an optimal fashion. Optimal in this case means in the manner which best serves the survival of our species. Fear is meant to be a short-term emotion that galvanizes action. It's not meant as a way of life. The negative impact that sustained fear has on the human physiological system is all the proof we need of this. We should not even have to wonder why heart disease, cancer and cerebrovascular disease have been the top three causes of death in our country since 1940.[69] A short burst of fear can save us. Living in a state of fear, conscious or unconscious, eventually tears apart our immunities, our organs and our ability to perceive real threats. We become our own worst enemy. We become the plague. We must consider the very strong possibility that the unconscious mind, which arises directly from the need to tuck away overwhelming stimulus in the interest of self-defense, is also in optimal function when its use is short-term—hours, days and sometimes months, rather than years, even decades—as a kind of holding tank to be emptied on a regular basis.

Dr. Christiane Northrup has a related take on this: "Healing can occur in the present only when we allow ourselves to feel, express, and release emotions from the past that we have suppressed or tried to forget. I call this *emotional incision and drainage*. I've often likened this deep process to treatment of an abscess. Any surgeon knows that the treatment for an abscess is to cut it open, allowing the pus to drain. When this is done the pain goes away almost immediately, and new healthy tissue can re-form where the abscess once was. It is the same with emotions: They too become walled off, causing pain and absorbing energy, if we do not experience and release them."[70]

Dr. Northrup's metaphor is helpful in further understanding why optimal use of the unconscious includes regular "drainage". When we are unable to empty ourselves of these locked away feelings, they fester. Our vision is narrowed to the point where gross blind spots can dominate our decision-making...and, of course, we *won't* see what we *can't* see and, consequently, our survival is not well served. We will confuse real need with all sorts of other things. We might get pregnant at a ridiculously young age because we want someone to love us. We might crave alcohol, drugs, sex. We might decide there are some people in the community or on the planet we hate because

126

they're different from us. We might "need" to hurt other people, take their belongings, kill them. We might hunger so much for money and power, we'll sell cigarettes to teenagers, or pollute an entire city, or knowingly build a flawed and dangerous product, or deceive the people who put us where we are just to fatten our own bank accounts. We might crave the esteem of others so much, we'll just work ourselves right into an early grave. We might feel so small inside, we just have to control, put down or physically abuse others—spouses, kids, workers. We might need love so much, we'll do nearly anything to grab the spotlight and command the world's attention. It doesn't matter how much money or power or how many diplomas we have. We can be intellectual giants and emotional dwarves. We might be so frightened inside, we'll develop a tool fetish in the desperate belief that such things will save us from terrible hurt. This is what we appear to have going on with technology today—a *colossal* tool fetish, a misplaced faith that the material products of our ingenuity will save us because, in the past, they have.

There's an extraordinary array of behaviors that might surface under the influence of the potent reactions frozen and tucked away within us. They don't just lie there quietly waiting to be drained. Their chill seeps into every corner of our existence. I've seen other explanations of the odd and violent history of our race, but none of them makes so much simple, resounding, elegant sense: we are driven by unconscious hurt that has very specific origins. We're not descended from killer apes. Nor are we predestined to live our entire existence on this planet amidst the violent consequences of habitual misjudgment. Or are we?

At this stage of our existence, is it realistic to believe we can ever empty the unconscious mind and keep emptying it as it fills? Maybe not. But maybe that's not entirely necessary for us to radically improve our lives and give us a much better chance of enjoying a long tenure on the earth. Maybe we just need to forget about ideal states and make a stand for the truth of what we feel, as we feel it.

What does this mean pragmatically? Nearly every single one of us in this nation and on this planet needed more of the benediction of parental safety, nurturance and love than we received. Nearly every last one of us, including those who insist they had a "normal" childhood, has unfinished business within, tears in cold suspension. And nearly every last one of us somewhere within ourselves longs for release, for genuine liberation. *The very myth that has revalidated the superman syndrome in our own time contains within its imagery the logic of a liberation strategy that has been hiding in the shadows of myths and dreams for centuries.* It's in direct alignment with the contemporary teachings of Dr. Northup, author/psychiatrist Alice Miller and a number of others. The Fortress of Solitude must be melted down, transformed from the frozen embodiment of unprocessed cataclysm to the warm, rejuvenating water of life— tears.[71] If the original pain was world-shaking, so will be the grieving.

The Weeping Species

Think about this. We are the only creature on earth capable of weeping. The leading authority on the subject, Dr. William H. Frey II, wrote in his book *Crying: The Mystery of Tears*, "Until evidence of other animals shedding emotional tears is well documented, I will continue to maintain that emotional tearing generally occurs only in humans. I agree with Montagu's view that 'the shedding of tears as an accompaniment to emotional distress has been attributed to other animals...The truth, however, appears to be that while some of these animals may on occasion exhibit the evidences of tears, this occurs very seldom, and is the exception rather than the rule...Psychic weeping is not known to occur as a normal function in any animal other than man.'"[72] Neurologist Antonio Damasio points out that while anger, fear and sadness all involve processes within closely located brain structures, and all three feelings activate brain-stem nuclei, only sadness appears to intensely involve two other important areas—the hypothalamus and ventromedial prefrontal cortex.[73] At the very least, this information leads us to take note of the elaborate effort Nature/God has invested in our ability to experience sadness.

It only makes sense to treat this as a substantial endowment and to ask why we have it. What is its purpose if not to aid in the processing of the unavoidable Raw Deals that come our way so that we can maintain the acuity and efficiency of our capacity for comprehending our experience? After all, to be the most conscious and sentient creature on earth *without* the capacity to process sadness would constitute a flaw in Creation's design so staggering we would be hard-pressed to avoid seeing it as anything but an outright curse.

Dr. Frey, a biochemist teaching at St. Paul University and directing research at the Dry Eye and Tear Research Center at St. Paul-Ramsey Medical Center in Minnesota in the first half of the 1980's has been the one scientist to take seriously the question of why we can weep. He examined tears produced by irritants (such as an onion), tears shed while watching an emotional film and tears shed in the thrall of powerful authentic grieving. ACTH, a well-known stress hormone, was present in all three kinds of tears. The sensible conclusion is that tears are part of a kind of stress-reduction orchestration of the body, equally capable of responding to an external or internal cause. The clear external stressor here was the onion. The film was also clearly an external stressor, although it's only natural to be curious about what it triggered internally to yield crying. Are we such profoundly sympathetic creatures that we cry whenever we see something sad…with no interior correlation from our own life? Doubtful. It's much more logical to conclude that the external stimulus touches something that's been tucked away in the unconscious. In the third case, there was no immediate external stimulus. The subjects were in psychotherapeutic sessions that constituted a safe environment in which they could reconnect and begin to complete the process of grieving over childhood wounds. So, in this final case, the stressor had been external years earlier, but had been held in cryogenic freeze. The empathetic counsel of another person helped to bring the thaw and the thaw literally brought tears. Substantially more tears were observed to be shed in the thrall of this grieving than in the other two cases. These tears contained the highest concentrations of ACTH as well—upwards of forty percent more than in the other two cases. Over all, the mean concentration of ACTH in all the tear samples was approximately five times that found in normal human blood serum.[74] Frey also found the level of manganese to be thirty times higher than the level found in normal blood,[75] apparent further validation that something akin to excretion is taking place through crying. This information would seem to instruct us that the most dynamic potential for healing is in weeping that is directly connected to the conscious processing of Raw Deals specific to the individual, rather than through an experience that is once-removed in the vicarious identification with a film character or someone else's story. This is only sensible, of course. When we experience the full impact of our own truth, its stark reality is not shunted off into sublimation but grips us completely, bringing with it the possibility of profound insight into our own development.

In one of Frey's studies, 286 women and 45 men ranging in age from 18 to 75 (mean age of 30.1 years) who were not under any psychiatric care or suffering from depression or personality disorders kept extensive records of their emotional life for thirty days. The women cried five times more frequently than the men. No big surprise here! Also not surprising that not as many men as women volunteered for the study. Interestingly, there was no age correlation whatsoever. Doesn't matter if you're young or old, you got cause to sing the blues. Eighty-five percent of the women and seventy-three percent of the men reported they felt better after crying. Dr. Frey believes "...tears are nature's way of excreting bodily chemicals that build up in response to stress. From a biochemical viewpoint, people who are sad or depressed could be suffering from a chemical imbalance...that is restored, at least partially, by the excretion of certain substances in tears." The secretion of tears, he concludes, "is *central,* not incidental, to the relief mechanism."[76]   More evidence of our essential nature as brilliant feelers.

Science is often fascinating and sometimes produces counter-intuitive conclusions. In this case, however, Dr. Frey's work confirms what many of us already know. Crying is as natural as any other bodily process. Why shouldn't the average person be tuned in to the basic truth of its function? Frankly, it's startling that the psychotherapeutic and psychiatric communities have not conducted comprehensive studies, not just of the chemical composition of tears, but of the full range of what occurs physiologically when we cry deeply in the throes of both physical and emotional hurt. You'd think there would have been so much research in this area, the information would be part of our conventional wisdom by now.   What happens to neurotransmitter levels, hormones, heart rate, blood pressure? What happens to our immune systems, our brain waves, skin electricity and moisture, muscle tension, vision, hearing, smell? Is there a predictable pattern of variation in all of these dependent on the specific kind of loss or hurt being grieved, as indicated by Frey's work? What is occurring electrochemically when we sob—when we experience that rapid contracting and releasing throughout our thoracic muscle mass, that rapid sequence of little convulsions which literally feel as if we are wringing sadness from our bodies? Is "excretion" or "drainage" the right metaphor or is there something even more complex and elegant unfolding which, in the end, has a similar result?

For all our materialist, empirical rage, you'd think any high school student would be able to find a nice, concise description of all this in any encyclopedia. You'd think, by now, as we move into the Twenty-First Century, we'd be undoing the hijacking and relearning how to let our tears flow when we're hurt. Instead, you'll have a hard time even finding "grief" "grieving" "tears," "weeping" or "crying" as serious subjects in much of the work being produced by therapeutic professionals. Like the Kryptonian leaders, they cannot see below the surface, to the core where sorrow gives rise to the water of life.

Yet, every parent has seen a child respond to a cut or bruise with wide open mouth, tears springing out of his eyes, his face flushed, veins standing out in his neck, his diaphragm pumping up and down. The attentive and sensate can see and feel that something important is happening here. The child's entire being is engaged. If he's allowed to complete his experience without parental invasion, he's done processing the hurt within a few minutes and back to whatever play occupied him. The pain has been excreted. Now, think about the fact that this basic, natural way of working through hurt quickly becomes off-limits, hijacked. By the time we're men, the cultural credo tells us we are not supposed to cry, even if someone drops a brick on our foot. Yell, curse, throw things, jump around, be angry, suck it up, be a Spartan...but no tears. Though this is not exclusive to our culture or our time, still the First Commandment of American Manhood seems to be, "Thou shalt not cry! Thou shalt be walled up in a Fortress of Solitude."

I have a very clear memory of falling down at the end of our driveway when I was about four years old. My knee was bleeding badly. My oldest brother, seven years my senior, put me on my feet and said, "Salute." He placed my hand up alongside my forehead. "Like that. Salute. Don't cry. Soldiers don't cry." Of course I love my brother. It wasn't his fault. Remember, this isn't about fault or blame. At age eleven, his own tears had already been hijacked and, as is so common in human life, he had shifted from being a victim of the culture to being an agent/perpetrator. He couldn't see the obvious. I was *not* a soldier. I was not a superman. I was a four-year old little boy with a badly scraped knee.

Multiply this vignette by a factor of millions and you have a very confused population of grownups scratching blindly across an icy landscape for exits to salvation, unable to see the doorways in their own eyes.

Phases

It is obvious that when we weep in deep emotion, something very powerful and important is unfolding, even if, as yet, scientists are unable or uninterested in discovering the full splendor of its physiological orchestration. What Elizabeth Kubler-Ross and others have done quite nicely is to observe and identify the full process of grieving.

Five distinct Phases have been described. In brief they are...

1. **Shock**: includes disbelief and denial

2. **Undoing**: includes guilt, shame, and the various forms of wishing, fantasizing and second-guessing, e.g. "If only I had..." or "If only they had..." or "If only this had happened instead of that..." or "I'm just going to imagine it didn't happen."

3. **Anger**: includes various forms of raging, e.g. "I've been cheated," and "How could you/God/Fate do this to me?" or "What have I done to deserve this?" or "I'll get even...somehow!"

4. **Deep Sadness**: includes profound sorrow, fear,

hurt, a feeling of aloneness, abandonment, rejection, betrayal and is accompanied by active weeping.

5. **Acceptance & Integration**: having "drained" enough of the hurt in Phase Four, involves truly being able to live with the reality of the loss/change. Includes an enhanced capacity to feel sadness/anger/fear/hurt when they present themselves and to work through them.

Of course, these Phases do not always unfold in a neat sequence. We often move in and out of them in a manner that has its own internal logic. Supermen and women have a hard time flowing with them, however, since its in their personality to try to control everything. This is one time when control is the strategy that guarantees limited success, if not downright failure. Grieving is not something we can trick or cheat our way through to get the certificate for our wall. It has its own pace, depth and direction. We just have to trust and surrender to it. Otherwise what happens is what some have called "premature acceptance" or "premature transcendence" or "premature forgiveness." We tell ourselves we're done, we're over it, because we're unwilling or unable to let go and experience the totality of our hurt. In reality, this is a return to the denial of the first phase or the wishful undoing of the second. As Alice Miller says, "The act of forgiveness will not help as long as it serves to disguise the facts."[77]

When we face the facts of our lives, we embark upon an inner odyssey which, as Thomas Moore points out in *Care of the Soul*, is not about a rush to closure or the accumulation of accomplishments and experiences we can add to our resume, but rather, "a deeply felt, risky, unpredictable tour of the soul."[78] In the midst of this navigation of our own wine-dark seas, we realize at some point with astonishing clarity that no one can tell us how many tears and rage we must feel before sailing out of a given storm. Only we ourselves can discover the scope and density of our own personal Fortress of Solitude. Yet, people will try to tell us we ought to be done with it. *We* will tell ourselves we ought to be done with it. Our internal critics and judges will come up with very "right sounding" reasons for us to stuff the feelings that remain, "stop feeling sorry for yourself and get on with your life." This is understandable. At times, grieving is an engulfing experience that may involve feeling physically spent, ill, even paralyzed. Yet, to truncate it, to allow the Jor-El mind to decide when it should be over, is to shortchange ourselves of the experience, its most profound lessons and richest benefits.

The grieving process is appropriate to far more than the misfortunes of childhood and the obvious losses of loved ones. Sometimes, the things we tuck away are quite recent. In our leadership workshop, it's common for our participants to begin grieving openly about adult events, sometimes things happening in the present moment. The following list is composed from actual experiences shared in the workshop. As comprehensive as it is, it's bound to be incomplete. Feel free to add your own.

Life's Raw Deals: The Middle and Later Years

1. Loss of a business.
2. Loss of a job.
3. Loss of a home.
4. Loss of financial security.
5. Loss of a great opportunity.
6. Seeing good friends lose their businesses, jobs, financial security, homes or great opportunities.
7. Departure of dear friends from the area.

8. Divorce.
9. Loss of custody of children.
10. Injury to a child.
11. Injury to any loved one or self.
12. Death of a child.
13. Departure of a child from the home.
14. Addiction by you or anyone you love to alcohol, drugs, nicotine, bad company, self-damaging behavior.
15. Sustained suffering of a loved one from cancer, diabetes, heart disease, AIDS, or any debilitating affliction.
16. Loss of vitality.
17. Loss of innocence.
18. Any physical or emotional violation of selfhood or property—including but not limited to rape, theft, etc.
19. Death of a family member.
20. Death of a friend.
21. Death of a pet.
22. Death of a beloved public figure (Princess Diana, John Kennedy, Jr.).
23. The trauma of social, political or economic upheaval, chaos, war.
24. The trauma of natural disasters.
25. A basic sense of being disconnected, alienated from yourself and your loved ones, walled up in a Fortress of Solitude, with all the really important things left unspoken.

Remember, the folks who attend our *LeaderOne* workshops are mainstream businessmen and women from more than a dozen different professions who come looking for something that will help them be better leaders. They're not high neurotics. Most of them are normal, every day "functional," "well-adapted" supermen and women. We're not looking for problems in them. We're just creating safe space in which they can rediscover who they truly are. We absolutely do *not* engage in any "in your face busting" such as has been and still is used by some so-called personal development programs. Our salutation says, in so many words, "Hello in there! Who are you? Come out, come out whoever you are! We'd like to know you." People respond in whatever manner they are ready for...at their own pace. Often, they discover there are whole pieces of themselves they've tucked away for years in that cold little back pocket of the mind, sealed up in the glass and steel of denial. When the environment naturally gives them permission to feel, the walls begin to crumble.

A former law enforcement officer wept in my arms over deaths of fellow officers that occurred more than twenty years ago. His body trembled with sobs for a good twenty minutes. In the midst of it, he shook his head in disbelief and cried, "I thought I'd put all that away. I thought I was done with it." Not long after his tears had dried, he openly acknowledged that the biting humor for which he'd become well known in his current organization was a direct part of his attempt to keep the hurt of those losses out of his consciousness. Once he felt through some of his grief (I'm sure, this was by no means all of it), he began to surrender that piece of his daily persona and was freer to be more caring and direct with his wife, children and coworkers.

A very cerebral middle-aged participant, who customarily worked twelve hour days, suddenly announced on the second day of the workshop, "I never express my feelings to anyone." Over the next few nights, he called his mother, his wife, and each of his grown children and spoke to them the words that never passed his lips, "I love you." By the fourth day, he told the group, "I've cried more in the last few days than I have my entire life...and I feel more real."

He also perceived the connection between his long hours and suppressed feelings. Upon his return to work, he trimmed his hours and actually started taking his days off. Those working under him saw the difference and were delighted. On several occasions, prior to his attending our workshop, I had made the point to this gentleman that an individual willing to work long hours is courting *inefficiency.* He's avoiding making the tough prioritizing and delegating decisions talented businesspeople make. He was never able to acknowledge the validity of my offering until he'd experienced his own deep truth. Herein lies a tale in its own right: there is a limit to what people can learn through standard training and education. The real energetic power for growth and change is in emotional insight...and this can't be "delivered" by teachers. It has to be catalyzed and/or facilitated through a safe process, one the individual chooses of his own free will.

Another participant who told me he doesn't cry and couldn't remember *ever* crying recently lost his mother in law. The whole family was gathered together as the poor woman, suffering from cancer, breathed her last few breaths. Suddenly, my friend felt heat rush into his face and his gut open up. He grabbed his wife and dashed from the room. Outside, he sobbed "as I have never sobbed in my entire life. I was just completely grabbed by it. It was like a convulsion I had no control over." He was stunned to learn he was capable of such all-encompassing emotion. "Now I know what it is people talk about. I thought they were just going off, you know, on some hysterical ride...or just exaggerating. It really just wasn't in my universe to understand until now. I feel so stupid...and yet, so smart now that I know. My relationship with my wife is so much better. I look at my kids and I just think I've got to be around more. I've got to change things in a big way."

A manager who had over two hundred people under him came to our workshop with a gnawing sense of missing out on his five year old son's childhood. His father had never been around and he was aware he was subjecting his boy to the same deprivation. We simply asked him to close his eyes and, with

138

the silent support of his colleagues, imagine that little sprite dancing into the room to see him. "What would he say? What would he want from you, Dad? What would you say to him? What would you do?" He just felt his love for his child so deeply at that moment. He wrapped his arms around himself as if embracing the boy. Of course he wept. He wept for himself and his son. So did a lot of the other people in the room. That man went home and changed his work life. No, he didn't make it perfect over night. In fact, he's still working at it. But he started paying attention to how subtly he could sacrifice his time with his boy . A year later, I ran into the owner of the business at a convention. He said, "I don't know what you guys do in that workshop, but you saved that man's family life and you saved us a great employee." What did we do? We just gave him a chance to feel how his hurt from his own childhood was converging on his son. It was just the truth of his life.

A health-care executive wept as she told us, "I'm a millionaire and I have nobody to love me. I just don't know how to do relationships." This was the first time she'd ever admitted this to herself out loud, having dropped her superwoman mask the day before. Till that moment, she'd been successfully convincing herself that she was happy, given the many choices she enjoyed with her big bank account. No, she didn't leave our workshop and walk into "Mr. Right" (another suspect concept in our culture). But she continued her personal inquiry, cultivated more balance in her life increasing the odds of her being perceived as more accessible by men. She also brought more sane judgments to her business.

A department manager who had a terrible time asserting herself shed a lot of tears over four days about her alcoholic father. She then went back to work, stepped up and terminated someone she'd been afraid to confront, someone who was long overdue for such action.

A couple that was on the verge of divorce attended, first her, then him a few months later. They opened up to each other, saved their marriage, and avoided the possible destruction of their business. Through her tears, she realized she did not want to be the hard-driving businesswoman she felt her father needed her to be. She wanted to have more children, a dog, family life on the farm. That's what she has today.

Two men who worked under the same roof and had never taken the time to get to know each other wept together as they discovered they'd both been brutally abused by their fathers. They forged a friendship that continues to sustain them. They actively support each other in swearing off cynical and submissive behavior.

A veteran wept for the first time over the killing he'd done "for God and country." Afterwards, he saw for the first time that never having grieved over these horrors had affected every major area of his life—his marriage, his relationships with his kids and his management style.

A young, soft-spoken department head who had been compulsively working eighty hours a week told us he hadn't cried in over twenty years. A few minutes later, as his eyebrows tensed, I asked simply, "Where is this feeling in your body?" "In my chest," he responded. "Breathe down into it...let yourself just feel it," I suggested. He took one deep breath and broke into sobs. Soon he was understanding without any coaching that he was working such long hours to keep himself numb, to avoid feeling the brutality of his childhood. He also understood that in so doing, he was depriving his own children of their father, just as his father had deprived him.

Time after time, the workshop experience confirms that most successful people are walking around with a lot of unexplored darkness, some from childhood, some from the more recent or even the immediate past. Their superman and superwoman masks have divided them from their humanity, from the truth of their lives. All the individuals whose brief stories I've shared here acknowledged they never would have believed the feelings they actually felt were in them if told in advance, no matter how

140

logically someone might have made the case to them. They also acknowledged they could not talk themselves or affirm themselves or will themselves into the changes that flowed quite logically once they did experience this depth of heart. Most of them had already tried self-talk, affirmation, medication or allegiance to a particular motivational guru to little or no avail. In fact, if prior to the workshop, you'd have recommended the benefits of grieving, most of them would have told you, "Leave well enough alone." Afterwards, no one had to explain the benefits of grieving through very specific Raw Deals. Nor did anyone have to make the case that their tears had broken free a great deal of energy and insight that could now be mobilized to live fuller and healthier lives. Finally, no one had to make the case for them that a substantial portion of the structure of their businesses and management styles as well as the customs and institutions of our society are colored or literally designed by the subterranean power of unprocessed feelings. Alice Miller is right. The traces left by childhood become visible throughout the infrastructure and superstructure of human society once our eyes are opened. As we say in our workshop, "It takes a long time for the obvious to show up." This insight leads to a magnum shift of mind such as Dr. Peter Senge identifies in *The Fifth Discipline. It allows us to imagine what a family or business or community on any level might look like if the dark colors of the past were gradually cleansed away by the water of life.*

Again, Dr. Christiane Northup describes with exceptional fidelity what we witness over and over in the crucible of each individual's transformation. "We have to give our bodies credit for their innate wisdom," she writes. "We also don't need to know exactly why something is happening in our bodies in order to respond to it. You don't need to know *why* your heart is racing or *why* you feel like crying. Understanding comes *after* you have allowed yourself to experience what you're feeling. Healing is an organic process that happens *in the body* as well as in the intellect."[79] Innate wisdom. Organic healing. Trusting and surrendering to the waters of life. Clarity and illumination will follow...touching the personal, professional and societal realms.

This grieving process should be common knowledge to school kids. It should be introduced in pre-school and deepened through practice all the way through college. It should be offered free to every adult in the nation through the full array of media so we can get about the critical business of raising children capable of becoming whole human beings and leading the rest of us to their truer vision.

Many organizations have experienced the rewards of this process. They send us streams of individuals who return to make important changes in their personal and business lives. Of course, these changes taken one by one, don't constitute a major societal restructuring, but they're important, sustainable steps, each one fostering a little more confidence and determination to continue discovering ways to rebalance the relationship between work and personal life. This is a gradual process that takes patience and compassion for self as well as others. We don't even mention a final point or destination to our graduates. Supermen and women are too hell-bent to achieve. We don't want them trying to become great feelers or great weepers so they can get some imagined trophy for their mantle piece. Instead, we emphasize the richness of the odyssey for its own sake and, for those who need more linear metaphors, the incremental gain over time—like compound interest in an investment.

It bears stating that our workshop did not initially include any explicit exercises, orientation or discussion about grieving. However, as we explored who we really were beneath our masks, a great deal of sadness kept coming into the room. By the third workshop, it was clear we had to take stock of what was going on. The first time I wrote the Five Phases of Grieving on the flip chart, most participants were readily able to find themselves somewhere in them. They were relieved to have a context that clarified what they were experiencing, and what, in many cases, they were resisting. They responded as though they'd been given permission to feel...which they had...and which they clearly needed. The quality of the sharing became far deeper and more authentic.

To be fair, there were and still are some who say, "Oh, man, I'd be afraid to lose control." So we have a poster on the wall that reads, *"You* are *not in control of what drives you to be in control. Until you reckon with that fact, you'll be more victim than creator."*

It doesn't take long before the most die-hard supermen acknowledge that anybody whose foot is on the floor in fifth gear at 7000 RPM's is not in control. We remind people about the sympathetic and parasympathetic states. A person cannot drive a sympathetic vehicle into the parasympathetic state. "You'll get stopped at the border," we kid. "Excuse me, sir, your license is invalid over here! If you're willing to toss it, leave your car and jump in that river, we'll be glad to welcome you."

Into the water of life. It'll take more than light dipping. But look at what you get when you come out down stream. No longer a Raging Materialist Sympath. Balance. Restoration. Time with yourself. Time with your family. You want to know where all the time is going right now? It's hiding in the shadows, in the freeze-frame of unfelt hurt, in the other half of your nervous system waiting for you to claim it.

Imperfection

It's true that sometimes we cry and don't feel better. Sometimes we actually feel worse. Perhaps we're really fighting the feeling, not letting it flow. Perhaps we need someone present to console us, to make it safe to completely let go. Maybe we have companionship, but the wrong individual. Being present to the sadness and hurt of another person requires patience, stillness, compassion. You have to accept the fact that your role is to provide safety and nurturance, to simply be there, witness, support the individual's right to feel bad. You can't play Mr. Fix-it. You can't play God. You're a friend, validating the feelings of a friend. Some people don't even want to be touched when they're in a feeling. They just want to know someone is there.

It's also not uncommon for a particular hurt to be so immense, we can't possibly process it quickly. The more emotionally powerful the experience was, the more time it's going to take. So it's natural that we not feel a sense of relief. We must remember that the very drive for it all to be "over and done with" is a *syndrome* dynamic. Supermen and women want to be healed, now, and fly off to lose themselves once again in action. That is simply an unrealistic expectation. Huge hurts don't yield easily. Our bodies may actually feel worse for a while, depending on the situation. In *About Mourning*, Weizman and Kamm describing major emotional travesty, write, "Mourning is all-encompassing and all-consuming. The intensity of grief wracks the whole body. It is a physiological event." They continue, "Some persons say they do not feel better after crying. 'My head hurts' is a common complaint. *Crying must be done with abandon, without any holding back. You must keep your mouth open and allow crying with your whole body.* You must not stop yourself prematurely and say: 'That is enough.' You must cry until you are all cried out of those minutes in time."[80]

Some early catastrophes may be particularly difficult to feel through and may not involve tears. They may be triggered by more recent deprivations and can confuse us. They may also present what appear to be exceptions to the grieving Phases. The more vulnerable we were, the greater the chances of being stuck in Phase One shock. Traumatic birth, infantile abuse or severe neglect and deprivation are all included here. Will integration be achieved through the same Five Phases? Through feeling, yes. Through those same five steps, perhaps not. This kind of pain usually has a raw physical aspect to it—deep hurt in the skin and muscles. It has to be experienced for what it is. Phase Four may be more dominated by experiencing all the various dimensions of this hurt. There may be a great deal of wailing and moaning as we burrow down through it, in the complete absence of tears. Of course, it takes a lot of self-trust to be willing to flow with such unfamiliar sensations. In moments such as these, it's important to have a compassionate, fully trusted companion in the room.

I'll refer the disbelieving to the works of Alice Miller, Frederic LeBoyer, Arthur Janov and Joseph LeDoux. I'll also tell you that I've been to these depths and know others who have as well. Sprawled on the bed, with my face in a pillow, I've gone down into the kind of full body hurt we normally associate with a virulent flu or dysentery. But I was not sick. The feeling was triggered by a gross sense of helplessness in a grownup situation. You might say, my button was pushed by someone in the present, but the offending individual did not put "the button" in my chest. Nor was he responsible for its hair-trigger sensitivity. It's extremely important to keep this in mind. We all have our "buttons" but the people who brush up against them in our adult lives did not build them into our chests. They were mounted and wired during our early development. Over the years, I've learned to trust what is trying to emerge from my body when someone "pushes" mine. The knowledge of its early origins becomes obvious at some point in the course of the experience when we trust and surrender to it. It reveals itself as any powerful insight does. Suddenly, it is there with certainty. It brings an understanding we simply can't acquire any other way, a grasp of what has caused us to have a given disposition and temper most of our lives. Processing these very physical early hurts goes a long ways towards rebuilding our capacity to be calm and present as adults. Some powerful physiology is unfolding and constitutes a sustainable gain in the core of our selfhood.

Some psychologists and neurologists have argued in the past that traumas in the first year to two of life cannot be remembered because the brain structures required for such memory are not yet myelinated or "booted up." However, scientists Lynn Nadel and Jake Jacobs have proposed a very logical explanation: only that part of the brain responsible for recording event memory— the hippocampus—is not yet functioning, due to a "prolonged period of maturation." The amygdalae, which mediate the storage of emotional memory, *are* operative in these early months. Professor Joseph LeDoux of the Center for Neural Science at New York University and author of *The Emotional Brain* also points out that people who suffer from severe trauma, whether childhood abuse or post-traumatic-stress disorder from war, may also experience a loss of event memory since stress can damage the hippocampus. In such cases, however, the emotional and physical memories are still present. In our view, this is more proof of the dogged determination of the body to preserve memory for future processing in order to rid the body of its suffering and benefit from its lessons.[81]

The Truth is Wired

Certainly, there are many folks who will dig in their heels and insist that this emphasis on the natural healing potential of the grieving process is over-stated or misplaced. Not only is there an active school of therapy that believes emotions can and should be controlled through thought or cognition. This is a popular belief among motivational speakers and millions of "average" folks. Why can't we just think our way out of what we were wounded into? Joseph LeDoux has provided us with a simple, elegant and inescapable truth. We're just not wired that

146

way. In his examination of the neurophysiology of fear—an emotion broadly attached to so much unprocessed grief—he notes the key role played by the amygdalae, two small almond-shaped structures, one present on each side of the human brain. He tells us that the pathways from these little emotional powerhouses out to the so-called higher cortical thought areas of our brains overshadow the pathways back from those areas to the amygdalae. This allows for "emotional arousal to dominate and control thinking...we are not very effective at willfully turning off emotions...telling yourself that you should not be anxious or depressed does not help much." In keeping with this biological truth, he notes that thought-driven efforts to extinguish phobias, fears and associated emotions can never be considered truly curative, since new stress and trauma are known to rekindle them. In other words, we can't build fortresses of solitude high or thick enough within ourselves to be free of our deep emotional truths. So convinced is LeDoux of the long-term futility of such efforts—and clearly understanding the vast implications of his research as it pertains to the history of human suffering and conflict—his only hope for our species is that we might undergo an evolutionary change that would expand the pathways from the cortical thought centers back to the amygdalae "allowing future humans to be better able to control their emotions."[82] What an ironic and forlorn conclusion for such a wonderful piece of work. LeDoux leaves himself and us dangling from a limb on the edge of an evolutionary cliff hoping for redemption, rather than embracing the truth he has uncovered: we are brilliant feelers. That's the way we're wired. Emotions are only destructive when they go unfelt, unprocessed at the time of occurrence. Yes, when they are compressed and compressed and compressed one upon the other over years of denial they subtly invade and distort our perceptions leading to dark life style choices *like the superman syndrome.* They also erupt into naked violence. On the other hand, if we honor our essential nature as brilliant feelers, we can grieve our way out of what we were wounded into.

Yet, in the interest of realism, it is important to acknowledge that we can be stuck in a given grieving phase for years. In fact, *the superman syndrome* is characterized by a kind of ricochet between denial, undoing and anger—Phases One through Three. However, what our workshop and broader experience have demonstrated to us is that, even after years of such an apparent vicious cycle, it's still eminently possible to break through and move forward through Phase Four weeping and into Phase Five acceptance and integration without a long term engagement in formal therapy. More than anything, it's a matter of providing a genuinely compassionate and supportive environment within which people can talk about their lives. In fact, so readily do people open up when safe space is provided, we can only conclude that though this adaptive gift of weeping and raging may be imperfect, it is more than anything else, under-utilized. So far.

Chapter Eight

Help

"Help! I need somebody. Help! Not just anybody..."

--The Beatles

Dr. Frey found that men were one fifth as likely to weep as women. Even given the small scale of his research project, we must ask if it's credible to conclude men are genetically only one-fifth as capable of weeping? Are our tear ducts one-fifth the size? Are our hearts one-fifth the size? Is our skin five times as thick? No. Our humanness has been molded into this form by our culture. Joseph Campbell quite rightly pointed out that societies do not want whole human beings. They want to cut, mark and mold people to serve their own unconsciously driven mores and customs. In our society, we do not stretch the earlobes or lips of men. Nor do we create patterns of burns or scars to mark them. Nonetheless, we have our own forms of scarification and the most notable visited upon men is the ripping of tears from their eyes. This mutilation is reinforced millions of times a day across our land with looks, comments and actions that implicitly declare, "The eyes shall not weep." Fortunately, this is not an irreversible mutilation. It can be changed. The piece of our selfhood that has been behaviorally and chemically disconnected from us can be reconnected. We do not have to hold to the belief that in order to provide for our families and attain success we must become symbolic survivalists willing to sacrifice our true nature as brilliant feelers. This is false thinking.

149

We don't have to choose between the head and the heart. It's all one system. We're not using it to its optimal promise. We can be open, feeling, balanced, clear, bright and wise. The full process of grieving and the rich insight, learning and communication that naturally flow from it constitute the dynamic that can grow us toward that optimization from the center of our selfhood outward. Over time, it re-connects and re-balances the sympathetic with the parasympathetic system gradually releasing into consciousness long frozen feelings and memories.

The availability of compassionate support is vital throughout life, but it's particularly important when we wish to include grieving as an important part of our day to day existence. Often, we need someone to listen and truly hear. Often, we need the reassurance brought by the mere physical presence of a compassionate other. Often, we need their capacity to play back to us without judgment what we are expressing. And, often, after grieving, we need their own life experience to enrich our learning so we can make positive changes in our lives. In other words, pure independence is an illusion. We need each other, but in authentic relationship, unmasked, tender, real.

I'm not expecting or advocating anything as trendy as a national "Grieve-in". That's what was triggered by Princess Diana's death—a worldwide "Grieve-in." We're in need of something much more sustained and real than a single outpouring over someone at that much distance from us (were we really grieving over Diana or what she symbolized for us?)

If we're going to substantially protect and nurture our selfhood and, along with it, our capacity to be real and present parents and enlightened business leaders creating a world around us that unequivocally reflects and leverages these values, we *are* going to have to open a national dialogue and come together in support groups across the landscape. These will spring up because ordinary folks decide they need them and want them and start reaching out to each other within their own families and circles of friends, neighborhoods and towns.

150

Unfortunately, many of us have abdicated our own central responsibility in creating such communities in favor of looking to so-called experts for what Deming referred to as "instant pudding." Given the pervasiveness and power of *the superman syndrome* in our culture, there just aren't enough counselors or therapists nationwide who understand grief sufficiently and are skilled in its facilitation to handle our need. In fact, my experience is that far too many professionals are trying to put us "in our heads" like the holographic Jor-El downloading into his infant son. Through an over-emphasis on cognitive techniques, they reinforce the prejudice of the neocortex towards our central brain. Unfortunately, in this field, you don't really know what you're going to get until you spend some time with someone. It's not a small paradox or challenge to realize that while giving enough trust to try working with an individual, you have to keep paying attention to the possibility that, at some point, you may discover he or she is not really trustworthy. *There is no unified theory and practice of healing recognized by the professional counseling community.* In fact, there are strong disagreements, a gaggle of relativistic views. So counseling, coaching or therapy is only as good as those giving it. When they're in their heads, they'll reinforce a divided selfhood, an internal tyranny, an entrenchment of the values of cataclysms. They'll talk about concepts, self-discipline or will, self-talk, behavioral modification and medication. Separately or combined, these cannot lead to an integrated human soul. The process may be complicated even further by the fact that we're so vulnerable when we're really hurting, it's easy to be deceived. When you've long suffered a theft of tears, it's not always easy to distinguish between clever counterfeits and the real deal. There certainly have been cases of people presenting themselves as "feeling therapists" who took advantage of the vulnerability of their patients to develop cult-like devotion in them rather than coaching them gradually towards authentic autonomy. Masks of denial abound in our culture. The professional community is no exception. Its own costumes can be so subtle, elaborate and enticing, we can be misled. As more than one maverick counselor has said, sometimes therapy *is* the disease it purports to cure.

We should be openly aware of the risks in seeking good help, but we must seek it nonetheless. There certainly are some good theorists and practitioners out there. We can take encouragement from the works of John Bradshaw, Aletha Solter, Alice Miller, Jean Liedloff, Vivian Janov, Arthur Janov and a number of other unsung heroes still quietly doing various forms of work under different names such as original pain work, bereavement or grief counseling, "re-grieving" therapy, Gestalt and Redecision therapy.[83] But there just aren't enough of them nationwide and our situation is too pressing to stand around hoping the universities of the country are going to start cranking them out. What's more, why would we believe the wisest and most compassionate healers will be recent university grads?

By all means, if we can find someone worthy of our trust—a good life coach, counselor or therapist—and afford his or her services, we should avail ourselves. By the same token, we ought to acknowledge that having to pay someone to listen to us with a wise and caring heart is a sad indication of how rank with alienation our world has become.

Beyond that, many of us will find we can also enroll our friends and (less often) family members in gradually increasing our skills in deeper emotional expression. Together, we can literally *practice* asking for an ear and a shoulder. Together, we can literally *practice* listening without judgment. Together, we can *practice* how to be present to suffering, to bear witness to it without absorbing it into our own cells and being overwhelmed by it. Together, we can *practice* learning to sense the difference between an emotional response that is appropriate to a present situation and an emotional reaction that is loaded up with unconscious energy that is seeking exit and integration into consciousness. Together, we can *practice* creating the sense of

152

safety necessary for each us to acknowledge and process these orphaned pieces of our selfhood.

I find a great deal of agreement across the span of professions that there are few masters of these skills in our culture, particularly compassionate listening. Yet, when it *is* given, people are capable of gaining important insights and making significant changes in their lives. Of course, if all this were easy, we'd have done it already. It's not. By the same token, consider how much time, energy and money we invest in practicing our golf game or tennis swing or sales techniques or computer skills or business strategy. How far can we travel in two decades if we invest equally in practicing the liberation of hearts?

Seek help. Search it out. Above all, take full responsibility for your life. Be demanding. Let people know what you need. If they can't or won't give it to you, move on. Trust yourself. Put in the time and effort. Most of us will spend more time buying a car than shopping for a good counselor or true healing buddy. Reserve the right to walk away when you sense your feelings are not being properly attended or they're being manipulated to make you dependent on the therapist. Above all, remember *the grieving process is accessible to everyone.* We were endowed by our Creator from birth with the blessing of tears. We still carry it within us—a great tool kit gathering dust in the often neglected workshop of the soul. If you must begin the work alone, so be it.

Just Say No...Except for These Pretty Pills!

No discussion of the topic of finding insightful, caring assistance in your inner work would be complete without commenting on the affinity of so many professionals today for drugs. Filling out a prescription sheet has become the new sketch art of the psychiatric establishment. The First

Commandment of American Manhood is "Thou shalt not cry. (Thou shalt just say 'no' to tears!) Thou shalt be walled up in a Fortress of Solitude." The Second Commandment is "Just say, 'No' to drugs, except *these* pretty little pills!" The new pharmaceuticals—a superman in capsule or tablet form—came along just in time to save psychiatry from the withering accusation that its analytic methods took too long, made patients dependent on them or simply didn't work. To be fair, such attacks were driven in part by economic and financial shifts in the health care system's own *syndrome* drive for faster and cheaper. But, by the same token, it's also correct to say that psychiatry aligned itself with a kind of mental chill, a detached analysis that would have been worthy of one of Krypton's Council of Five. Psychiatrist Dr. Peter R. Breggin has taken his profession to task over its detachment from its clients in favor of an attachment to drugs. He points out that the term "psychotherapy" comes from Greek roots meaning "ministering to the soul or being of another." "It is psychiatry that has medicalized and corrupted the word to mean 'the treatment of mental illness.'" He emphasizes the importance of caring and love on the part of anyone who would engage in ministering to souls, encouraging them in the safety of a compassionate relationship "to look inward, to experience and to express their feeling." Yet he adds, "Nowhere in my formal psychiatric training was there a serious discussion of caring, compassion, or love. Psychiatrists, more than most nonmedical therapists, are taught to be aloof...Modern psychiatry is suffering a moral decline under the psycho-pharmaceutical complex."[84]

In terms of our myth's messages, Dr. Breggin is telling us that the purity and innocence of the pre-cataclysmic child and the uncritical, unrestrained love of the mother is being disqualified in favor of the austere frost of imperious father energy. No amount of fancy intellectual footwork on the part of psychiatrists should dampen our astonishment at this insight. The pharmaceutical companies, with billions in revenue, are able to stimulate and mobilize the media and the doctors, on whom they spend thousands of dollars each per year. So-called miracle drugs lend themselves to magazine covers that fly off the shelves and over-worked doctors trained to address symptoms rather than systemic causes. But then, they're only playing to our societal obsession with being happy, beautiful, young and pain-free—as bullet-proof and immortal as the Krypton Kid.

The popularization of the belief that legal drugs can and should fix just about anything that's wrong with how we feel is a new phenomenon. As Dr. Breggin points out, it wasn't so long ago we outlawed and vilified drugs that were taken just to make you feel good.[85] In fact, as I passed through my teens into my twenties during the Sixties, my entire generation was being asked in outrage and indignation by our parents, "What's wrong with you that you can't just feel good without smoking marijuana?" Today, it's okay to depend on chemicals for our happiness—especially if they are not an obvious direct derivative of a naturally occurring plant and the drug dealer is an M.D. Strange logic at best, particularly when we consider that most of the hundreds of thousands of prescriptions written every month for so-called antidepressants are authored not by psychiatrists but regular M.D.'s who have had little or no training as counselors or psychologists.[86]

On the other hand, why not? Apparently everything has to do with chemicals in the brain. If we're unhappy, compulsive, distracted, irresponsible, addicted or just twitchy, it's because of chemical imbalances in the brain, right? Isn't that just the sort of thing doctors ought to minister to? What's the problem?

Well, the problem is that explaining everything in terms of brain chemistry is a very convenient way to remove all serious inquiry about root cause. Of course there is a chemical "imbalance" if you're chronically distressed in some way. Personality *is* chemistry. But what caused this imbalance in the first place? Looking at the raw volume of prescriptions, we can logically ask if the doctors are trying to tell us they believe our species suffers a genetic defect of disposition that can only be righted through drugs. Now that's a tough pill to swallow! Isn't it more likely, in fact obvious that experiential factors in our early years are usually the cause? What happens to the delicate developing brain of a child when that child suffers a Raw Deal—is neglected, abused or has to endure war, famine, disease or flood? Isn't it eminently probable it's going through its own microcosm of Jasper's experience? This "imbalance" is actually a survival strategy that allows the suffering child to somehow tunnel through to adulthood without total psychic annihilation. So, perhaps the use of the word "imbalance" is, well, unbalanced. The question now is, "If this particular survival ploy now limits the grownup individual's happiness, and, consequently, his chances of surviving and thriving, can the earlier adaptive chemistry be reversed through some means other than drugs?" After all drugs only "correct" the situation as long as we continue to take them. They are band aids that must be continually changed.

We ought to be calling loudly and clearly on the scientific community to give us due diligence in answering these important questions directed towards discovering the inherent healing potentials within the body before we resort to popping pills like so many teenagers tossing popcorn at each other's open mouths. We should be striving to understand if the capacity of the brain to secrete neurotransmitters in such a relationship to each other that we feel genuinely good about life can be reclaimed through a regimen whose core piece is grieving, drawing water from the rock-hard ice of incomplete sorrow, and augmented by exercise, massage, support groups, good counseling and some natural food supplements—all of which have been found to aid in the treatment of depression.[87]

There may be a place for some medications in severe conditions, but Dr. Breggin makes a strong case that sufficient compassionate, non-pharmaceutical *innovation has not really been sufficiently attempted even for these disorders*. He cites persuasive evidence as far back as the mid-1950's that caring, non-credentialed volunteers can readily be trained to have a significant beneficial impact on suffering souls.[88]   Recent research by Tirril Harris, Ph.D. in London has confirmed that volunteer "befrienders" interacting with chronically depressed women contributed to a remission in depression basically equal to that achieved through the use of antidepressants or cognitive therapy.[89]   Since this was true of severely afflicted individuals, how much truer is it for those of us suffering from more conventional wounds?   Yet "organized psychiatry, under increasing biopsychiatric domination, rejected the widespread use of volunteers...we find that the psychiatric monopoly and the psycho-pharmaceutical complex must be broken before significant progress can be made in developing humane, caring, nonmedical alternatives.   We have a blueprint for easy-to-develop, effective programs, if only they could get funded."[90]

Teacher In Waiting

The problem with medication as a core strategy is that it elevates our mood, or calms us *without our having learned anything.* Though the happy prescribers would have us believe otherwise, it's not really all that different from cracking jokes while stoned on marijuana.   We really don't know if we're genuinely funny or just stoned. On mood-shifting drugs, there's a kind of disembodiment. We can't know if we're really better, if we've really learned anything and own those lessons in our protoplasm with the force of insight and conviction that can drive innovation in our life or if we're just, well, drugged. The truth of our personal history is out of reach, a teacher waiting in the unilluminated classroom of the unconscious. Sure, we can talk about what drives our sadness, craving, yearning, anger and fear and our speed-demon brains. We can analyze it, but we can't feel its real potency in shaping our current state. Without

157

such full involvement of our entire array of senses and emotions, we're bereft of the force of profound experiential insights and the *sustainable* energy they yield to enable us to bring about significant and liberating change that nurtures our selfhood. We'll just cope, adapt to crazy situations and relationships we ought to be challenging, altering or leaving. We'll get better at doing the *wrong* thing. When you've been stuck on a merry-go-round, there's no gain in learning to spin faster. The gain is in jumping off, just saying...er...um, "No!" If you're already taking a psychoactive prescription drug, it's not quite that straightforward, of course. Dr. Breggin points out that it can be as dangerous getting off it as getting on. A gradual approach should be taken, with the guidance of a physician who really knows what he's dealing with.

We don't need drugs as our central strategy for personal liberation. They are a last resort and generally only to be seen as temporary. Dr. Breggin tells us, "The dangers of biopsychiatry for the individual and society cannot be exaggerated. Beyond causing physical side effects, drugs almost always blunt and confuse our emotional responses—our internal signal system." He goes on to share this wise perspective: "Our mettle is forged in the heat of human emotion and conflict, and drugs dampen and put out the fire."[91] To put it more simply, if we can't *feel* hurt when we *are* hurt, we can't stop living in ways that *cause* hurt.

We are suffering a theft of tears, an enslavement of the heart. The appropriate strategy is to get back those tears and unshackle that heart. This, of necessity, means a great deal of weeping and raging. It is not a pleasant experience, but then the very idea of trying to make pain into pleasure is insane as is the idea that we can and should only live in an invulnerable state of happiness. As Thomas Moore warns us, "...modern psychology, perhaps because of its links to medicine, is often seen as a way of being saved from the very messes that most deeply mark human life as human."[92] We should not expect or demand that we can grasp the promised treasure of our humanity without walking the mileage. To be limited by such a mentality is to be stuck in the second phase of grieving—undoing or wishing—with the medical establishment complicit in the conspiracy of unconsciousness. We can and should seek support, comfort, sympathy, consolation and guidance from those possessed of an authentic wisdom of this process.

There are many wonderfully intuitive, gifted people among us with great listening hearts well-suited to nurture us along. A lot of them don't have a certificate on the wall. What they do have is the purity and innocence of the child, the uncritical love of the mother, the strong, positive protective intention of the father. They bring their genuine selfhood to our hurt, a capacity to be present to sorrow without being submerged by it. These skills flourish in them in part, *because they haven't been schooled out of them.* Compassion and altruism are natural human impulses which actually manage to survive in many people even as they endure their own journeys through Life's Raw Deals. Somehow, they emerge into adulthood with an intact capacity for true friendship. They've never bought the red boots and cape. They move comfortably out of speed into depth. Regardless of how bare their walls may be of official social validation, their salve is often preferable to that of professionals. The thousands of people who participate in Hospice are stellar examples of this. As a society, we need to actively support such individuals and exponentially multiply their numbers while broadening the scope of their ability to apply their learning to the full range of Life's Raw Deals. We ought to bring their gentleness and caring wisdom into our education system beginning with teachers, parents, children, siblings, relatives and friends *at the pre-school level and continuing all the way up through life.* In twenty years, there shouldn't be a twenty-five year old in our country who can't recognize and appropriately attend to his or her own feelings and those of others. There shouldn't be a boardroom or boss's office in America where unconscious cataclysmic residues masquerade as accepted business practice.

Ask almost any anthropologist or philosopher what it is that most clearly distinguishes us from our higher primate relatives—the chimpanzees and gorillas (with whom we share about 97% of our genes)—and they will tell you it's our capacity for rich, subtle, varied, fine communication through language. Yet, today, in the Information Age, there's not much depth of value to the shower of babble we coin. Our words may buy us a little time in life's parking meter, but so do clever plug nickels. So we could easily argue that this extraordinary gift of the ages—the ability to speak with such complexity—is largely misused in our culture...just as we can readily argue that the other gift which most poignantly distinguishes us from our primate relatives and provides a superb navigational tool for the inner journey—weeping—is largely unused. I invite you to imagine a people in whom both these treasures are cherished, honored and practiced.

Chapter Nine

PERSONAL JOURNAL

"...a spirit is characterized not only by what it does, but no less, by what it permits, what it forgives and what it beholds in silence."

--Leo Baeck

Whenever someone recommends a particular course of action that promises to radically change your life, you have a right to ask where his ideas come from and to what degree he actually lives them himself. I believe I've already gone a long way toward answering these queries...but not quite far enough. It's appropriate that I share in more detail the manner in which I navigate my own journey through the water of life. Toward that end, in this chapter I'm going to present two autobiographical episodes which, hopefully, will sufficiently answer any questions about where my point of view originates and to what degree I live it.

Father

When I was fifteen, my family moved from the suburbs where we'd lived all my life, into New York City. I hated the city and had a terrible time adjusting. I felt I'd been robbed of my entire world. Both my older brothers had been permitted to complete high school in that suburban town, but I had not. Crying was not part of our family culture. We just didn't do it, at least not visibly. Both my parents' mothers passed away by the time I was fourteen. My folks may have wept, but I never witnessed a tear. There was certainly neither implicit nor explicit permission for me to grieve over being wrenched away from my friends, my neighborhood, my town, my dream of graduating from the same high school as my brothers had before me. The idea that my parents should include me in discussions of why a move might be necessary or highly desirable was not even on their mental map. When I objected as I saw the plan taking form, I was told, "You'll come with us and you'll damn well like it."

When we settled into our New York apartment, I tried my best to find the bright side of my new environment and to put on a happy face, but it just didn't work. I had terrifying dreams night after night and was overwhelmed with dread in daylight. Before long, I refused to go to school. I really wasn't trying to be a brat and have my way. I could not physically bring myself to stay in that school. It was a dreary all-boys institution, entirely different from what I was used to and needed. One morning, my legs refused to go there any more. That's exactly how I experienced it. It wasn't an act of willful defiance. It was an utter absence of will that seized me for the first time in my memory. My father was outraged. He thought I was trying to ruin the family with my "stubbornness". At one point, in a pique of anger, he threw me on the floor yelling, "You're not my son. My Bobby died! You're not my son." He was seething over me, his hands around my throat. That was the worst moment of my teens, one of the worst of my life. Fortunately, a kind of moratorium took over when we got some help from a sympathetic psychotherapist. For the better part of the next two years, however, my father and I hardly talked. I was persona non grata in my own home. Even my compassionate counselor gave me no support for crying. He helped me endure, but grieving was just not on the radar screen. I gradually built a shell around my sense of loss, went back to school, on to college and into adulthood.

About fifteen years later, I was living in California while the folks had settled in Cleveland (yes, a very comprehensible distance). With the help of a grief-oriented support system, I had recently managed to process much of the rage and tears I'd held within me during those teen years. Coming out of that particular stretch of my inner journey, a number of lessons were truly mine. Specifically, I realized I'd become an angry and somewhat cynical person because I hadn't been able to feel to completion; also, that a parent should take the time to engage his child on an age-appropriate level in a discussion of the reasons for any major decision that will affect him. Even if a major change *is* necessary, the child's feelings matter and should be ministered to. A sense of loss should be expected. The child should be given a great deal of support in working it through at his own pace.

A few years after I'd honestly put this behind me, the greatest beneficiary of all turned out to be a son who wasn't even a thought in my mind at the time. My wife and I moved from Los Angeles to San Luis Obispo, California (from the city back to the suburbs, dear Kal-El!). Ben was two and a half but had already become quite comfortable with his L.A. world and his friends there. I took a month off before starting my new job for the express purpose of helping him with the adjustment. We spent a lot of time together, more than enough for him to get very comfortable, even enthusiastic about the possibilities of his new digs. I can't image that I would have had this sensitivity to his needs had I not felt to the bones how my own had been violated years earlier.

But the benefits were broader still. I was finally able to accept what my father had done back when I was fifteen and genuinely forgive him. This set up the possibility of a reconciliation. After four years without any face to face contact between us, I visited for a week.

Dad had managed to get a couple of tickets to a Cleveland Cavaliers basketball game. We drove out early one evening and with about forty minutes till game time, sat in the car eating sandwiches Mom had made for us. I could sense there was something going on with Dad but I couldn't quite read it. Then he started telling me about how he'd recently been given an opportunity to work in the State Department under then President Jimmy Carter. Government was not his realm. He was a journalist and had been since he was sixteen. Listening, I felt excited and proud for him that people in Washington were aware of his talents and saw a need for them. But I quickly understood he wasn't relating this to inform me that he and mom would be moving to D.C. Not by a long shot. He said that once he had moved past feeling flattered by the offer, he fell into a deep funk and became terrified, so terrified, he couldn't exit the fear. Everything in his adult brain told him he had all the talent and intelligence necessary to do a great job in this new position, but he'd been waking up in the middle of the night with cold sweats, completely out of control. He knew it was from his childhood, which had some frightening periods of which I was well aware by now, but he just couldn't get through it all to take the job. I sat nodding in obvious understanding. Now he looked into me and said, "I never understood what you were going through back when you were fifteen. I thought it was so much bull. I'm so sorry, my son. I'm so sorry." He fell into my arms and sobbed.

Until that moment, you could have lined up fifty of the smartest, most articulate people in the world to explain to my father what had happened to me back in my teens and he would've listened and nodded and walked off grumbling under his breath that I was basically just a stubborn, spoiled brat. But in one crisis, as a menacing unprocessed fear from his own childhood rose and snarled before him, he got it. Unfortunately, he didn't get the kind of help that might have girded his courage to work through these engulfing memories. Yet, he had waded in deep enough to gain a compassionate insight no one had been able to give him for fifteen years. We had our moment of

164

genuine acceptance and integration. We were dipped in the water of life.

Son

As I've mentioned earlier, in 1984 I left my superman job, napped like a baby for a couple of weeks and then assumed my new position, well rested and physically restored. Over the next few years, my organization was increasingly successful. My hours were tolerable, leaving time and flexibility for me to stay close to my son. There was also time for me to stay healthy and fit. I jogged, rode my bike, hiked, worked out with weights, paid more attention to eating right and getting plenty of sleep. I often went home for lunch and slipped into a five or ten minute nap. My health and vitality rose to new levels. I rarely had a sniffle.

All of this prepared me for a new and more secure grasp of the old cliche that you can't run away from yourself. First Corollary: *Restoration of physical health is necessary but not sufficient for wholeness.* Second Corollary: *When you get your act together in the present, you'll be even more ready to feel some of the past; when you feel some of the past, you'll be even more ready to get your act together in the present.*

Despite a very gratifying working life, far more time with my son than my previous job had allowed, and restoration of the body, I was still definitely what any outside observer would call a "driven" person. This was somewhat evident in my behavior but I experienced it more in my mind. I had a very hard time achieving any kind of mental peace for more than a few moments or, at most, a day. I was constantly thinking about work and my future. Those close to me would probably have described me as quite competent but I felt wholly *in*competent in penetrating the present because I was so busy with the near and long-term future. Experience tells me this is true of most committed business people, particularly entrepreneurs. The tendency and talent to think strategically--which assumes a focus on the future--is critical to success in a competitive market place. *I didn't wish to disown this ability. I wanted it in balance.* I wanted to develop the capacity to slip out of it, to escape Time to a place where the only thing that mattered was being—truly knowing the beauty of my son, my dear ones and nature. I'd visited this province of tranquility, but not often enough, not long enough. To the degree that I have any understanding of what wisdom and love are, I believe they come from having access to this state. If you ask me my number one goal in life, I'll cite you my favorite proverb. It commands, "Get wisdom." Wisdom and love—life's ultimate prizes. I want them. I'll give much more to get them than I will money or glory.

So there I was, doing very well in worldly terms and feeling very physically healthy but having a hard time turning off the buzzing of my mental beehive. I had time for me and time for Ben, but the quality of that time wasn't on the level I sought. When I *was* fully present to Ben, I had the most delectable experiences of my life. I wanted more. I thought I was capable of getting it. I knew Ben deserved it. Yearning to be worthy of him, I was a Raging Sympath seeking silence.

I began checking in with myself physically and emotionally on a regular basis, taking time to ask, "What's going on with my body? Where am I tight? Why? What am I really feeling? What do I need to do for myself?" These simple queries led me to a far more intimate knowledge of what I was really feeling at any given moment. Specifically, I gained a far greater appreciation of the degree to which the surface frenzy of my high-velocity mind was operating as a defense to keep me from feeling something pushing from a deeper level. In such instances, the entire process we usually refer to as "mind" seemed more like a diversionary tactic. What were the feelings from which I was being diverted? It was difficult to abandon the analytical approach and, instead, "allow," "sink into," "be with," "trust and surrender" to whatever feeling was trying to emerge.

Taking a few slow deep breaths would help, but then I'd often hit a secondary defense level—an impulse to eat something or have a glass of wine or flick on the TV or read or go somewhere or call someone and just jabber. In other words, when thought no longer worked as an effective defense, the secondary mode was behavioral defense.

As I gradually learned to breathe my way through these impulses, too, I hit another level of discoveries. I felt hurt in my body in a way I rarely have. It was both physical and emotional. More often than not, it began as anger in the belly and temples and concluded as a jagged sadness arising out of my solar plexus. In other words, my body was trying to express something. The high velocity thought, the rush to stuff food in my mouth, to dump anger on someone else—my son, an employee, a girlfriend—all of these were some sort of attempt to escape from or cover a deeper feeling. I'd gone to this level of awareness in the past, but I couldn't seem to *own* the knowledge with the kind of deep, dynamic force that purposefully impels a positive shift of both experience and behavior.

One afternoon early in January 1987, I sat alone at my favorite beach, trying to slow my mind and just enjoy being on the earth. Working my way down through levels of defense by breathing and allowing things to percolate to the surface, I suddenly found myself saying out loud to the voices within me, "Just let me be! I just want some peace. Shut up, dammit!" Without warning, a sadness presented itself to me, centered in my chest like a dark knot. It literally hurt in a physical manner...not as a pain, but more a twisting ache. I lay back on the dune, took a deep breath and submitted to it, having no idea where it would lead. A few tears came, then a few more, then a lot more that lasted several minutes.

The essence of what I felt on that sand dune was this: I had spent much of my life working hard to catch up with the rest of the world. I was the youngest of three sons. My parents were both extremely articulate people. In fact, I'm blessed to be their

167

son, growing up amidst their high verbal fluidity, intelligence and curiosity. However, the down side in being the youngest of a family of impatient, high-speed thinkers and talkers was that, prior to the development of strong verbal skills, I experienced a sustained period during which I was the only one in the family who could not easily engage in the banter that was such an important part of our household culture. Until my day on the sand dune, I never truly understood the powerful effect this "outsider" feeling around ages two to four had on me. Though very small, I was struggling hard to master thought and expression so I could belong to a family that prized both. As an adaptation, my mental velocity revved up. When this strategy succeeded for me, it became an essential component to my operating mode. But, as is so often the case with such things, what was designed to serve actually came to dominate me.

During those moments on the dune in 1987, I actually felt very young, helpless and alone, the smallest soul at the far end of the dinner table. I grieved over having pushed myself so hard at such an early age to compete in the race to connect with my family. I cried experiencing the dark side of their brilliance and the price I'd paid trying to catch up with it. Mind you, to many outsiders, we might well have looked like a model middle-class family living in a good, safe middle-class neighborhood. We had none of the more visible raw deals or cataclysms as I grew up. No drunks, addicts, molesters, no terrible accidents or unexpected deaths or acts of God befalling our family or town. Many of my current clients have had it much worse. In fact, there was a lot of magic in my childhood, but there was also this subtle, cool fog of isolation that moved in around our feet and seeped into our cells. It left me with a stealthy form of denial, slightly dazed, confused and of course, driven. I wept on that sand dune as the full realization came up through my body that for all our verbal gifts, the one thing we could not speak about freely and openly in our family was our feelings. Sure, we could emote about our sports heroes, movie stars and movies, books, political heroes and events, art. But the simple words, "I'm lonely...I'm scared...I'm angry...I need you" were iced in, beyond our view or hearing. There was a potent unspoken rule that forbade such simple, direct and true communication. I wept as I returned from that slow motion flashback and felt some of the fog dissipating, revealing the truth that all too often in my adult life I had not been the person I knew I could be to my dear ones and my employees—simple, direct and true. I'd pushed and prodded or held myself back from them when they weren't giving me what I needed, rather than responding with a stronger, calmer, more lucid and generous spirit. The invisible isolation had often mastered me. Unable to truly be my better self, I was unable to help them be their better selves. Finally, I wept with a sense of gratitude because this breakthrough shed so much light on my entire disposition, I felt gifted, in a state of grace. I'd shattered an icy wall of solitude within me. A piece of my soul had been restored.

Outcomes and Insights

This being a true story, I must tell you I did not fly away and live happily ever after. I felt very good, though. I had a sense of passing a threshold and making sustainable inner shift. Open and utterly relaxed, I watched the waves breaking for a long time, my mind bestilled. A Sympath in a state of silence. Whoa! No voices in the head? Whoa! Sounds impossible! Let me check….No! Hello, Silence, my new friend. It happened. And it's happened many times since.

A number of things began shifting in me as a result of this experience and other related feelings that surfaced in the following weeks. I did indeed find myself to be more easily immersed in the present. I also found myself turning away more readily from acquiring stuff—material proofs of my worth such as plaques, clothes and gadgets. I just wanted to be with Ben. It was much easier to wholly enter his world. In other words, more grieving, more clarity, more *presence*, more balance, more reality.

The Payoff—Peru and Beyond

Given the emphasis I've put on the danger that awaits our nation if we do not turn from *syndrome* speed and materialism to rediscover the pure purpose of parenting, a specific example of exactly how the inner journey transformed my relationship with Ben is in order.

Around eight-thirty one evening later that same month, January, 1987, Ben, then twelve years old, was stretched out on the couch reading his Social Studies book. I sat nearby reading a book of my own. Ben heaved a deep sigh and asked, "Could you read me these two pages? I'm really tired and I have a test tomorrow."

"Sure, Ben. What have we got here?"

"It's about the Incas."

"Mmm. I haven't read about them in a long time."

I took the book and began to read. His eyes started to close.

"Hey, Ben, are you gonna be able to stay awake for this?"

"I'm listening. I just need to rest my eyes."

"Okay. Here we go." I resumed reading. The first paragraph was about how the Incas built thousands of miles of roads but had no wheeled vehicles. Wheels would have been useless in such an up and down world. They also had no substantial pack animals. A llama was far inferior to an ox, for example, since it could only carry about a hundred pounds. I stopped to comment.

"Man, all those roads and no wheels. Think about it. No really good beasts of burden. Imagine what those trains of llamas snaking through the mountains must have looked like!"

Ben opened his eyes and smiled, imagining. "Yeah, a

thousand loaded llamas snaking through the mountains."

I read on. The Incas had relay runners called "chasquis" to take goods and messages through the mountains. They could get fish up from the coast so fast, it wouldn't spoil.

"Wow," I marveled. "Can you imagine the legs on those chasqui guys?"

Ben pulled himself upright, growing more alert. "Yeah. Those guys must really have been strong."

"I'll bet they had calves like rocks," I said, holding my hands out to show the size I was envisioning.

Ben nodded and shook his head. "Isn't it hard to run high up in the mountains? Isn't the air thin?"

"Yeah, and these guys, some of them were running up over ten, twelve, fourteen thousand feet. I've heard those people down there in Peru today have larger lungs than people like us who live mostly at sea level."

Ben took a big breath, expanding his chest and exhaling loudly. "I'll bet they could swim about a mile underwater!"

I laughed and agreed. "And, Ben, could you imagine these guys running all alone in the night, with nothing but a torch or the moonlight to guide their way? What do you think was going on in their minds? What did they think about?"

"I don't know," he said. "I don't have any idea what you'd think about running around in those big mountains."

"How old do you think they were?"

He was silent for a good ten seconds, then said thoughtfully, "Sixteen to twenty-five."

"You know, I think that's a really good guess. They'd have to be young and strong, wouldn't they?"

"Yeah, really in good shape, like Olympic athletes."

"You bet." I paused a moment to consider. "Think about this, Ben. They might have only been four years older than you. If you'd have been an Inca boy, you might have an older brother running through the mountains."

Ben's lips pursed as he contemplated this possibility. He

171

swung his legs over the side of the couch to sit fully upright. He was wide awake now. His eyes shone. "I'll bet those guys saw gods in the sky, like in the constellations, you know? I'll bet they weren't at all afraid of the dark. I'll bet they just danced over snakes in the night and just breathed and breathed and breathed."

I put the book down to look at him. His face was luminous. "Read more," he commanded.

Who was I to disobey? Now we learned that the chasquis carried a thing called a "quipu." This was a whole web of strings tied together in a very particular manner with different colored knots positioned very carefully in relation to each other. It was the Incas' way of recording information—population, agricultural output, numbers of livestock and so on. The quipu was so advanced, it was even used as a mnemonic device to aid the passing of oral tradition. Only very expertly trained people could decode it. They were "quipu camayocs" and enjoyed a status equal to high priests. So, if an enemy succeeded in stopping a chasqui, he might take his quipu, but the chances of his being able to decipher its meaning were slim and none. There was a picture in the book of a six-foot long quipu at a museum in Lima.

"Wow, Ben, can you believe this? I don't ever remember reading any of this when I was your age? This is incredible. Who could think up such a thing? A bunch of strings!"

He stared at the picture. "That's so cool!" he exclaimed.

The next paragraph told about the stonework of the Incas, how each stone was beautifully shaped and fitted to the others around it without the use of mortar. We stared together at a picture of an Inca wall. The caption said that even after five hundred years and numerous earthquakes in the area, the stones were still so tight, you couldn't fit a knife blade between them.

"I can't believe that!" Ben exclaimed. "Earthquakes and stuff and no mortar to hold them? Look at the shapes of those stones, Bob. They're beautiful!"

Something inside me just busted wide open and I said, "Ben, let's go there and see those stones! Let's go to Peru! Let's go see that six-foot long quipu!"

He looked at me with delight and a touch of disbelief. "Really?"

"Yeah!" I said emphatically.

"When?" Hey, he was a salesman's son. He knew how to close the deal!

I thought for about two seconds and said, "This summer."

"All right!" he squealed, and we slapped our hands together.

I started making plans the next day and we made that trip to Peru in the middle of his thirteenth year on the planet. We also went back again when he was twenty-one and again when he was twenty-five, this time taking more than a dozen of our *LeaderOne* graduates...but those are other stories.

Now, let me ask you this: back then, in January of '87, how do you think he did on the test the next day? Of course he aced it. But was that "A" a good measure of what he had learned? No. It was wholly inadequate. And we had never discussed the test from the moment he gave me the book or the next morning on the way to school. We hadn't spent one second memorizing facts. We had been totally connected to each other and the subject matter. We were in a state of pure flow together. Mind you, I wasn't operating under any conscious theory of teaching or parenting. *I just loved my kid and was not entangled or subjugated by finger-pointing scripts from the past because I'd been doing the work of grieving I needed to do.*

So, let's look at what I did *not* do that night that I or many other fathers might have done under the influence of old unconscious prescriptions.

I might have refused to read to Ben. I might have told him he should have planned better. I might have asked in an intimidating voice, "How long have you known there was going to be a test? Why did you wait till the last minute to study?"

I might have shamed him for not doing his job while I was working my butt off doing mine.

I might have lectured him on responsibility and sent him to bed with a stiff warning that he'd better get up early and study those pages.

On the surface of it, these may not seem such dire alternatives. Ben might have still achieved the A. However, look at what would have been missed!

When I think back now, it's so clear that in my total openness I was cultivating a love of learning in Ben, and not just any kind of learning, but shared learning, learning as relationship with a loved one, learning as opportunity, learning as adventure, learning as a connection to something in the world you could go see which would, in turn, lead to more learning, more seeing, more adventure—an endless journey of discovery and delight.

You may be a more evolved person than I. You might have been there for your child as I was for Ben without thinking twice about it. But for me, it represented an important liberation from authoritarian parenting impulses grounded in the past. It became eminently clear to me that merely spending more time with our kids will not, in and of itself, constitute a qualitative leap in parenting. *When crazy parents are more involved with their kids, their kids just become crazier.* The inner work of the grieving process is what frees us to be the real, sane, present protectors and nurturers our kids need us to be. When we give ourselves over to it, quantity and quality of time together begin to merge.

Gut Check

It's important to temper this description by stating the obvious. Not every gut-check or internal scanning leads to weeping, raging or life-changing illumination. We often don't know in advance *what* we're going to feel. There's a wide range of possibilities, all the way back to birth. We often don't know in advance *how much* we're going to feel, either. I've gone into a restroom at work and cried for ten seconds and reaped benefit (…and no one had any idea what I was up to.) We often don't know in advance whether or not we need a compassionate companion or can go it alone. At any given moment, what emerges may be no big deal—just a bit of stress reduction, for example—but, by the same token, it may be a very big deal.

Those dune insights were definitely a big deal for me. They brought illumination and closure of some long-troubling issues. They constituted a prelude to a series of opportunities to permanently change the way I lived. This convinced me all the more of the benefits of the inner expedition. I've come to see this as my way of taking responsibility for my life. I don't "blame" my parents for anything. I recognize their place in the causal cascade of generations that made me who I am up till this moment. Some of the waters they poured into me were pure, fresh, effervescent. Some were dark and roiled. That's my life. I can change it. I can learn to let the darkness clear and free myself of the silt of centuries.

During the many years that have passed since that day on the dunes, I've walked a lot of inner turf *I didn't even know was there.* How could I? It was unconscious, tucked away. There have been times when I felt the great full-body ache of birth or infancy. Believe me, it's not a great way to spend a weekend, but when a truth is moving in the body, it should be experienced. We go into that vice-like pain when we must…and guess what? As horrid as it is, we emerge with greater clarity, strength, integrity, freedom and calm.

This exploration of inner space has been the principle source of my strongest innovations as a leader. It engendered in me a rock solid determination to transform a business that was grossly inhospitable to sentient human beings. My team and I managed a fair amount of success in that endeavor. We renovated the architecture of how we engaged our customers back early in

1991 with the development of what we called "Haggle-free, Stress-free Car Buying". We created a team-based sales compensation plan that was unique in the industry at the time and has been imitated by many nationwide since. We designed work hours that were unique and are still envied in the industry. People had time for personal restoration and for their families in a business that has long given nothing more than lip service to such needs. We created several dynamic advertising campaigns from which my current clients are benefiting many years later. We consistently had the highest Customer Satisfaction in our franchise line in the seven western states. In a speech at the 1992 National Automobile Dealers Association Convention, I stated publicly that I was trained to lie in this business and called for us to declare the Nineties "The Decade of Ethical Renewal." Though there's still plenty of room for improvement, considerable progress has been made. I never would have had the self-confidence to stand before the industry and admit I was trained to lie, did lie and trained others to do so, if it hadn't been for my grief work.

Now, others may have created humanizing business innovations without engaging in any kind of intense personal reconstruction. For me, and for many, judging from my consulting experience, it is eminently necessary and desirable. I was a pretty good manager and leader before I fully integrated the grieving process with my professional life. People wanted to work for me. More often than not, I treated them well, helped them make money and tried to make it all fun. So far, so good. But that was the problem. That was the limit. So far, so good. I was a good leader doing business in a bad paradigm. I wanted to go further. I wanted to be better...for the simple reason that I knew I had it in me. So, if you're good, really good, *in spite of* limited self-knowledge, imagine the possibilities beyond your current operating mode.

It's also important to establish that what most people seem to fear about such inner work never came to pass. I wasn't a burbling idiot at work. I didn't roam the business preaching the benefits of grieving, giving demonstration break-downs. In fact, most of my colleagues never had more than the slightest clue what my personal process was. By and large, I wasn't ready to share it and it was my judgment they weren't ready to receive it. Nonetheless, they reaped the rewards.

Feeling, recovery, integration, action. More feeling, more recovery, more integration, more action. This has been the major dynamic nurturing the integrity of my vision of who I wish to be as a person, a father and a professional. Beyond certain limits, we can't change the world out there without first changing the world in here. It's time for our leaders—all of them—to face this truth.

Chapter Ten

Anger at Work

"Blow, till thou burst thy wind, if room enough!"

--Shakespeare, *The Tempest*

If we never really see Kal-El engaged in the fourth stage of grieving—deep sadness and weeping—it's because he lives within the first three stages—denial, undoing and anger. Especially anger, but not generally the hot kind with which most of us are familiar. Since he is not exactly the most feeling fellow on the planet, it's understandable that he would become the embodiment of a cold, controlled, righteous fury. Anger masquerading as the instrument of justice. Its central importance in his behavior only confirms the obvious—that anger is endemic to the American male credo, the breakfast of champions. Tears are the breakfast of wimps. Consequently, it's important we examine this potent emotional and social force. It may be the third stage of grieving when the process unfolds neatly (which, as we said, it often doesn't—it has its own logic) but men often move into it quickly and get stuck there as a defense against feeling something deeper. It's the safest place for most of us to hang out. But, of course, anger is simply another aspect of the sympathetic nervous system's orchestration of fight or flight behavior. When we genuinely must fight, it serves as optimally designed. It's certainly better to protect ourselves than be wounded or killed. However, when anger becomes a life style, vaunted as "the competitive drive" or "a mark of winners," it is merely girding our addiction to the self-fulfilling prophecy of symbolic survivalism.

Within such a context, it's not surprising that flash temper is common in our culture, readily visible as a disruptive force in parenting, spousal and workplace relationships. We're not referring here to anger that moves us to appropriately express and assert ourselves against day to day social or physical transgressions. We're talking about rapid emotional escalation, an engulfing personal experience that fires on a hair-trigger, is disproportionate to the actual situation and abusive to others. The fundamentals of resolving its destructive force are the same at work and at home. In the ensuing pages, we're going to examine how these apply to you if you are the individual in question, followed by a look at how to confront and convert colleagues and employees who are productive, talented, even ingenious and yet leave a wake of the wounded behind them wherever they go.

Seven Truths

First, you must be bluntly honesty with yourself. Exploding in anyone's face—a child, spouse, friend or employee, belittling and embarrassing him or her is unacceptable, immature and certainly unprofessional behavior no matter how hard you work for your family or how much bacon you bring home or how lofty your position at work or how long and hard you labored to get there or how noble you believe your cause to be. Such outbursts do not arise from personal integrity, but from an inner rift. Furthermore, very few relationships can tolerate them without sustaining major damage. Let me repeat, there is no "executive privilege" in this situation. It doesn't matter if you're the boss or the patriarch. It doesn't matter if you're a billionaire. No amount of money or prestige can buy you a license to bully. What's more, the way things are developing around the general issue of work place harassment, it won't be long before bullies are being sued for psychological abuse. So wake up and face reality. This is a no-win situation.

Second, the person(s) who appears to trigger this verbal violence is *not* responsible for the rage you feel. It is *not* their job to make it all better for you by taking your bullets in the chest. People make mistakes. *You* make mistakes. People also just flat disagree sometimes. There must be room in any relationship for error and constructive discord, for making great big messy mistakes as well as small ones. That goes as much for business as it does for personal relations. A vibrant family or business boasts an environment that encourages experimentation and creative risk-taking. There are important lessons to be derived from errors and plans that fall short. If someone in the family is "incompetent" either teach them or stop expecting them to do the job. If someone is totally incompetent in a business, ask, "Who's responsible? Who hired him? Who's supposed to train him? Who has the obligation to admit a mistake and terminate the person if necessary?" Flights of caustic acrobatics cannot conceal limitations in your ability to work this truth and provide meaningful leadership.

Third, nearly *everyone* but you knows you're out of control. In other words, nobody is buying your sanctimonious mask. You're doing serious damage to whatever respect others might have had for you. You're ranting that they just don't get it, that you've got to do everything yourself if you want it done right, but you're the one who really doesn't see. You're the one who goes around unconsciously making everyone else wrong. It's a vicious cycle. It makes you a loser with the delusion of being a winner, just like Kal-El. It makes your family and your employees losers because it deprives them of the opportunity to admire you and connect with you on an authentic level. It also deprives them of the kind of appreciative, supportive and open environment that is hospitable to meaningful relationships and optimal creativity. Children, spouses and workers quite literally will learn far less and come up with far fewer good ideas with grenades exploding around them on a regular basis.

Fourth, *you* are responsible for your rage. No one else can be. There is little doubt its origins reside in early experience, which means that most of the time, the issue is *not* the present situation but rather how you've been "programmed" to respond. Your folks might have loved you dearly, but *something* happened to make you so thin-skinned. To put it another way, *someone in the present may have pushed your button today, but they didn't plant the button in your chest.* Acknowledging cause is very important, but it's not the same as taking responsibility. Until you take responsibility for the presence of this brutish force within you and the devastation it causes, until you acknowledge there are more mature and effective ways to relate to and motivate people, until you genuinely long to be free of its power nothing will change. I worked with an extremely intelligent man who had all the right intellectual answers concerning the cause of his hair-trigger. He had been through extensive conventional counseling centering on talk and self-control. None of his insights helped. He followed the classic pattern after an outburst—apology, genuine remorse, commitment to change, attempt to change and, alas, within a few hours or days, repeat of the offense. Only when he found someone to help him feel the teeth-gnashing depth of his fear of rejection did he begin to make real, sustainable shifts in his behavior.

Fifth, your flash temper is costing you money at work. It limits innovation, productivity, efficiency and employee loyalty. If none of my other remarks ring bells for you, this one should.

Sixth, you probably wouldn't want to work for or be married to someone with your temper. In fact, if you were being judged as harshly as you judge others, you'd probably be outraged at the injustice of it. By what twisted logic can you rationalize subjecting others to something you wouldn't tolerate?

Seventh, if you want to grow as a person and a business leader, it's absolutely necessary to develop the self-guidance techniques that will gradually dissolve the affliction of flash temper.

Down, Through, Out

Flash temper seems to have a life of its own, rising suddenly "out of nowhere" to take you over. What are you to do? Expect the strategy necessary to tame this beast to be difficult to apply. If it were easy, you'd have already handled the situation. If it were easy, there'd be consensus among counselors, psychologists, psychiatrists, coaches and common folk. There isn't. So if you find yourself squirming as I present my own take, just hold onto your seat. Take some time. Feel and think your way through it. Without bold action, you and your employees (and probably your loved ones) will continue to be victimized.

Here's some very good news. *It's okay that you get angry.* There's a reason for it. It's probably not a brain tumor. You're not possessed by the devil. There's a cluster of unattended feelings trying to emerge from within to achieve conscious resolution. Still, blasting someone is unacceptable. You need to find a neutral place to let it rip. At home, that's usually the bedroom. *Go somewhere safe* and rant. Take a ride in your car to a park that provides some privacy. Keep a pillow in your office so you can close the door and yell into it. Bite the darn thing if your rage is that strong. Sound silly? Better to bite off a chunk of pillow than the head of an employee. Put a small exercise room in the building...with great soundproofing and a full-size punching bag and a lock on the door. Seems off the wall? Levi Strauss has a "quiet room" in its San Francisco headquarters where anyone can go scream or nap or read or listen to music—the ultimate multi-purpose room. The point is to find or build a safe place where you can let the steam out. In my experience, the various "management" techniques like deep breathing, reciting an affirmation, counting to ten or ten times ten, focusing on a single point, listening to a particular piece of music or a taped spoken message—all have some limited value. They may temporarily work to control or dispel a mild flash, but beyond that, they're likely to fail you. Frankly, the whole country would be markedly better off if every business and every home had a room or an extra "walk in" closet sufficiently sound-proofed and padded for a person to just let go.

During most of my working life, I've chosen to live a short distance from the office so when I was on the edge of something I didn't want to swallow, I'd go home and work it through. Of course, that proximity isn't available to most folks, which is why I support the "private room" idea. Again, if you think that sounds weird, I'll tell you what's weird—a society that tolerates extraordinary stress and abuse without having a basic understanding of it or a realistic, curative strategy readily available to everyone. All of us are carrying around our own pieces of cataclysm. All of us can benefit from an accessible safe place where we can work through them when they get active. Clearly, having a correctly trained counselor available on-site or by phone represents important additional assistance.

The only obvious caveat concerning this method is for people with serious blood pressure problems. This is a thorny area, indeed, and requires great finesse. Allowing unrestrained venting might be hazardous to your health under these conditions. Consulting with your doctor is a must. On the other hand, in my experience few doctors have a unified understanding of human nature sufficiently complete to allow for optimal counsel in this situation. It's quite possible your blood pressure problem is the direct result of stuffed, disconnected feelings whose expression would lead to its resolution. Perhaps the best strategy is to find a counselor who works with the grieving process and maintains a close relationship with an MD. However, in the end, each of us must be deeply involved in the critical decisions that direct our healing process. They're too important to simply abdicate to someone who does not have our body and our life.

Not the Next Olympic Event

A key point about safe venting: it's one thing to have a padded wall or punching bag around for the more violent moments of this experience, but let's not elevate it to a sport. We have to stay with the present and, eventually, the earlier context of the real hurt erupting within us rather than allowing ourselves to get lost in a fantasy world imagining throngs cheering our Rocky-like fist work as we defeat all foes.

When we take the flash temper out of its "triggering context" in the present social setting and really let it rip somewhere safe, we're far more likely to turn that potentially destructive force into a very constructive and specific lesson in the dynamics of our own personality.

If this is leading you to envision a household or company full of oddballs running off to padded rooms, think a little harder. These feelings don't generally surface every day and when they do, they're often very brief, concentrated eruptions. When we work down into them and get under the anger, the result is usually relief along with increased clarity and focus.

So which do you prefer to experience and have around you—distraction, hurt and hidden psychological agendas or a maturity that owns up to its frailties? Personally, all other things being equal between you and me, give me the padded rooms and my company will out perform yours and my family will surpass yours in the riches of intimacy.

It generally comes as a welcome revelation when people learn they have every right to be mad, but not every right to act on it. One client of mine engaged in a great deal of self-hatred over his anger at a relative who played a significant part in his business. When I simply told him his anger was important and he had a right to it but had to find a safe place to experience it, he wept. When I told him it wasn't helpful for him to beat himself up over his rage, more water of life flowed. Since that day, like the other individual mentioned earlier above who was saturated with rejection as a child, he's steadily made good progress in ending his self-abuse and abuse of others. The two are often connected, of course. If you feel you're a bad boy, you're going to enlist others in your conspiracy to be one. When you accept that there is a reason for your anger, a specific cause that makes sense, you have the chance to deal with it.

It's only fair to state that there have been limited-scope studies that seem to indicate there is no benefit to "safe venting." In fact, they argue, it actually increases the individual's belligerence. The reason for this, in my experience, is a lack of clear guidance as to the real nature of the erupting feeling. *The anger that emerges in a flash episode is not generally the root feeling.* Particularly for men. It's the energy of the root feeling transformed into something more socially acceptable within the person's family culture, fed by the wider culture. This is a critical point. At the risk of being redundant, let's again consider the evolutionary purpose of our capacity for anger. It is to protect us. It activates the sympathetic nervous system so we can fight when we truly must. When it operates appropriately, it is proportional to the threat. In a life or death situation, we make a quick judgment to fight or flee. If we stand and fight, the proportional response is to mobilize every ounce of ferocity of which we're capable. On the other hand, if some neighborhood kids carelessly kick their soccer ball into our front yard and do mild damage to our favorite rose bush, the appropriate proportional response is much smaller. The rose is not us. Our life is not in danger. There is no intentional threat. By the same token, if an employee takes an action or decision that falls short of our expectations, there is no life-threatening reality. Yet, those of us afflicted with flash temper consistently respond in a disproportionate manner as if there were. Why? Assuming we're not sleep-deprived or in the midst of some present crisis that would temporarily lower our threshold of pain, there can only be one basic reason. The present situation triggers an unconscious Raw Deal (or series of them) from the past when we were unable to protect ourselves or fully process the helplessness of our reality. Helplessness. During what period in our lives are we most likely to be overwhelmed by such an experience? In infancy, when we're utterly dependent on others, when we can scream our heads off in an attempt to bring their attention to the satisfaction of our needs and *still* get no help, until we've exhausted ourselves, are overwhelmed with hurt and tumble into the solace of sleep—a way for our bodies to chemically go unconscious. When such experiences are repeated over and over, one possible response is a chronic "fussiness" whose adult form is a "thin skin" or flash temper. Infancy, of course, is not the only possible arena of origin for the kind of Raw Deals that can yield a hair trigger, just the most obvious.

The point is, anger itself is not the end of the feeling. Anyone allowing himself to vent should be attentive to the probability there's a deeper feeling of helplessness and/or fear trying to emerge from the chest or solar plexus. When it does, rage dissolves into tears. Helplessness and fear are terrible feelings. They hurt. A lot. One of the reasons we become obsessed with control as adults is to avoid them. However, when we are courageous enough to trust and surrender to the small, pained voice within us, we do get some resolution. Even if we only cry a few tears for a few seconds, we have a truth in our possession we lacked a moment earlier. Even if we can't consciously connect this feeling to any memory, we know it is about helplessness or fear and the extraordinary sorrow and physical hurt that are integral parts of them. Some relief comes when the gateways open in our eyes and waters emerge, even a trickle. Suddenly, we realize the breadth of our over-reaction to the present situation and are free to remedy it. Next time a flash feeling comes over us, we have a little better sense we need to get away to a safe place and surrender to the deeper wound. By consistently going down into and ultimately through the anger, we will find our way out of it.

We've seen many graphic examples of this in our leadership workshop. Men begin by stating their anger with limited expression. After a day or two of our work, there is more physicality—clenched jaws and fists, bent body. Once they feel safe in our environment, we commonly ask, "Where is this feeling in your body?" The answer is generally, "In my chest and stomach." We invite them to sit back in their chairs, close their eyes and simply breathe down into the feeling. Time after time after time, the posturing angry adult dissolves into the tears of little boys suffering from a poverty of fathering.

All of this should make it eminently clear why the so-called anger management techniques referred to earlier are so limited. To the degree that they train us to get away from the trigger person or situation or attempt to gain some immediate control when we can't exit the situation, they're helpful. Toward that end, self-talk may work for a while, as may dissipating the energy in the body by immediately engaging in five to fifteen minutes of vigorous exercise. Moving major muscle mass brings a temporary shift in our physiology and may calm us. However, to the degree that these or any other techniques tend to make the whole strategy about control or "management" and discourage us from *actually feeling down into our truth*, they're still expressions of the warrior archetype. They may be nakedly exalted as such or thinly masked in athletic, political or other business-friendly buzzwords. They purport to foster "high performance" but that's precisely the problem. High performance and optimal living are too very different states of being. The "high performance" credo subjugates depth to the service of speed. More *syndrome* behavior. The alternative I'm suggesting here puts speed in the service of depth, which is exactly where it belongs.

Riveting support for what I'm suggesting comes from

psychologist Lydia Temoshok. She has presented convincing evidence in her book, *The Type C Connection*, that an inability to express emotions, *especially anger*, is an apparent major risk factor for the development of cancer as well as resistance to recovery from it. She cites specific case histories of cancer patients experiencing significant improvement after deeply cathartic sessions in which they relived Raw Deals that had gone ungrieved.[93] She tells us, "we must recognize that years of repressing anger has indeed turned it into a potentially harmful force. This is all the more reason why we have to find a safe place in which to explore the irrational side of anger, with compassion for ourselves."[94] Again, down into it. Through it. To the root feeling and ultimately out.

So, if you manage to gain some competence at "safe venting," don't be at all surprised if you discover a wrenching sadness beneath your anger. We've touched in general terms what that might be about but only you can discover what the specifics are for you. If the idea of shedding tears, even in total privacy, is tough for you to swallow, just work on safe venting for now. *But don't just jump up after a short blast and head back to work.* In such cases, it *is* possible you will be every bit as pugnacious as you were when the incident began because you haven't yet reached a resolving depth. Give yourself time to tune into what's going on in your body. There's a whole world happening in there. Do you have the courage to explore it? Perhaps it's time to realign your sense of the heroic. You think football players are tough? You think boxers are tough? Find me a man with the courage to face his own black and blue heart. That's tough. That's heroic. Take some time to be a hero to yourself before you rush back to work. The payoff can be enormous.

A very important point about venting: do *not* address the issue with the "trigger" person or situation until you're calm enough to have a clear view of how to communicate in a constructive manner, even if it takes several hours, days, even weeks, unless it's absolutely urgent. How do you know you're ready? When there's no tension in your body. No tight jaw, chest, stomach, neck, back, fists. No curling toes. When authentic calm and openness settle in your solar plexus. When this state arrives, we often realize we've made a mountain out of a mole hill. Sometimes, there's really nothing to say other than, "I'm sorry. I was temporarily insane." Try practicing that in the privacy of your bathroom. "I'm sorry. I'm sorry. I'm *really* sorry." I guess American mothers weren't as insistent on instilling that phrase as "please" and "thank you" because we don't hear anywhere nearly enough of it.

Yes, of course, it's possible that in your case nobody ever pushed you or bullied you or abused you verbally or physically. Perhaps no one neglected you in infancy. Maybe you've just allowed your job to get the better of you. You've taken on too many responsibilities to the point where you're constantly on the edge of stressing out. Still, you need to take a couple of days off for a retreat and perhaps you ought to make that a regular part of your year—two, three, four long-weekend retreats to rethink the entire configuration of your business and your life. It's also quite possible you can delegate enough of your work so you can calm down and your trigger won't be so hair-sensitive.

It might be equally desirable to sit down for a heart-to-heart talk with everyone in your family. They may need to hear more about your genuine desire to grow and be a better person and your hope they have the same approach to life. You might need to tell them not to be alarmed if you remove yourself in the middle of something that's obviously upsetting you and go into another room to vent. Your kids, especially if they're small, probably need to be assured for a while that "Daddy isn't falling apart and he isn't hurting the bed. He's just having a big feeling, like when you fall down and hurt yourself." Little kids are usually quick to grasp this when it's explained clearly and calmly because they're still so in touch with their own feelings. My son never had a problem with my going behind closed doors and beating up the bed. He certainly never had a problem with my tears. When he cried, I held him and, sometimes when I cried, he held me. Our age and role differences didn't matter at those moments. We were just two human beings who gave each other love and consolation in the face of life's sharp edges.

Perhaps it would also be an excellent idea to have a similar discussion with your workforce. It's possible there would be great benefit from your publicly apologizing for every dressing down you've engaged in. I have clients who have done this with their staffs with excellent results. Make yourself totally, publicly accountable for your behavior. Why should others be accountable if you're not? Tell people this is not the person you want to be for them. Empower them to walk away from you if they see you starting to lose it. Ask them to give you the time-out sign or inquire whether or not you shouldn't go for a walk and talk about this later when cooler heads prevail. Put your self on the line and watch how much they'll help you. The wilder this suggestion seems to you, the more astounded you'll be by the results. Oh, sure, some employees and colleagues will be skeptical at first. After all, you may have peeled the skin off them a number of times. Now, suddenly, you're the kinder, gentler you? Not so fast! But there will be those who can see the sincerity in your eyes (assuming it's really there.) Take the chance. This is real leadership. Having the guts to be open about your own shortcomings and ask for help. This is where dynamic growth begins. Remember, courage in the service of feeling.

If someone in your life, a spouse or an employee, has the courage to stand up to you, to tell you straight out they're not going to take your maniacal bull, you'd better scramble to find a way to embrace that individual because what they bring to the party is exactly what every person and every company needs—a friend with integrity and character who will give you the straight truth.

Of course, it's also generally beneficial to focus on health and fitness. Get regular aerobic exercise, go for long walks, hikes, bike rides, whatever turns you on. Vary it but don't obsess over it and turn it into one more *syndrome* activity. Get seven to eight hours of sleep a night. Don't buy the argument that some people really only need five hours. I have direct experience with quite a few folks in my own life who have claimed to need far less sleep than "the average." These are classic supermen. Every single one of them. They're so flashy and brilliant, they breathe a kind of ether into the room wherever they go. So great is their "star power," people walk away impressed and stoned without knowing why. But such individuals consistently make gross errors in judgment because they are strung out for lack of rest and are usually taking a variety of stimulants to compensate. So opt for exercise and plenty of sleep.

Limit your intake of stimulants like caffeine.

If you're tired in the middle of the day, your body is telling you something. Listen to that small sweet sleepy voice. Learn to master the brief nap.

Learn about nutrition and take care of your body.

Try meditation or yoga.

If these activities help even two percent, that's a good gain.

Is there music in your life? It's true...it can soothe the savage beast. Its evocative power can actually help you feel some of those deeper hurts before you ever get triggered into fury.

Do you have a rich, vital life away from work?

Do you love someone and welcome their love in return?

Are you really accessible to your children? Are you carrying around huge guilt about not being with them?

How much time do you allow for yourself to experience the invisible realm within you, the spiritual realm around you? Remember, Superman is a prisoner of the material world. Maybe you're punishing others because you feel so pushed inside, because you haven't made a stand for what ought to be non-negotiable in your own life. *What are you waiting for?*.

If all this fails, shop hard for a really good counselor, psychologist or life coach—someone who won't do the Jor-El Trick of putting you in your head. Beware of people who want to help you "master" or "manage" anger. Find out what they mean. If they have a lot of neat self-discipline concepts but there's no encouragement to find or create a safe space to really feel down into and through this emotion, keep shopping. As indicated earlier, you're just as likely to find the right person if you seek out a grief specialist. Expect the whole undertaking to be an effort of some duration. Remember, too, it's not your fault you're a rager, but it *is* your responsibility. Take it from one who's been there...and changed.

Saving Prima Donna's

You may be a pretty level, patient person, not given to hurtful outbursts yourself but rather directly facing or indirectly witnessing it in someone else in your organization. In my experience, it's all too common for companies to tolerate psychological and verbal abuse on the grounds that "he's so gifted and productive." This deserves a sub-category of its own within *the superman syndrome*. It's distinguished from *syndrome* behavior in that Kal-El is not guilty of this sort of bullying. Consequently, we call this *the prima donna syndrome*, because it is based on a distorted inner logic that posits talent as justifiable grounds for being less kind and civil than the rest of us poor average folks ought to be. Not only is there increasing likelihood of legal vulnerability in allowing such behavior, it carries immeasurable costs in depressed morale, productivity and employee loyalty among those who are victimized. It blows a hole right through any discussion of corporate integrity. It reveals "bottom line thinking" as the only thing that really matters.

But, once again, there is good news. It is not necessary to

tolerate *prima donna*'s. It is quite possible to confront and transform them. In fact, it's the fear of losing them and the lack of firm engagement that reinforces their disruptive behavior and makes you, their boss, look like a, well...hypocrite, to put it diplomatically. Everything we've covered so far in this chapter is good background for understanding what you're facing. However, you can't force that understanding on others any more than you can force them to seek counseling. You can and must put forth clear definitions for everyone in the business delineating what behavior is out of bounds. You can and must make sure everyone respects those definitions. Here is a tried and true method for confronting and saving most *prima donna*'s.

Make sure you've got the goods

In this case, we're going to assume you have a file of notes or lengthier descriptions of the behavior in question from a variety of sources—those who have been the direct objects of unacceptable behavior and those who have witnessed it. The absolute best-case scenario is when you personally have witnessed it. We're also going to assume that you or others have had less weighty, formal chats on the same topic with the offender. In other words, this is not the first time. But it *is* going to be the last. We're also going to assume that if you have any legal concerns whatsoever about the situation, you've called the company lawyer for the appropriate guidance. In almost every *prima donna* situation I've dealt with, the individual in question has been in the organization long enough for his or her behavior to be one of the great open secrets of the day.

This is not a debate

You prepare yourself mentally and emotionally to be compassionate, clear, direct and firm. You invite the individual into a private office and sit face to face with no desk to divide you. You maintain eye contact throughout the process.

You speak as follows, "Jack, it's very important that you listen to me with everything you've got and I don't want you to interrupt me. Okay? I'm telling you up front that the next ten minutes are not going to be a pleasant experience for you. What I have to communicate is going to upset you. But I want you to know that my intention is to be constructive, and to avoid your having to leave the organization. Here's the long and the short of it. You are one of our stars in productivity. That's no secret. But for some time now, you have engaged in behavior that is unacceptable (be specific here—it may fall under the category of verbal and psychological abuse or may be more readily described as rabid gossiping, down-putting, negativism, covert insubordination). We're not here to debate whether or not you do it. You do it. We've talked before but not forthrightly enough. I can't believe in my heart you want to be this kind of person. I do believe in my heart you are essentially a good person. But you're doing damage here and we're not going to get into a knit-picking debate over details. That will not serve any good. We have numerous complaints on file from your fellow employees/subordinates to this effect. Frankly, we have probably made too many allowances for you because of your talent. But that's a double standard and it's wrong, Jack. You have to be as much of a person, as civil and as courteous and as kind as everyone else around here. Your performance, like everyone's, is being assessed in two major areas—the operational area, in which you excel, and the interpersonal area, in which you are failing. A success in one area doesn't offset failure in the other. We need you and everyone in our company to achieve certain thresholds in both. *We need people, at the very least, to be kind to each other.* You run far too hot and cold...so, given your unacceptable performance in the interpersonal realm, we're here to discuss your choices. There are only two. The first is that you recognize this behavior to be negative and genuinely want to change it for the better and honestly believe you can. If that is your choice, we want to help. We want you to tell us how we can help. We want to suggest you seek some outside help as well. There's no shame in that. We're all unfinished works on this earth. We're all students learning how to live. So, we're hoping you honestly believe you can change, want to and will commit to take action to effect that change."

If the individual jumps in here and begins making testimony that he wants to and will, hold him off. "It's premature, Jack, for you to make such a commitment to us. Hear me out. The change can't be a thirty, sixty or ninety day miracle that gradually erodes back into the same old stuff. It's got to be permanent. People don't go around hurting others, cutting them down as you have unless they've got some powerful unfinished business of some kind within them. This is not easy stuff. In fact, this may be one of the toughest learning curves you've ever had to work. So we want you, I want you to think this through and talk to your loved ones and anyone else you feel you can confide in. I want you to take forty-eight hours to really do some soul-searching on it. Then, we'll meet again and you'll tell me if you're going to change and stay or if you honestly think you can't or don't wish to, in which case your choice is to leave us."

Allow some seconds of silence. Let it sink in. Then ask, "Any questions at all?"

If the person gets into a "don't I have the right to face my accuser" mentality, the answer is, "*I* am the person who is assessing your behavior, Jack. I'm the one you've got to deal with and I've laid it out as cleanly as I can. We're not going to have a debate." If he begins to lose it, you say simply, "We're done, Jack. Take the forty-eight hours and think it through." Get up. Open the door and walk out.

What's more likely to happen

Did I suggest you have a box of kleenex nearby? Do. It is common for people to weep in these situations. Yes, even the big, burly tough guys. They know they've got a problem. They usually do want to change. Like a child, they've unconsciously been yearning for someone to firmly but compassionately set the boundaries so they can find within themselves the motivation, the sense of urgency to confront this demon in them. By all means, if they open up and share their hurt and what's driving this behavior, be one hundred percent present, compassionate and quiet. Let them pour it out. You don't have to comment other than to ask empathetic questions or make empathetic comments. You've already established the boundaries. When they're finished, you might want to repeat them one last time to be sure they didn't get lost in all the emotion. Stick to the plan. Get back together again later.

So far, my clients are batting about 900 with this technique, meaning that most of the folks in question come back within forty-eight hours deeply committed to changing. It's common for them to seek out those they've hurt and make heartfelt, often tearful apologies. It's also common for them to seek help or get more actively committed to a current counseling relationship.

How you help sustain the change

You keep a close eye on this person, catch him doing something right, as Dr. Ken Blanchard says in *The One Minute Manager* or let him know you're hearing positive feedback about him. Give him a pat on the shoulder or, if you're comfortable enough—which you might well be, given that this person has generally been with you a long time—put your arm around his shoulders and tell him you're proud and that he should stay the course.

197

In some cases, it's quite workable and appropriate to get some of the person's peers together, even subordinates and let them know you've drawn a line in the sand and that he's really committed to change. Ask them what they think they might be able to do to help. Facilitate a little brainstorming session on the subject. You may be surprised at how some people will take ownership of the fact that they've played a co-dependent role (not all that dissimilar to the people of Metropolis) in allowing themselves to be victimized. They commit to stepping up and giving the time-out sign if they see trouble brewing. They agree on some simple, direct non-incendiary language like, "Jack, time-out, man. This is not who you want to be. Let's break till cooler heads prevail." By the same token, they can also encourage Jack and give him a slap on the back every time he gets through a day as a "new person." I've seen employees walk right up to a man and say, "I really liked who you were today. Keep it up. You're actually a nice guy when you relax a little."

It's also legitimate and highly effective in some cases for the original confrontation to be done with a group of the offended people rather than just you. Hold on before you reject this out of hand. I've facilitated this process and it can bring wonderful results, far beyond what can be accomplished by you alone. Of course, the offender has to be willing to trust you enough to believe that the whole purpose of the meeting is to move beyond a kind of "stuckness" he and his colleagues are experiencing around his behavior. You take on a facilitation role. You stipulate the purpose and guidelines at the outset. The language runs something like this: "We're here because a number of you have asked if there isn't some positive way for us to help Jack end his habit of using cutting put-downs towards you. I'm convinced that it's not fair to deprive a man of the unadorned truth. In fact, I'm convinced that sometimes sharing it with him in simple, straightforward language, is the best chance he has to fully grasp what he's doing...because, frankly, I think Jack is a decent human being at his core, but he has not yet realized what it is he's doing and what the extent of the damage is because we haven't taken complete responsibility for telling him. So, let's be clear. We're here to tell the truth, but this is not going to be a beat up session. Each of us will have a turn to speak. There will be no interrupting. The rest of us will listen really hard. When you speak, stay with how you feel as a result of Jack's behavior. There will be no profanity. If anyone violates any of these guidelines, he'll have to leave the room. Everybody got it? Okay, who wants to speak first?"

If you don't have sufficient confidence in your facilitation skills to handle this, consider either bringing in someone else from the company who is a disinterested party and has those skills or hire a professional counselor. As I've said, I've personally facilitated this group process and found it to be an extraordinary experience that yielded far more than the immediate desired results. This is an act of community. You see, the truth is this was never just Jack's problem anyway. It was the work community's problem as well because the "abusees" have been participating in the problem by accepting a co-dependent role with Jack. When the members of that community really take it on, they play an ongoing part in the solution, increasing the likelihood it's going to stick. Morale gets a transfusion of esprit de corps, openness, honesty, co-authorship and enhanced communication skills.

We are great in this country at innovating on the level of operational performance. We should aspire to bring the same caring, guts, determination and insight to interpersonal performance. We'll be the better for it and, yes, so will the bottom line.

Chapter Eleven

Renovating the Workplace

"It is a characteristic of wisdom to not do desperate things."

--Henry David Thoreau

As individuals, we can reclaim the ability to give our children the safety, nurturance and love they need by dedicating the next few decades to releasing ourselves from a heritage of cataclysm. As the Superman story instructs us, this storm of the heart has its origins in our personal history. We will each accomplish this by gradually coming to trust and surrender to the restorative water of life that springs from the center of the grieving process.

Of course, the teaching does not end there. It places our individual challenge in sweeping context, addressing past and current conditions of our nation and our race. Its heavy chords accent the dark consequences of a society trapped in the theater of the unconscious, where the audience dutifully applauds...with its eyes closed. However, Art, whether through music, dance, acting, painting, sculpture, story-telling or any other form, often conveys important meanings as much by what it leaves out as by what it leaves in. This is certainly the case here. The very absence of a humanistic vision of community calls to us from the silences between the notes of its mythic song. Here absence does make the heart grow fonder. We sit at its feet to discover through our yearning the fundamentals on which an authentic visionary community of any kind must be based. Above all, it must celebrate our true nature as brilliant feelers with profound needs for safety, nuturance and love on the social level. No organizational form can be exempt from honoring the essential character of human beings. Having taken its rightful place at the center of our consciousness, respect, trust, honesty, integrity, cooperation and affection then inevitably emerge and take their rightful places. In such a community, each person is beautifully suited to his or her role, contributing willingly at the appropriate time in the appropriate way without lectures on responsibility or accountability, without coercion, without obeisance to authority, without fear. In such a community, even as individuals do their inner work, they share a deep connection to a common purpose that needs no articulation. Everyone is truly present. Everyone is heard. Relationship has become artful.

This sounds a bit Utopian. It is. However, it's also possible. I've seen it. In enduring moments of actual reality. So have you. Our forefathers and mothers were not cynical about such visions. They built the foundation of a republic with the clear intention that such a society would one day be realized. We must restore within ourselves their special brand of enlightened optimism. If we attend deeply to the absences within Superman's biography of endless action, wise guidance continues to stimulate and clarify. Consider that only a few hundred years ago, when we were largely an agrarian society (the setting of Kal-El's recuperation), work did not generally divide families in the way they're divided today. Mothers and daughters labored with fathers and sons in the fields, in the barn, in the kitchen, in whatever had to be done. If there was a division of labor, it tended to be within visible proximity. Sweat was mingled by all ages, sizes and genders. In fact, for most of our species' time on earth, men have not flown off every day to a separate place in order to provide for their families.

Industrialization and the Information Age, have certainly brought benefit, but they have also brought cost. The *dis*integration of the family is not a minor transgression in the long chronicle of human life. It is a gross violation of the sacred.

It is a sin of the first magnitude. From out of its silence, as well as from the image of Metropolis' woeful ineptitude, the Superman myth urges us to imagine we are bright enough to reweave what has become frayed and to do so in a new and unique way. No, we can't "go back". It would be fatuous to imagine Americans totally relinquishing their affection for the material aspects of our contemporary lifestyle. However, we can respond to the myth's message with courage and a faith in the possibility of building broader footings out of greater depth. Within this architecture, materialism takes its appropriate place as one component, rather than defining and dominating the boundaries of personal identity and social interaction.

Clearly, this will not be accomplished by men who think we must "learn to swim with the sharks," and "do lunch or be lunch."

To change America, to reunify our families and reconcile the nation's soul with the patriarchal brutality of its past so that it might finally transcend it, we will figuratively and literally have to bring the innocence and purity of the pre-cataclysmic child and the untainted blessing of the mother's unconditional love into the workplace.

On a pragmatic level, this is going to require a lot of heart and brain power by people everywhere in our culture. However, I want to zero in on one particularly influential segment of the population by sharing with you a question I've been asking more and more people across the country. Here's the question:

"What is the one group of people in America who have the most influence on the quality and quantity of time parents spend with their children?"

When I ask this of front-line workers, about seventy-five percent will respond "Employers." When I ask it of managers and employers, about seventy-five percent will respond, "Parents themselves." In both cases, each will give the other's answer as the second choice, but it takes managers and employers longer to get it out of their mouths.

203

Let's be totally honest. We're not very good at parenting in this country. We're far better at making movies, building bridges, airplanes and databases, inventing new drugs, advancing technology, increasing agricultural yields per acre, creating new businesses and besting athletic records. We're far more committed to excellence in those realms than in raising our children. To argue otherwise is to fly in the face of the evidence. Each of us as an individual must seize responsibility for the disintegration of parenting, even those among us without children…for the fate of our culture is directly bound to it.

Having acknowledged this, let's talk now about the special power and responsibilities of employers. Who really sets the agenda that establishes the basic structure of life in America? Employers. Sure, if a person doesn't like the texture and length of a given job, he has the freedom to look elsewhere. But the fact is, most jobs in America increasingly involve the manipulation of technology. This means there is generally less and less choice about the texture of work. It's bound to involve intense volumes of electronically-driven tasks. Furthermore, most full-time jobs range well above forty hours a week on up when you throw in commute time, work performed at home and The Distraction Factor. It's also a fact that whereas, by law, many other countries give even entry level workers four or five weeks a year off (Austria five, Belgium four, Switzerland four, Norway four, Sweden five—and many give more by agreement—Denmark five weeks, France five to six, Great Britain four to six, Italy four to six, Sweden five to eight[95]), the standard fare in America is a tiered system that starts with one week off at the end of the first year and gradually, over seven to ten consecutive years on a given job, moves upwards towards three weeks total vacation, four for some. There is little or no portability, which most Europeans have by law. With diminishing job security, the percentage of people who will ever see four weeks of paid vacation in our country is likely to shrink.

The texture of work, the length of the work week, the

204

amount of time off, the unspoken expectations that keep people working in their heads even when they're home—all of this is largely in the hands of employers.

Business has long tried to exist in its own stratosphere, separate from social obligation. That's what the phrase, "business is business" means—the belief that business has nothing to do with you, personally or with society. It serves its own end, which is to make a profit. This point of view always had serious limitations but it is simply unacceptable now, in light of the parenting deficit. Employers have an enormous obligation to the society that comprises the very matrix within which they exist.

Every smart businessperson knows that one of the key responsibilities of leaders, perhaps *the* key, is to identify the area of greatest positive leverage potential and invest the bulk of the company's power there. You're looking to get a thousand feet of movement from an inch of push. The one point in the system of any society where there is indisputably the greatest leverage to build quality in, reduce costs, remain competitive in the world and create jobs is the parent-child relationship. *It's a no-brainer.* Without Total Quality Parenting, Total Quality Management cannot possibly assure the success of the country.

To raise one healthy, well-loved, well-rounded American human being is a political, economic and social act of unqualified importance.

A commitment to exert such leverage for the greater good requires a long-term perspective and a profound capacity for caring. Both of these have rarely been given priority in the basic arithmetic of business strategy, but that's exactly why we're in this fix. To assure our nation's continued preeminence in the world, we're going to have to abandon the old amoral paradigm. The new paradigm is as basic as an ounce of prevention being worth a pound of cure, but it's not going to be easy to implement. The good news is there are plenty of short-term benefits that accrue from the effort, most of them measurable in increased productivity, reduced absenteeism, enhanced workforce loyalty and customer loyalty. Where do we start?

Theory

First, we must have a comprehensive theory of business, not a "by the seat of the pants" reactive approach. Most of the businessmen I've encountered in my career have a philosophy but not a theory. The philosophy is a construct of values and conclusions based on their personalities and experience. This is desirable and necessary. But a theory involves more. It not only embodies assumptions about the future. It actually has verifiable predictive power. You might look to Deming, Drucker, Senge, Bartlett and Ghoshal, Collins and Porath or a number of others who regularly share their learning in the Harvard Business Review. A theory allows us to construct a whole series of sentences which state, "If this, then that…" Deming's theory, attending to our nature as brilliant feelers, could be expressed as follows: "If we really drive fear out of the organization, then people on all levels will want to contribute. If we honestly invite their contributions under these open, trusting conditions, in brainstorming and decision making, then we'll come up with better ideas. If we come up with better ideas contributed from all levels and departments, then we'll build more quality into our products and services. If we build more quality into our products and services, then we'll drive down costs and drive up productivity. If we do that, then we'll enhance our competitive position, gain market, improve net profit, create a lot of jobs and have a secure future."

Of course, a valid theory will also take into account the amount and quality of effort and time necessary to get results. It will tell us, "If we've been managing with mistrust and fear, then it will take a lot of sustained safety, nurturing and love to convince people we're serious." Peter Senge and James

O'Toole, to mention only two influential business thinkers, stress the critical importance of patience in shifting the way an entire system operates.

For the purposes of what I'm about to suggest, a specific, well-formed theory of business is called for. It must include two tightly inter-related assumptions. First, business is a system and the more we build quality into it from the beginning, the lower will be our costs and the more likely we are to be consistently profitable. Second, trust *is* a form of quality. The more trust you build into the workplace, the more people will contribute and the more they contribute, the more innovative and competitive you'll be. When you take the combined real-world success of Deming and Senge, you have ample evidence this theory is valid.

Now you might have a theory of business completely opposed to the one cited here. Your theory might largely be built around this basic assumption: "If I trust only myself, I'll be able to control the destiny of my business." You might be willing to be "Answerman" all the time—just another incarnation of a superman—running around putting out fires and calling that leadership. You're entitled to that opinion, of course, but the suggestions I'm going to make here are not likely to find favor in your eye, nor will they work for you. Supermen create self-fulfilling prophecies that lead to the failure of any trust-based operating system. If you really want out of that spin-cycle, a leap of faith is called for.

The Limited Approach

Some of us may be amenable to the self-description "cautious optimists" or "realistic idealists." We see the logic of the theory I've suggested. We see the seriousness of our social dilemma. Still, we are unwilling or unable to envision a comprehensive strategy to address it. Is the choice, then, to do nothing? Hardly. Companies, like individuals, do not all move at the same pace. Faced with the magnitude of our challenge, any progress is welcome in the hope that the compound effect of millions of incremental improvements across the nation will yield the necessary leverage to shift the balance. So, there is plenty that can be done, even by small businesses, in the service of a future that places humanistic over materialistic values at the center of our lives.

Leading Examples

One of the most common complaints I hear from middle-level managers and front line workers is, "the boss doesn't really walk the talk." Since we've already spent considerable time looking at the inner journey, it should suffice to state here that to lead any transformation, you have to practice what you preach. Best of all, is to practice it *before* you preach it. If this is true of bosses, it's just as true of those deeper within the organization who wish to wield leadership influence. So, if you're passionate about creating a genuine win-win between work and personal time and you're not already a stellar example, you must begin attending to your own need for balance. Set some clear boundaries for yourself around time, energy and stress and let them drive you to innovate in managing your day so you can take care of yourself and your family. Let people see both your efforts and their results.

The Right Stuff

If it's self-evident that leadership by example is a high-leverage behavior regardless of what kind of program, process or strategy we wish to implement, it's equally self-evident that regardless of what kind of strategy, program or process we wish to implement in a business, we need the right people in the right positions in the right physical environment, the right compensation and reward, the right on-going training, the right technological and staff support and the right management style. A comprehensive exploration of all these "rights" is a book in itself. Fortunately, there are a number of good titles at your local bookstore devoted to them. However, I do feel obligated to concisely address the first "right" here since I so commonly run into an inadequate understanding of how vital it is to be highly selective in determining who fills every single position in a business, including the fellow who changes the light bulbs. Here are the six critical practices as I see them.

First, to build a great workforce that is so effective and efficient it can create an array of realistic family-friendly choices for itself, we must hire people with the character capable of developing into great players for their respective positions. Which would you rather hire, someone short on skills but long on character or someone long on skills but short on character? Skills and knowledge can be learned. In fact, when the right character is present, they'll be acquired with optimal diligence and speed. Character, on the other hand, is not something we acquire quickly. Its basic dynamic is largely set in childhood and is likely to expand only gradually through experience after the first five to seven years of life. This means we ought to be *hiring* character and *developing* skills. If we can get both, great, but character traits such as integrity, honesty, energy, sensitivity to others, a strong desire to contribute, persistence, loyalty, responsibility, imagination, humor are all far more essential to long-term success than knowledge or skill. Every real story about an individual who started at the bottom and worked his or her way into a position of leadership over time is a story of character. This seems plenty logical. Yet, clients are quick to show me their nicely printed job descriptions but not one has ever pulled out a *character description* to go along with it. Consequently, a far from ideal choice is made in hiring. Then, the problem is compounded in a failure to acknowledge and forthrightly deal with a poor choice as soon as it becomes evident.

It's imperative we invest some time looking at those people who have been our best performers in every given position and distill their core character traits into a description that can be shared with prospective hires. As part of this inquiry, we want to achieve clarity about why these folks fit so well in the company culture because cultural fit matters a great deal. We're not looking for *prima donna*s who are highly productive on the operational side and highly destructive on the cultural side. Seen through a wide angle lens, these folks actually hurt us more than they help us.

If we doubt our own ability to perceive the necessary traits for a position, there are "predictive index" assessments available through a variety of companies—Profiles International in Waco and Niemann in Salt Lake City, to mention only two. These assessments are very helpful but in my experience there is no substitute for clarity and straight talk during the hiring interview. One simple tool we can develop to facilitate these discussions is the "*This not That*."

When a candidate has impressed us sufficiently that we're close to offering a position, we look him or her in the eye and say, "We like what we see in you and we're inclined to offer you a place on our team. Before we do that, however, there's something we want you to give very serious consideration over night. Then we'll talk again tomorrow. We have a very definite sense of the kind of character we want in this position and in our company in general. We think you fit the bill, but it's important we err on the side of being absolutely explicit about this so you and we can make the right decision. It will be disruptive of your life and ours if ninety days from now, either or both of us have to decide we've made a mistake. So, please give your most honest consideration to what I'm about to share. For this particular position, we're looking for individuals who are...

This not That

(Elaborate concisely on each as you proceed.)

> Solidly ethical, not creatures of convenience
> Sensitive, not cynical
> Team players, not lone eagles
> Quick learners, not plodders
> Consistently energetic, not easily fatigued
> Assertive, not aggressive
> Readily responsible, not shirkers or blamers
> Totally honest, not dissemblers
> Self-confident, not ego-maniacs
> Good at handling set-backs, not easily defeated
> Well-rounded, not workaholics
> Ambitious with integrity, not just ambitious

Now, we know this is a tall order and we don't expect any one person to be able to honestly say, 'That's me 110 percent. Sign me up!' We all have our shortcomings and every single one of us on this planet is a work in progress. So we don't want you to think this is an absolute 'all or nothing' proposition. We invest in our people. We really help them grow. But, by the same token, we've got to have the right stuff to work with. That means these character traits matter. What we're asking is that you go home and think about this tonight. Do some real soul-searching. If there is any one of these criteria for which you feel you may not be a great fit or with which you aren't really comfortable, we should have a very frank discussion about it because we don't want to find out three months from now that either we made a mistake or that if we'd have known you needed a certain kind of support, we could have been further down the road already helping you fulfill your potential...rather than having lost three months or so in discovering it. Does this make sense?"

When the "*This not That*" is delivered with the proper blend of sensitivity and directness, it's extraordinarily helpful in hiring the right people. Yes, some candidates are intimidated and end up doing everyone a favor by withdrawing. Far more of them, however, are grateful for such clean definition and return the next day eager to have a full and frank discussion about who they really are and what they need in order to fulfill their potential.

The second practice is creative recruiting. We must cast a broad net in our search for character and talent, not just keep working the same old fishing grounds. We can and should go anywhere there's a reasonable possibility we might find the kind of person we're seeking, starting with right here in the ranks of our own organization. I've consistently been able to help clients discover talented people right in front of them. Beyond exploring within, we can reach out to high schools, colleges and universities, service organizations, all kinds of clubs and other professions. We can search and advertise through the Internet. We can use tried and true employment agencies. We can hold career nights to expose our business opportunity to a large number of possible candidates in one fell swoop. Great teams actively scout for talent, whether they're in the athletic or business arena.

However, if we do reach out into the community for exploration and exposure, yet fall back on the same old language we see recycled through employment ads across the country, we're blowing the opportunity. We must create marketing and advertising phrases that speak to the specific character we're after. This isn't hard. It only calls for a few creative inventions out of our authentic vision of the candidate. For example:

Highly supportive manager/coach seeking person to fill
_____ position. Prefer ___ years experience but,
above all, we hire ethics, talent and character, not a
resume, so if you think you've got the stuff, call us.
Family-friendly, wide-open culture. No heavy-handed
bosses here!"

Third, to further ensure we get the right people, it's highly desirable to have each candidate interviewed by at least two of his or her potential peers in addition to whatever managers initiate and are responsible for the process. Front line workers can be trained to do effective interviews and abide by all the appropriate laws. In smaller companies, they can be taught what to look for in employment applications as well do reference checking. They should each have an equal vote in the decision. When all the interviews are completed, an in-depth discussion among all the interviewers should take place, followed by a vote. If it's not unanimous, I generally counsel, "Keep talking until it is or, if you're just not getting there, pass." We must be optimistic. There's someone out there for this position we can all agree on. Patience is required in building a great team. Time and time again, I've seen employers who were convinced, "I just can't find good people," be happily surprised when patient commitment to this process brought a great individual into the business.

Fourth, we must execute the *90-Day Cut or Keep Decision*. This is an obligation so many organizations neglect. By so doing, they undermine their own values and vision. The deadline comes and goes. No review is held. Everyone is busy, the excuse goes. No decision is made, which means you keep individuals who might be clearly unacceptable, but because they have warm bodies and because so many managers dislike hiring (foolishly seeing it as an interruption of their work) and because they often aren't very skilled at it, they just let the *90-Day Cut or*

Keep Decision slide. This omission is a tax levied on your company. It costs you dearly. A good personnel lawyer will tell you that about ninety-five percent of the disruptions and legal actions brought against a company are caused by five percent of the workers—people whose character weaknesses were readily recognizable within the first ninety days. When the red lights line up on someone, make the tough decision now, rather than a year or two after mediocre performance and a whole host of other possible problems. Besides damaging yourself, you do a terrible disservice to the good folks who comprise most of your workforce by allowing unacceptable behavior and performance to be institutionalized.

Fifth, having hired the right people, grow them as if you were an inspired gardener. Set up skill-mentoring. Buy them books and tapes. Send them to school and bring in teachers. Know where each person wants to go with his or her career and life and actively, consistently facilitate the journey. Make nurturing talent a top priority.

Sixth, but not least...even with the right people on the front line you must have the right leadership style around them if you want to realize the full potential of the business. The right people are strong, even when they're janitors, couriers, doorpersons, receptionists or porters. They want to be educated, supported and given appropriate autonomy as soon as they're ready for it. They want to be told the truth in a timely manner—both good and bad. They want to be treated with trust and respect. They want to be asked for their input on a consistent basis. They want to co-author the company's future, not be dominated by Control-Freak Management.

You *can* get good people. They're out there. Follow these fundamentals with due diligence and you'll find them. Let me assure you, it is completely worth the extra effort. *There is a dramatic difference between an organization that has about seventy-five percent of the right people and one that has upwards of ninety percent.*

214

So, now as we proceed more deeply into The Limited Approach, we're going to assume we are doggedly implementing these six hiring practices. We're moving towards a critical mass of excellent, sensitive, caring, responsible, dedicated folks with solid integrity on our roster.

EAP's

Employee Assistance Programs, also known has EAP's, have proven themselves highly effective over the last fifteen years. These are provided by specialized companies such as LifeWorks in Boston, formerly known as WFD, and Working Solutions in Portland, Oregon. Both have national reach. Companies such as IBM, Starbucks, Eddie Bauer, Boeing, AT&T, Xerox, Aetna and Reynolds and Reynolds use such services. However, don't let the size of those companies throw you. The actual cost of the broad array of offerings we're about to discuss generally runs from a dollar and a half to three and a half dollars per employee per month. One of my clients covers all 80 of his employees for $250 a month.

EAP's offer 24-hour 800 hot lines to provide referrals for sick child care, general day-care and summer care needs, parenting advice, marriage and personal counseling, substance abuse counseling, psychological and health crisis intervention, stress management, house cleaning services, elder care, estate, retirement and general financial planning, educational counseling—just about everything within reason that can support the full array of an individual's needs, bringing more peace of mind so he or she can go to work and focus on the job at hand.

The number one cause of unscheduled absence, as well as late arrival and early departure from work, is lack of available care for a sick child. EAP's quickly put the employee in touch with competent, trustworthy providers in these situations. If that were the only reason people used the EAP, it would pay for itself, given the extraordinary cost of unscheduled absences. If you want to go further, the EAP can assist you in setting up Decap Programs—pretax dependent care accounts that assist employees in setting aside the necessary financial cushion to handle the cost of care during the inevitable illnesses. EAP's can also advise you on establishing subsidies for lower wage employees' sick child needs.

Independent studies have shown about seventy-five percent of those who used an EAP service reported taking less time away from their job than before the service was available and doing a better job as a result of feeling less stress and worry—which just stands to reason. Again, consider this: less stress, better focus, leading to increased efficiency and productivity, yielding the very real possibility of reduced and/or more flexible work shifts.

Given the low cost and its obvious contribution to employee focus and loyalty, the EAP requires no grand strategy or elaborate decision-making process. It's a no-brainer as a first step to begin demonstrating your commitment to the families of your workforce.

Mentoring and Coaching

No formal structures and no additional expense outlays are necessary for you to have heart to heart talks that begin to make a difference in people's lives. You don't have to be the boss or a manager, either. If you're actively committed to keeping your life in alignment with your most deeply held values, you have something greater than authority to share with people—authentic influence. So, share it with those who are hungry for encouragement and ideas. Gradually engender a neighborhood of commitment within your own work area or department.

If you are the top man or woman of the organization or of a department, you undoubtedly have some great employees who have a tendency to get caught up in The Momentum Function.

They get carried along by the surge of work and stay unnecessarily long after they should have gone home. You can start by identifying a few of these folks and having heart to hearts with them. Let them know there are no brownie points for excessive hours. The same goes for people who suffer from an "Over-pleasing Complex". One Over-Pleaser said to me, "I just can't say no to people" meaning his boss, colleagues and customers. I replied, "Well, you don't seem to have a hard time saying no to your family. You do it constantly." He got the point...and took immediate sustainable action to rebalance his life. Let Over-Pleasers know explicitly that they can please you the most by giving you a good day's work and going home to give themselves and their families a good evening. They'll bring more long-term value to the business if they're more fulfilled as total human beings.

A lot of Momentum Functioners and Over-Pleasers never stop to consider that their willingness to work almost any amount of hours *actually breeds inefficiency*. People who are so willing to work harder aren't likely to work smarter. I've literally pushed both types out the door at the end of their shift. Yes, that's exactly what I'm encouraging you to do, *with humor and affection*. People will respond with profound gratitude when you put your arm around them, and walk them out of the office, saying, "Please go home! Read your kid a book. Actually listen to your wife. Go for a walk or a work-out. Take care of yourself. Take care of your family." Few behaviors speak more loudly and build more loyalty than this kind of active support in helping people re-establish their non-negotiables.

Imagine if you help a family gain a half-hour a day. That adds up to about 115-120 hours a year. Imagine if half of that time were spent reading a child a bed-time story. What would the impact be on that child's life—*fifty-five to sixty more hours a year listening to dad read a story?* A few of my clients have assisted employees in moving closer to work, cutting upwards of *two hundred hours a year* out of their commutes. This is how we must begin to think. We apply this sort of approach to traditional time-management of work tasks. Why wouldn't we mobilize the same technique to do a better job being with our kids?

There are other ways to mentor as well. I have clients all across North America who care enough about helping their people, they send streams of them—front-line as well as management—to our leadership workshop, whose whole purpose is to help them grow from the inside out, to bring more depth and less speed to their lives, to make greater contributions to creating a genuine win-win between work and family. These organizations see such developmental learning experiences as a key component of their extraordinary success.

Individualized Management

There is a traditional school of thought to the effect that policies should and must be uniformly applied to everyone in a business. However, there is another school of thought being referred to as "Individualized Management" which in essence says we ought to tailor every aspect of a job as closely to the individual's need as possible if we want optimal performance. In other words, if "mass customization" is good for the external customer, why shouldn't it also be good for the internal customer? Those who fear this will lead to chaos should remember there are always limits to choice, for consumers as well as workers. The point is to push the envelope on both fronts. We don't know what the ultimate possibilities are without stretching our current reality. It's precisely this kind of stretching that leads to innovation.

Liz Dodd, the office manager at Crystal Valley RV of Crystal Valley, Illinois, the largest RV dealer in the greater Chicago area, gave birth to her boy Alex in November of 1998. Liz had originally planned to go back to work after three weeks and put Alex into some form of day-care. She attended our leadership workshop when she was five months pregnant and the experience radically changed her relationship with the whole idea of motherhood. Fortunately, her general manager, Bill Mirrielees, had attended the workshop several months before her. With his full blessing and the support of the rest of the organization, she began bringing baby Alex to work with her only weeks after his birth. Bill set aside a special room for them so they'd have quiet and privacy for breast-feeding. Liz brought all the necessary baby paraphernalia, including a motorized swing to help Alex sleep.

Now a lot of employers and managers at this point in hearing the story are worried about "screaming babies" all over the place. The fact is, however, when babies get their fundamental needs met—nursing, cuddling and cooing, timely changing of diapers and temperature-sensitive clothing—they are far less likely to cry. Would the papoose have been as popular in days gone by if those babies were screaming in their mothers' ears all day? Hardly. Well, as it turned out, the entire workplace was enhanced by Alex's presence. During breaks, it was common for colleagues to come knock on the door to see how Alex was doing, offer to hold him for a few minutes and just generally give Liz a great deal of support. Nearly a year after this Individualized Management began, Bill reported to me Alex was still coming to work three days a week with Liz. The whole experience had given the culture at Crystal Valley RV a beautiful way to become more tightly bonded.

Individualized Management or Management by Exception is something I'm familiar with from the inside out. My single fatherhood lasted for thirteen years, beginning in 1979. Initially, I was a salesman and the only single parent on our sales force. When Ben was six, my child-care support system was in constant flux. My bosses came to our aid by encouraging me to bring Ben to work whenever necessary and put him in our meeting room. He spent many a Saturday or weekday afternoon there with legos and coloring books. My sales colleagues welcomed him into the environment. They loved watching the progress of his colorings and constructions. In fact, Ben frequently sat in our mid-week morning sales meetings before I'd take him to school. Those meetings took on a far more civil, light and positive air because of his presence. In fact, our entire department was uplifted by this practice of Individualized Management.

Single fathers were an utter anomaly at the time, but no one complained about my getting "special treatment." My manager actually encouraged me to become more efficient so I could work my shift and go be with Ben. That's exactly what I did. I mastered my selling and appointment-making skills. I built genuine relationships with my customers and, more often than not, they were quite willing to come back on *my* time. Our schedule alternated from morning to afternoon during the week. By improving my skills and sticking to it, I frequently had the time to sit in on Ben's pre-school and elementary classes. In fact, Ben's pre-school teachers celebrated my spending more time involved with his class than any other parent.

This was all made possible by the active Individualized Management of my boss. He came out a winner, too. My deeper purpose in giving Ben the lyrical childhood he deserved made me a more disciplined and creative professional. I was the top salesman four out of five years and did it in less time than the others. I was the Yoda of time management. So my boss won. My colleagues were enriched by Ben's presence and, clearly Ben and I won. This was not a win-win. It was win-win-win-win.

There are numerous lessons that can be derived from my brief story, but I want to emphasize one above all others. It was not a need to be number one that made me number one, nor a hunger for material things. It was not competitive drive that made me more competitive throughout my career. We humans are more marvelous than that. We must believe this. There are more powerful motivators available to us than material hunger, fear, ego and external goals.

What made me a devoted father also made me a devoted professional. Each nourished the other and created an integrity within me. Integrity is a word whose root means "touching." An integrated person is one whose various parts or pieces are literally in touch with each other. They fit together snugly, like a complete puzzle. When you have integrity, you have purpose. When you have purpose, you have unfettered creative energy. But, how can the pieces of a person fit together in a state of integrity if he is more accountable to work than to his own health, personal development, marriage or children?

We have been mistaken in thinking the most dynamic drivers of business achievement have to do with money or exhortations to be number one and so forth. Such calls actually appeal to a relative minority of workers in any sustainable manner. If we want to break through to the untapped motivational depths of the large majority, we've got to think bigger than business. We've got to help people live lives of joyful balance, lives that honor and protect their non-negotiables, lives rich with integrity.

Ben is a grown man now, a beautiful, balanced, responsible, self-starting, curious, funny and compassionate person who has just become a father himself. He's already begun giving his own son the lyrical childhood *he* deserves. I also have an eighteen-year old stepdaughter whom I've been helping to raise now for a decade. Through her and her friends, I see how much more difficult it's becoming every day to be a child or a parent...so the issue is very much alive for me. Please don't make the mistake of thinking that my example is somehow too special to be of value. Having been a married parent, a single parent, a step-parent and now a grandparent makes me quite representative of today's culture. What's more, in my many years in management, I surrounded myself with responsible people of integrity from all sorts of family structures. I gave them a supportive work environment. I managed them by exception as much as possible and almost *without exception*, they more than repaid the organization.

At the very least, take some of the basic steps, the very small risks we've been touching on in The Limited Approach: Leadership by Example, Employee Assistance Programs, Mentoring and Coaching and Individualized Management. If you've done your job hiring and developing the right people, there will be definite business gains. However, your sense of personal gratification in contributing to the healing of our culture by enhancing the well-being of specific families with specific children will go well beyond the business.

The Comprehensive Approach

The Comprehensive Approach involves a substantially different way of viewing your business than is traditional. It should be taken as a given that each of the ideas presented under The Limited Approach should be folded into The Comprehensive Approach. However, to execute on this broader strategic basis requires a greater willingness to move beyond the edge of your comfort zone. It calls you to a higher level of leadership and a deeper level of personal inner work. Taking this Approach means you have the vision on both the moral and pragmatic levels. It means you see the huge potential of *openly engaging* every member of your workforce in the quest to enhance business performance *and* reduce hours and stress while maintaining or even increasing pay. It means you're willing to take a number of good risks in the service of this vision. Of course, it also means you know that you can't control what people do in the increased spare time you're going to create. Some may go to the bars! But you *can* wield considerable influence by consistently communicating and coaching and having structures and processes in place that all speak the same message: "Business is a wonderful enterprise but there's more.

Go home, be a person, be a mate, be a dad, a mom, a son, a daughter…make a full, rich life!"

More Leadership by Example

As with The Limited Approach, you must start with yourself…you must begin practicing what you're going to preach and let people see you doing it. Let them in on the difficulties as well as the successes. Then, pull together your managers and let them know of your serious intention. Assure them this will be a measured, step by step process. It won't happen over night. Encourage them to examine the lack of balance in their own lives and begin taking some baby-steps to bring more depth, less speed. Pledge your support and ask for theirs in doing the same for the entire workforce. Characterize the undertaking as, in many ways, no different than any other business undertaking…because in many ways, it's not. It mobilizes a lot of the same talents and resources.

Next, hold a series of grass-roots meetings that will run from a half hour to an hour each. In each meeting, you'll have a portion of the entire workforce across departments and levels of responsibility. In these meetings, you start by declaring your conviction that tending well to personal health and development, marriage and children are not negotiable. You have no desire to build your success on someone else's parenting deficit or time poverty.

Now, you're going to show a specific structure and process that will guide the unfolding of a comprehensive plan. You'll have to state and restate through each grass-roots meeting that you know this is a heck of a challenge but you're convinced that reductions in hours and stress without reductions in pay are possible for virtually every position *if* we mobilize all the ingenuity of the organization toward that end. Progress will come slowly at first, baby-steps, perhaps…then longer strides and longer...over time. You'll point out that a daily gain of a half-hour yields about 120 hours a year...a gain of an hour 240 hours a year...imagine the impact if half that time were spent reading to children, or going for a hike with them, or just hanging out in their room.

Some people will respond with immediate enthusiasm. Most will be interested but cautious. Some will be convinced it's just a scheme to cut their pay or benefits. You'll consistently encourage discussion. It will come slowly at first. Over weeks and months, if you lead by example and keep the conversation going throughout the organization in formal and informal settings, you'll gradually experience a level of openness and honesty you didn't think was possible.

The Vision Team

My relationships with my clients are measured in months and years, not weeks. I'm brought in as a transformational coach, not a trainer or "installer." In each of my client organizations, we establish a team that becomes the central engine of change. We usually call it The Vision Team. It's permanent, meaning it will exist in some form indefinitely. Its purpose is to drive continuous improvement and innovation by developing formal and informal structures, processes, policies and learning opportunities that grow the business by supporting the balance, integrity, knowledge and skill of all workers. It explicitly looks at ways to create a healthier distribution of time and energy between work, personal and family life. It will often instigate the formation of process improvement or project teams, whose life-spans are generally terminated when a process has been duly improved or a project successfully completed.

Composition

The Team is comprised of a cross-section from all departments and levels democratically elected by their peers. If the boss wants all department heads on the team, fine, as long as the elected members equal or exceed them in number. If he wants to exercise an "option" to appoint a couple of people, just a couple, who weren't elected but whom he believes have something important to contribute (other than raw political leverage), he should do so. Sometimes our most creative thinkers aren't all that popular. We need them to stir us up. All elected representatives will serve for a minimum of a year. Anyone who's worked in a team setting and has first hand experience of the "forming, storming, norming and performing" phases described by Peter Scholtes in his *Team Handbook* knows it can take considerable time and trauma before real dialogue is achieved, particularly when the issue at hand is one that so openly involves personal values.

In addition to elected members, the Team will regularly invite spouses and children of employees to participate—a calling in of the spirit of the child and the mother-blessing. Decisions will affect them and they may have some important input and ideas no one else would come up with. Experts on various topics are also brought in on a regular basis to keep the Team learning.

Clearly, the larger the organization and the more spread out it is geographically, the more creative we must become in configuring this team. Representatives per population unit diminish in order to avoid establishing a Vision Team that is unwieldy and ill-suited to finding the optimal balance between deliberations and decisions particular to the business world. In such cases, a Virtual Vision Team may be called for or smaller local Vision Teams with clearly delineated authorities. They may conduct frequent (once a month or every two months) town hall style meetings in order to sustain openness and the flow of ideas. They, in turn, send their own representation to the larger Team. There are a number of ways in which the whole structure can be arranged. The operative guideline is to err on the side of assuring effective representation from all corners of the company.

Leadership

Initially, managers may lead the Vision Team by virtue of their comfort with such responsibility, but for no more than three or four meetings. The company's top man will make a major impact on the Team when he states unequivocally that he will not be the leader and it is also his strong preference that this person *not* be a manager. The Team will then elect a leader who's primary job it will be to facilitate the meetings. This means this individual has to possess strong interpersonal skills and not be the least bit shy about disagreeing with or giving a "time-out" sign to someone in a higher position than himself. We've seen some wonderful people emerge among my client organizations. Managers scratched their heads wondering why they didn't know these individuals had such gifts. In situations where the Team feels there is no one ready to assume this responsibility, the best bet is to bring in a consultant to fit the bill until talent begins to emerge. The consultant can be involved long enough to nurture the facilitating skills of these people. This is eminently achievable within a year or two—a short time considering the Vision Team is forever.

Decisions

The Vision Team does not supersede management's right and obligation to act in a timely manner on those issues for which such action is clearly called. However, even in such cases, the Vision Team often provides a valuable advisory and sounding function equivalent to the cabinet of the U.S. Presidency. For most of the matters that clearly ought to be given over to the Vision Team, its principle method of decision making is generally either consensus or super majority, or both, depending on the situation. Consensus decision making means that when an idea is offered for a vote, *everyone* agrees with it at least 70% and will give it 100% support if it's adopted. The 70% is obviously a gut call, but having used this in many settings I can tell you people relate to it quite well. The 100% support means that even if you were barely at 70%, if the team adopts the decision, you're shoulder to shoulder, all of you. There are no water-cooler mutterings or rebellions. This is admittedly a slower way to achieve closure, but once you get there, you have a higher quality decision.[96] By super majority I mean 67 percent of the voters agree with an idea. Personally, I prefer consensus because of the depth and breadth of unity it creates. Of course it's hard work. When there's one hold-out telling us he's only at 65 percent we have to listen hard and work to help that person come on board. This can and usually does lead to a marked improvement in communication skills and a higher quality decision. What's wrong with a simple majority? Imagine we have thirty people in the room and sixteen of them vote for and fourteen against. Do we walk out with any real unification? No. We get a lot of divisiveness, water-cooler mutterings and rebellions. Better to build quality into the decision-making process. Take the time to get it right. Whichever method we use, the intention should be to walk out of the room on any decision day with everyone feeling the topic was well researched and each person was given an ample opportunity to speak his or her mind.

Before we look at a method of working the specific challenge at hand, a few words about teams in general. Teams are *not* the be all and end all for the simple reason that there is *no* be all and end all, period. But they can contribute a lot in mobilizing the energy and ideas of the front line. People want to contribute. Teams are a good way to facilitate that. More often than not, the collective IQ of a team will far exceed that of any one individual. Not always, however. It's important to be up front about this. Sometimes, the opposite occurs and the group sinks to a lower intelligence than anyone in the room! Let's not forget that every tyrant in history had large "teams" of highly intelligent individuals around him supporting his insanity. There's no substitute for leaders who have the mother-blessing within them. They have mastered the art of proximity, intuiting when to move forward and when to step back. To foster that kind of development, there's no substitute for the challenging inner work I've already described in detail on earlier pages. Bill Gore of Goretex has an idea he calls "antimanagement". He believes in finding great people, giving them what they need and getting out of their way. That's the desired state. No question about it. But there's a lot of road for most organizations to travel before they're even near the border of such a responsibility-rich province.

Just remember that if you seriously doubt the proposition that most people will do a good job given the right tools, education, trust and support they need, you're casting your lot with dark pessimists who are doomed to *the superman syndrome*. No one will ever live up to your expectations. You'll be arresting the miscreants forever.

Purpose and Parameters

Put together a team but don't expect perfection. Nurture it along, give it loads of support, access, resources, outside facilitators and all the learning opportunities you can find, whether they involve bringing people in or sending people out

Initially, you may define the purpose of the team as follows: "Redesign an entirely new workplace that represents your best thinking about how to put it all in balance with personal and family life. Start with a totally clean sheet. Nothing is off limits. Don't just get outside the box. Get outside the idea of even relating to boxes. Stand on your head. Take off your head! Get loose. Get bold. Get wild. There must be ways to increase efficiency, productivity and profits, shorten hours, maintain or even boost wages and benefits. Someone is going to come up with them in our country. Why not you? When you do settle on an idea, any idea you truly believe in and you've worked it down into the details, bring it to me. Let me repeat, *the real litmus test is your depth of conviction.* If you believe in something, come to me and I'll try to say, 'Yes.'"

Why is the depth of conviction the real litmus? *Because conviction makes the impossible probable.*

If you think your people are ready for an even grander orchestration of purpose, you might use "The Moonshot Challenge" as a context:

"Some of you will remember that President Kennedy challenged the nation to mobilize its resources to put a man on the moon before 1970. We did it, with time to spare. Here's our equivalent...and it's probably a lot more important because it concerns the quality of your time in this life, and that of your children and spouses. It has to do with undertaking a creative adventure right here on earth, right here in this business by finding ways to customize work situations so that you can achieve optimal happiness and effectiveness. We can imagine a ten-year horizon, but I'm confident we'll make substantial headway very soon. So, here's our Moonshot Challenge. I want to invite you to approach your task as a team with the following question:

'How can we redesign our work environment so we...

1. sell more product/service
2. grow the company—meaning more revenue and more jobs
3. increase wages, benefits and net profit while driving down costs
4. have more fun and much less stress
5. increase workforce loyalty so we basically only hire people because we've created new jobs, not because good folks left existing ones
6. increase customer loyalty
7. increase our security in the marketplace, which may mean increased market share or increased share of customer, whatever the strategic preference might be
8. constantly improve our operation
9. become more responsible citizens to our community and environment
10. accomplish all this while trimming and molding the work week throughout the organization—not just for a few—gradually down towards thirty-five hours, then thirty, then...who knows?' "

If this sounds outrageous to you, wait till you see how it invigorates people in a *sustainable* manner. Under common management practices today, a great deal of workforce commitment and vitality remains untapped, due to the cancerous hypocrisy eating at the core of the organization's integrity. It's essence is, as mentioned earlier, that we ask people to give high accountability at work while abdicating their accountability to themselves and their families. Further, we give yards of lip-service to respect and trust but we're afraid to hear what the workforce does *not* say, what it is really feeling in its heart of hearts. When you truly respect and trust someone, you invite them into the creative design of the company's destiny. You listen hardest to the issues that rankle you the most, because they hold the greatest potential for innovation. *Where there's pain, there's possibility.* No, what I'm proposing here isn't the least bit outrageous. What *is* outrageous is failing to make every effort to align the company's strategy and processes with the most cherished values of its workforce. When people are fully aligned, their talents are liberated.

To ignite the launch of the Vision Team, bring in someone who has an excellent grasp of the real essence of Deming's work and Peter Senge's extension of it. Spend a couple of days off-site for an introductory course in the 14 Points, Diseases and Obstacles or Senge's Five Disciplines of The Learning Organization. Deming's method has near endless depth. There are top leaders from business and the armed services who attended his four-day seminar numerous times. So you have to be prepared to keep studying his work, actively using it in the Team meetings. You'll be riding a vibrant learning curve together, even as you begin brainstorming. You'll have to maintain an open spirit of experimentation, which is exactly what Deming's work is designed to help with. His Plan, Do, Check, Act model encourages us to Plan and Do on a limited scale initially so we can eliminate a lot of the bugs and kinks before a broader roll out.

As imperfect as a team-based operating system can be, it's what I've seen work best.

People frequently ask consultants about "best practices." It's often out of their supermanly quest for quick fixes. I'm going to share a handful of ideas that particularly appeal to me. They're out in the "real world" being used to positive affect. But I can't overstate this: the two best practices on the planet are 1) making the inner journey to the water of life that creates authentic leadership and 2) collaborative effort in the workplace. Collaboration constitutes a kind of regathering of the fullness of our humanity. People are called to serve a higher purpose than their paychecks. They re-learn to listen to the pure, innocent voices within them. They re-learn to communicate with each other from the heart. None of this happens without the total commitment of a leadership that works its theory of business day to day and is possessed of a genuine willingness to give any team conviction a fair try. I've seen previously quiet and unassuming individuals flower in these settings. I've seen surprising ideas emerge, things I myself or the leaders of the company definitely wouldn't have thought the group capable of. Over and over again, I've been moved by the magic of desire and cooperation.

So, if you're hoping for an in depth catalogue of best practices, sorry to disappoint you. That's not my intention here. Navigate your own personal journey of grieving and, at work, support the gathering together of people who genuinely yearn to combine their talents to co-author a new destiny for the organization. If you do that, you'll create the kinds of innovations Tom Peters, Bob Kriegel and others like to write about.

Having made myself clear on this point, following is a handful of ideas that make a lot of sense to me and which I offer to a Vision Team for stimulation and consideration. These are evolutionary, not revolutionary. My belief is that through the persistent work of Vision Teams in implementing programs like these, we'll look back in just five years and see that we've gained substantial ground moving towards a balanced life. Each of these ideas has been written about in the general press, the business press or in business books. But, again, the key here is not a specific concept but *the development of a work environment based on genuine openness, profound trust, a shared vision and consistent contributions from all levels towards making that vision real.* People came up with every one of these ideas, people in businesses somewhere. The next round of innovations beyond these could truly just as well come out of *your* organization if you foster the depth and breadth of honesty within yourself and your business culture that I'm recommending.

Two brief warnings. First, if your mind is quick to reject a given concept, see if you can cultivate a second response before you read on. Your rejection only means the idea challenges your assumptions, not that it's a bad idea. Almost everything you think can't work *is* working somewhere because people cared about it enough to figure out how to make it succeed. Second, every idea *must be customized* to the needs of the individual organization. There's no such thing as a turn-key transformation. The Team drives the transformation, not some clever "plug and play" concept.

Reconfiguring Work Time

By "reconfiguring" I intend a broad set of possibilities that has to do with mass customization of work time in a manner different from the standard continuous cluster of eight or nine hours, five days in a row. This includes...

- fewer hours in the same number of days
- the same hours but fewer days
- the same hours but more days
- earlier or later hours in the same or different days
- alternating early and late shifts from day to day
- alternating longer and shorter periods in a given month
- job sharing and flextime
- the "Bank of Days"
- E-Holidays

Some of these ideas are so obvious and well-known, it's not necessary to elaborate on them. The underlying rationale to each of these programs is that when a company involves workers in designing their own schedule, a common outgrowth of a Vision Team, they become more focused, responsible, efficient and productive. Today's trendy lingo espouses involvement creating "buy in." I'm not particularly enamored of this or any language reducing every meaningful transaction to a buy/sell relationship. When managers have to "sell" workers, there's too much management persuasion and too little genuine exchanging and learning going on. When workers are treated as "stakeholders," "associates" or "partners" and honestly enrolled in determining and navigating the destiny of the company, there's no sale, just a lot of communication that awakens and invigorates people. They don't just "feel part of something". They *are* part of something. When it's done with sincerity, empowerment is not a technique. It's a way of infusing an organization with the oxygen-rich atmosphere of integrity. It says, "Father-boss-superman" does not necessarily know best how we should go about our work. We have faith in you. You figure it out. Try some stuff. See what works best." In my own consulting practice, I have yet to see any reconfiguration of work come out of a well-facilitated team process that did not increase efficiency, productivity, stakeholder morale and the quality of customer engagement.

The common sense of this approach is confirmed by economist Juliet Schor's findings that when hours are reduced incrementally—one or two at a time—and pay is *not* reduced—*a critical factor that initially challenges the paradigms of many employers and managers*—"a shorter workday has been shown to pay for itself." She adds, "Workers appreciated the company's willingness to schedule fewer hours and raise pay. As a result, they conducted more personal business on their own time and showed up for work more regularly."

Tardiness, absenteeism, unfocused and downright wasted time are all antivalues whose cumulative and exponential effect are difficult or impossible to measure with confidence. We have no way of knowing how the mishandling of just one customer multiplies its loss to us through negative word of mouth. *How many additional customers will not even give us a try because of this one?* What would the revenue have been? How would those relationships have enriched us? What might we have learned from those people? The same kinds of questions can be posited about one serious design or production line flaw. Consider the cost to an automobile manufacturer of a single recall. What was its real root cause? Was it stress, fatigue, arrogance, a lack of trust, a lack of conscientiousness? We don't get to live the parallel universe that would show us what might have been, but these are exactly the kinds of things Deming had in mind when he said that many of the most important numbers relevant to a business operation are "unknown and unknowable."[97] They clearly do have the potential to create serious drag on productivity and growth and we must attend to them.

There's nothing revolutionary about the idea that trimming hours without trimming pay will result either in the maintenance or increase of productivity. It's a gradualist approach that assumes that when you err on the side of trust and generosity, most people will be more trustworthy, conscientious and responsible.

When I became a manager under a man who respected my integrity needs as a single father, I gave him more quality in less time than most managers in the industry. I actually had eight days off every four weeks—a rarity in automotive retail. I also enjoyed sufficient trust that I could come in a few hours later or leave a few hours earlier when I judged that it wasn't injurious to business. Those extra hours added up to my being able to exercise regularly, stay fit and have the energy and focus necessary to be extremely effective when I was on the job.

Specifically, what I'm suggesting here in keeping with Deming's Plan, Do, Check, Act model is that the Vision Team might come forward and say to the entire workforce, "We believe there's real benefit in finding out if we can all do as good a job, or even a better job in one hour less per day, with no cut in pay. Others have done it. Why shouldn't we? If we succeed, we'll all have more time for ourselves and our families and the company will continue its success. We're going to start on a trial basis with X department, with whom we've already discussed this. They've been working 9 to 5. They're willing to be our 'trial run'. They're going to work 9 to 4 (or 10 to 5) for six months and see what happens. We'll monitor and measure their improvements, their efficiency, productivity, job satisfaction—including changes in stress levels—impact on customer loyalty and financial performance. We'll report back to the rest of you at the end of the six months. If the plan works out, we'll gradually fan it out through whatever other departments or areas it seems likely to work for."

Six months is probably the minimum time necessary to try most ideas. It's long enough to get people past the "honeymoon"and begin to live with the new program day to day. Once a commitment is made to a time-frame, it must be honored, barring a catastrophe. As mentioned earlier, I've seen managers rush in to find fault and cancel an idea. This is devastating to the spirit and creativity of the organization. Managers, grit your teeth and leave it alone. Drive to a nearby wood and scream if you must! But let it stand or fall on its own merit over time. More often than not all that will be called for is some minor adjustments. The front-line, given the freedom to experiment, will usually err on the side of protecting the business. One of my clients called me after I'd guided his sales force through a compensation and schedule redesign to report, "I was surprised they didn't want more. They really erred on the side of generosity to the house, when I was prepared to err on the side of generosity to them!"

Remember what this is all about. If it's possible to trim one hour a day from work, we have potentially gained back more than half those forty plus hours a month with our kids that have been lost since 1960. What else have we to do to gain back all that time? Eliminate a few "busy" things from our own weekly schedule. Eliminate some of our kids' rushing here and there to various lessons that may seem worthwhile but are just adding too much speed to their and our lives. We could grab back forty to fifty hours a month pretty quickly if hanging out with our kids were truly our top priority.

A few words about longer and shorter shifts based on predictably busy times. The general model to think about here is the life of a typical independent CPA. It's predictable that his workload will be greater in the months clustered around April, given the IRS's deadline for tax filing. Even during this admittedly busier time, it may be possible to spread hours, take longer lunch breaks and work later into the evening, for example, in order to maintain the opportunity to eat right, exercise, take a nap, visit with the family and keep stress at bay. But, under the current system, it appears to be unavoidable that there will be more total work hours invested around the April 15 deadline. So, during the remaining months of the year, maybe you work five or six hours a day or four days a week or even both.

The same kind of approach can be tried in a variety of ways in other businesses. Whether you're wedded to a month paradigm, a quarter or a year, there are predictably busy and slow periods. In fact, this is also true within the structure of an average day. Build hours around the busiest times and give people a break during the slow times. Let the schedule breathe with the business.

You can also create staggered or alternating schedules—morning shift one day, afternoon the next—to get the coverage you need and build variety into people's lives.

We can't mention these issues without bringing up the question of total operating hours. Clearly, a market place that is increasingly consumer-driven is going to generally offer more hours. But extended hours should not be seen as a necessary good in all cases. I've come across a number of situations in which a business or a group of businesses has been open late or very early "because we've always done it that way." It's been years since they actually measured whether or not there is sufficient business to justify these hours. Often, there isn't. The only remaining reason to keep the status quo is, "Our competitors are open." Yes, but they're not doing any business either. Why should we compete with them to see which of us can be more wasteful? Shortening the day allows for more family-friendly possibilities.

When you have the right folks, you can count on them to work hard when necessary. By the same token, they should be given extra hours or days off when possible without loss of performance. When you make the mistake of consistently scheduling too many or too few people, the work force perceives you as either disrespectful of their lives or out of touch with the front line realities of your business. In either case, you undermine their confidence in you. You can apply this concept to just one department or the entire business.

Another area for potential innovation is the flextime mentality that realizes there are twenty-four hours in a day and there are jobs in many businesses whose time of operation has no specific bounds. If there are a few people who are night owls and want to work weird hours, why shouldn't they, as long as it doesn't create unworkable disruptions for others?

Job sharing is another possibility. I've seen it work in an area where the conventional wisdom is it simply won't. Two veteran salesmen decide to team up with slightly over-lapping schedules so they can both get plenty of time off and still take good care of their customers. Automobile sales has traditionally been a hard-core "every man for himself" game. Yet, I've seen two gentlemen with sufficient maturity ask, "Why?" When I approach one of them towards the end of a month and inquire, "How's your month going?" he replies, "We're going to do about forty units." An authentic "We" on a car dealership showroom! Forty cars between the two of them, helping each other, handling each other's customers, both men making an excellent living and both having time for a life! If it can be done in a car dealership showroom, there are undoubtedly plenty of other settings where it will work, in spite of the conventional wisdom to the contrary. Encourage people to imagine the conventional wisdom to be wrong. You never know what life-serving plans will emerge.

Stimulate your Vision Team to ask over and over:

- Where can we cut hours?
- Who might benefit from a schedule that breathes with the month's or year's activities?
- Where might staggered or alternating schedules open up choices?
- Who might be interested in and benefit from flextime and job sharing?

When we engage people in this kind of co-creation, an essential truth is verified repeatedly around the country— mobilizing everyone's intelligence and passion to free up time to be better human beings will result in their paying back the company with increased focus, efficiency, responsibility and loyalty. The right people really appreciate such a commitment to integrity and balance. Remember, there are plenty of right people in the market place, many of them already working for you but half asleep under the numbing weight of an old system. When the system awakens, so do they.

The Bank of Days

This is an approach that is beginning to find favor but is still relatively unknown, so let me define it for you. It is also referred to as "paid-leave" or "time-off banks". There are a number of variations on a common theme. For me, the most interesting is the most comprehensive. The Bank of Days concept can eliminate distinctions such as sick days, floating personal holidays, grief leave and vacation and, instead, literally give the employee a Bank of Days which can be used for any purpose. If the company deems it workable, these days are also available to be split in halves. I suppose it's equally possible to split them in thirds or quarters, though, of course, all of such decisions are up to the Vision Team. Chubb Insurance in New Jersey gives its people a bank containing between 17 and 33 days, depending on tenure. Let's say a person has twenty days—neither a newcomer nor an old-timer. Ten of those days could be split and taken as twenty half days and still leave two weeks of vacation. So a person would have plenty of time to get and stay fit, have some personal restoration time, be with the spouse for a morning or at school with kids. You could get involved in extracurricular activities with them, take a daughter to dance lessons and stay and be present, or a son to soccer and stay and be present or just go to the beach as I did with Ben. You might make twenty weekends into two and a half-day weekends. Use your imagination.

According to a study done by Hewitt Associates, widely considered the preeminent consulting firm in the field of employee benefits, seventeen percent of all companies in the U.S. currently have some form of paid-leave or Bank of Days program. A quarter of these programs were initiated in 1993 or since. Thirteen percent of companies report they are considering a Bank of Days type program. Among those who have such policies is Hewlett-Packard which offers fifteen days to employees with one to four years tenure. H-P, like Chubb and many of the companies with such programs, allows the employee to carry days over into the next year. Avista Hospital in Louisville not only has a Bank of Days program. It has a unique component that actually allows employees to purchase an additional twenty-four hours a year to add to the bank and have the cost deducted in small amounts from the year's twenty-six paychecks. We're talking creative, here!

So far, in Hewitt Associates' study, such programs have been rated effective by eighty-six percent of those using them. They've yielded a decrease in unscheduled absences by nearly half of the employers who've implemented them. Only two percent of the companies surveyed reported an increase in unscheduled absences, which tells you what I've contended all along. Most people are trustworthy. Do right by them, they'll do right by you. The savings in decreased unscheduled absences is not small potatoes. Figuring the cost of sudden absences is nearly as challenging as calculating the cost of employee turnover, but one company, CCH, an Illinois-based firm specializing in human resources law, in a May 1997 study, found the annual costs of unscheduled absences in salary and wages as high as $1012 per employee. Multiply that out by your workforce population!

Look at what the Bank of Days encourages.

Let's start with honesty. A worker needs or wants some down time, regardless of the reason. What does he do in most companies to get an unscheduled day or half day off? He lies. He tells you he's sick. Why would you want to design any system that makes it necessary for people to lie to satisfy such a common need? What does that say about the company? How does that align with the company's espoused values, its lofty vision or mission statement? Any aspect of any system that tends to encourage lying is a direct assault on the integrity of both the company and its individual workers. The Bank of Days supports the truth. "I'm taking a day from my Bank." That's all that's necessary. The Vision Team, of course, can decide on the exact way to execute this, with a high degree of attention to the integrity issue.

The Bank of Days enlists the responsible participation of the worker in the general flow of his work. This is likely to have positive spill-over into his day to day performance.

241

The Bank of Days also invites more healthful living. Why would you want to squander your days laying in bed with a fever? Take care of yourself! Stay home and rest for a day. Get some exercise. Eat like a sane person. Take your vitamins. You could be skiing, rafting, scuba diving, hiking, laying on a beach, making a theater trip to the city, strolling the streets of Florence, or just working in the garden, for heaven's sakes.

The Bank of Days allows for real human flexibility. You can use it for joy and for sorrow. Maybe you're trying to finish a home improvement project. Maybe you're writing a book. Maybe you just want to have a "you and the kid" or "you and the spouse" day completely uninterrupted by any concerns. What if you're really devastated by the loss of a loved one? Some companies have no bereavement leave, some have a few days. Who knows how much time you need? You think you're going to be back on your feet in a few days if you lose a child, a spouse, a parent, a best friend, even a cherished pet of many years?

The Bank of Days is a big morale booster. It says to the employee, "Look, you're a good person. We know you have a life, needs and desires and you don't have to explain them to us. We trust you to follow the basic rules of the program. You'll have more choices and you'll feel better about coming to work...and we'll feel better about having you."

It may be too soon for conclusive research, given the recent implementation of most plans, but clearly there's a high probability we'll find that productivity will likely be enhanced, as will employee loyalty by this mass customization idea, The Bank of Days.

E-Holidays

One of the most common complaints I hear concerning the violation of any possibility for genuine restoration on a day off is, "Well, I've gotta check my e-mail," or "I'm taking the kids to the zoo, but I've gotta take my cellphone." Leaders are going to have to step up and acknowledge the benefit to the company when each individual employee, regardless of his or her position, experiences a complete absence of electronic intrusion. They're going to literally have to tell people, "Turn off your cellphone and beeper. Don't check your email. Take a *real* day off!" They can go further and declare specific days throughout the year, especially the national holidays, individual birthdays and vacations as absolutely off limits for any work-related activities. It is a riveting moment when a leader openly acknowledges and defines for his employees the boundaries beyond which they have every right to say to their colleagues, managers or the CEO himself, "Time-out. I have a life!"

More Possibilities

There are numerous other ideas currently in practice or experimentation designed to develop more mutual respect and integration between work and family.

Entertain the possibility that you can hold far more "virtual meetings" using the new technology so each person can speak from his or her own home. If such a meeting bought people an extra hour before leaving for work, it would have a substantial cumulative impact. Even if only a half-hour were gained, multiplied out across a year, it can make an important difference if the time is used wisely. Increasing numbers of companies are seeing that certain kinds of work can be performed as well or even better from home with the assistance of new technology. Home-based work can also make it viable for people in a variety of "constraint" situations to contribute at least part-time if they wish: soon-to-be or recent mothers, fathers taking partial paternity leave, those taking partial leave to care for a sick child or parent, those recovering from surgery.

Hal Morgan and Kerry Tucker did a yeoman's job providing a catalogue of concepts for your Vision Team. They're drawn from companies such as AT&T, Fel-Pro, HBO, Johnson & Johnson and Stride Rite, to name just a few. Among the ideas offered in their excellent book, *Companies that Care*[98], are...

- child and elder care consulting
- in-house child care and day camps
- referral or income set-aside services for child and elder care
- paid disability leave for childbirth with additional unpaid leave negotiable
- unpaid parental leave with same-job guarantees
- adoption leave
- financial gifts for newly weds, for newborns and for newly adopted children
- paid time off for care of ill family members at the discretion of management
- no-charge, on-site fitness centers
- on-site health centers
- subsidized emergency home care
- lunch-time seminars on a variety of family and health issues
- tutoring services for kids with learning challenges
- college scholarships
- subsidized legal services, tax preparation
- subsidized meal services, including on-site deli's or cafeterias that enable workers to eat a healthy lunch without having to drive somewhere, so they can get back to work more quickly and, consequently, go home sooner.

There's no shortage of ideas. Remember that none of these

is "plug and play". Each concept must be vetted and massaged through the Vision Team process.

Wild Imaginings

I want to suggest four possibilities that may seem like wild imaginings given the disposition of our present culture, but which I think are common sense and ought to be tried. Please keep in mind Deming's use of the Shewhart cycle—Plan, Do, Check, Act. It reminds us that we can experiment with bold concepts on a limited scale without putting the business at risk. If you really understand PDCA, you must believe there are very few ideas which, if they enjoy the conviction of the Vision Team, should not be attempted. Even if they don't succeed as designed, the learning we derive from them is often invaluable.

My first suggestion is an expansion of the vignette shared in The Limited Approach concerning Liz Dodd and her baby Alex. Let's call this "The Return of the Papoose". It's pretty much self-explanatory. Babies and mothers need to be connected. For literally millions of years, they were. The workplace as we know it is a very new environment, not the one for which we were designed by evolution. There are many jobs that women perform which do not involve danger. These positions should be identified by the Vision Team. Your business insurance company should then be consulted. Knee-jerk rejections by such providers should be challenged. Once the possibilities are clear, common sense guidelines should be established around each. On-site high quality child-care may well be a must, so the participating women can get a break when they need it. Students majoring in child development at nearby colleges and universities make enthusiastic on-site babysitters, as do many retired folks. A quiet, private, pleasant area for breast-feeding is also called for. To *whatever* degree it's possible and desirable for a given individual, some form of papoosing and on-site breast-feeding should be supported. Honoring the need for this early connection between mother and child can make a substantial difference in the development of the child. Babies don't create much ruckus when they get their essential needs met. This can also enhance the health, well-being, loyalty to the business and long-term contribution of the mother. Finally, the presence of babies in the workplace will facilitate the formation of happier, more tightly woven relationships. Babies make us feel good. They bring out our gentleness and humor. They evoke in us a desire to help, to reach out. They remind us we're a community that must pull together, a community with a life beyond any one individual. They restore dimension to a flattened world. They rejuvenate in us the spirit of the child and the blessing of the mother.

My second suggestion is what we can simply call, "The European Lunch". Most workers are not experiencing anything that can legitimately be called a lunch "hour." This is all the sadder when you think there are people just a plane ride away on the other side of the Atlantic taking three hours! It stuns even more when you consider that virtually all mammals nap. Frequently! That fact alone gives the lie to *the syndrome* belief we ought to be able to go nonstop for ten, twelve or more hours at a crack. The European Lunch concept is really worth the Vision Team's giving a good chew. Imagine the impact if you could have a genuinely healthy, leisurely lunch, go for a walk or workout, take a nap, do some reading, have a good chat with someone who matters. Fill in the blanks! A lot of people would be willing to work later, as do the Europeans, with a longer lunch break to moderate the whole flow of the day. It's not necessary to start with three hours, of course. Most people would likely be thrilled with an hour and a half or two. You can stagger the leave and return times throughout a department so there's coverage. Remember, try it on a small scale first. Fine tune it. Work the problem. Gradually lengthen the time. Set aside the thousand reasons you think of why it can't or won't work. Let

246

the Vision Team digest the possibility. History is not made by the people of a thousand no's.

My third suggestion is to close on the Sabbath. The English language may not have the words to express the weird irony of the fact that in our predominantly Christian culture, staying open Sundays is considered by many business people to be a *sacred* cow. Eliminating the Sabbath from the week is one of the most blatantly sacrilegious acts of American society. We're supposed to be a Judeo-Christian culture. The Ten Commandments are supposed to matter to us…not just a little. They're not rules to be bent or broken. They were handed down as the non-negotiables of a cohesive and righteous society. I can find no passages in Exodus where God says to Moses or anyone else, "Well, look, my personal favorite Commandment is the first one and some of these others are not such a big deal so I'll cut you a little slack if you mess up." What I do find in my dear wife's King James version of Exodus, Chapter 31, 12-14 is an absolutely unequivocal statement of the importance of the Sabbath. "And the Lord spake unto Moses, saying, Speak thou also unto the children of Israel, saying, Verily my sabbaths ye shall keep: for it is a sign between me and you throughout your generations; that ye may know that I am the Lord that doth sanctify you. Ye shall keep the sabbath therefore; for it is holy unto you: every one that defileth it shall surely be put to death: for whosoever doeth any work therein, that soul shall be cut off from among his people." Again in Verse 15, the Lord says "whosoever doeth any work in the sabbath day, he shall surely be put to death." There's no wiggle room here. There's no invitation to deal. There's no tiny little opening for you to ease your great big toe into with some gloriously tortured interpretation. Violation of the Sabbath will lead to a spiritual death—"cut off from among his people". The physical execution that will follow is almost a formality. When you are severed from your people, you might as well be dead. But just to be sure, you actually *will* be! But the cup is at least half full.

This Commandment represents God's gift of a sacred ritual to his people. It's supposed to keep us together *across generations* through consistent, deep connection to the values that define and invigorate our integrity as individuals and as a group. We're meant to take a day together, not to have a third of the workforce off this day and another third that and another third this. This ritual is a direct manifestation and expression of our biological need to bond. Without it, we devolve from a cohesive tribe into The People of the Golden Calf, raging materialists who can only understand value in actions and transactions, deals and dollars, not in dreams fulfilled. Like the leaders of Krypton, we are disconnected from the deeper meanings at the core of life, from each other, from our heritage and from the great rejuvenating mysteries. Incapable of authentic union, our most enduring ritual becomes the annual watching of the Superbowl.

You don't sand the edges of the sacred. They're sharp and uncompromising for a reason. The Sabbath Commandment, like all of them, is haggle-free, yet it is far more pervasively violated than "Thou shalt not kill" or even "Thou shalt not commit adultery." A small percentage of our nation engages in murder and promiscuity, but nearly all of us are complicit in the weekly strangulation of the Sabbath.

I have my own ideas about magic, power and intelligence in the universe. They don't easily match up with images offered by institutionalized belief systems. Regardless, I must tell you, I believe we Americans need the Sabbath.

In our leadership workshop, we take a hard look at our need for restoration. We invite our participants to consider that it's not an issue of specific religious belief. When a profound truth beckons, we must listen with a hearing beyond the filters of our family or cultural experience. We don't have to be Jewish or Christian to appreciate the words of King David in Psalm 23. "He maketh me to lie down in green pastures; he leadeth me beside the still waters. He *restoreth* my soul." The king, the most powerful man in his world, is telling us across the ages that being a king, possessing power, wealth and prestige, will not bring us goodness and mercy. It's all for nothing if we do not seek restoration amidst the sacred. As I repeat the verse of this psalm, I'm always particularly struck by the verbs: "He *maketh me...he leadeth* me..." David is telling us that no matter how high we may fly in the world, to maintain the wholeness and vision of a true king *we must be compelled by an even greater power* to leave the court—the workplace. Its seductions are so potent, so enveloping, we need help to get away, a voice from within or without, a voice with firm conviction *to make us* shed the material mantle of royalty and worldly illusion and be as we were as children, as David was as a youth, stretching out to rest in the lush meadows to dream, gazing up into the sky or down into calm, water. There is something to be felt there, something to be sensed that cannot be sensed in the hurly-burly of the working world, something so critical that without it we will *not* be able to transcend fear or find nourishment in the face of adversity. Our cups will *not* be full. They will *not* run over. We will *not* know goodness and mercy. The house in which we dwell will be merely ours, a material possession, with no meaningful connection to God or Creation or Nature or our fellow humans. Though David does not specifically mention the Sabbath in his poem, he has superbly described the essence of the Sabbath experience to which the Commandment calls.

Certainly, I don't favor putting people to death for sullying the Sabbath. Neither am I looking for Congress to legislate the Sabbath back into our lives—after all, depending on your creed, it's a different day of the week. Any movement in this direction will have to come from the ground up, one personal epiphany, one commitment at a time.

A huge percentage of those businesses that stay open on the Sabbath are in some form of retail. If you have the courage to be the first in your area to honor it, *you can actually gain competitive advantage* by explaining through whatever media work best in your market that you just decided enough is enough.

Something has to be held sacred. It's time to stop talking about family values and make a stand. A good copywriter would have a field day with this concept. He or she could create sheer poetry for you, calling for the public's support. Once again, before you conclude there's no way to garner sufficient support for this, speak from your heart to the Vision Team. Find a way to try it out on a limited basis. Give it three months in your off-season and see how your sales numbers stack up against previous years. Call your customers (during the week!) to see how they're responding to the message. Measure the impact on employee happiness. But never forget, as you measure, that you're trying to reinfuse your life and the lives of those around you with something that cannot be measured—restoration of the sacred.

*   *   *   *

Many of the ideas shared here are already in place at hundreds of businesses. A Hewitt Associates survey of 1000 major U.S. companies found in 1998 that 72% offered flextime, 36% job sharing and 20% at-home work. Yet, other research has shown that men substantially under-utilized these programs. Why? Largely because of a lack of active, visible, credible support by leadership. Leaders preaching one thing and practicing another.

In fact, a study by the Ford Foundation showed that even though employees who did use these various family-friendly programs were generally more efficient and productive than their counterparts, they also were more likely to suffer negative impacts on their careers...because of their commitment to a more balanced life. There is powerful pressure, both visible and invisible, within *the superman syndrome* credo to equate quantity with quality of work. This is ethically wrong. It's also dumb from a hard-core business perspective. A study by the University of Chicago of Fel-Pro Incorporated, a gasket and chemicals manufacturer in Skokie, Illinois, found that with

250

active support by leadership for such programs in place highly autonomous and participatory job designs yielded workers who used the family-friendly programs more *and submitted twice as many quality improvement suggestions as those who did not use these programs.*[99] This only supports the contention of economist Juliet Schor who states in *The Overworked American*, "Study after study shows that reforms that humanize the work environment, respect employees, or give them more latitude turn out to be very profitable."

Remember, a relatively small percentage of the workforce will be sustainably motivated by competitive challenges to outsell the guy down the street or become number one in some form. However, nearly everyone can be sustainably enthused about an employer who helps them be as accountable to their personal and family needs as they are to work, *someone who unequivocally supports the balance and integrity of their lives.* Again, if you have no children and don't even like kids, go ahead and be a cold pragmatist. This is still about higher efficiency, productivity, innovation, reductions in absenteeism, employee turnover, unemployment claims, workman's comp, litigation, theft, training and lost customers. What's more, raise really sane kids and after a generation, your taxes will drop significantly because we'll spend far less on law enforcement, lawyers, courts, prisons, health-care, social services, education and protecting the environment. This is the ultimate realization of the third of Deming's Fourteen Points which counsels us to build quality into the process up front.

Finally, and at the risk of being repetitive, remember that to try *any* idea that initially strikes you or your co-workers or managers as weird or wild requires the ability to set aside the first reaction, the quick put-down. We all have those reflexive reactions. Fair enough. You just told me why it can't work. Now tell me why it can. Take the other side of the debate. Walk in the other side's shoes. *Explore before you judge.*

251

You Say You Want A Revolution...

You could legitimately argue that each of the ideas touched on in this chapter represents a small improvement to the current socio-economic system. You could, in fact, argue these are awfully tame after some of the dire statements I've made earlier in this book. You could further argue that if we're truly going to realign our culture and actively center it around developing authentic selfhood and raising sane children, we'll need more than incremental improvements to the current system. You could design a whole new system from the ground up, a new alternative never before seen, more dedicated to the enriched cultivation of leisure than to work. It would be a system that is not driven by the relentless insistence on competition, productivity and growth, on "do and get", but rather on "provide and become". The entire organizing logic of such a system would be markedly different from what we currently experience and yet, it would be far more genuinely integrated with the core values of the Judeo-Christian tradition which we claim as our spiritual essence. This would not just represent an ordinary paradigm shift. It would be a PARADIGM SHIFT on a massive scale. It would crack the pillars of secular power and send its temples and their high priests, the CEO's, tumbling from their Olympian pinnacles. You could argue all this with substantial validity.

But there are a few hitches. Such grandiose plans are usually articulated by supermen and call on supermen for their implementation. Yet, supermen represent the biggest obstacles in effecting any meaningful change. No matter how well intentioned, their thinking tends to be shot through with the affliction they seek to cure. This may not completely nullify their ideas but it definitely makes them suspect and limits their value. To offer an example and metaphor rolled into one, whatever plans tobacco company executives come up with, they're not likely to include the elimination of their entire industry, which is the greatest public service they could provide.

This is not to say that there aren't exceptions, of course. Millard Fuller, the founder of Habitat for Humanity is probably the best example. He was a millionaire by the age of twenty-nine and yet soon found that his wealth did not bring him happiness. He and his wife, by their own public admission, went through a substantial transformation of their marriage and their sense of purpose before the idea for Habitat came to them. Aaron Feuerstein, President of Malden Mills is another example by exception. When his factory was largely destroyed by fire during the approaching Christmas of 1996, he kept everyone on the payroll at the cost of millions out of his own pockets. Perhaps Feuerstein had always been more caring and sensitive than the average business owner, but he'd also gone through a substantial transformation in the early Eighties under the tutelage of Dr. Deming's work.

These fine individuals notwithstanding, it's only prudent to be suspicious of supermen who promise to abdicate once they've led us to the new land somewhere away from Metropolis. Anyone with a master plan is arrogating to himself god-like choices. We could help these folks a lot if we made them stay home with the kids for six months and provided them with a good counselor.

When people start talking in terms of megalomaniacal grandiosity, I want to hold up a screaming, neglected baby and say, "Here! First figure out how to make this kid feel good." We don't need more etherized flitting from these folks. We need them to get real and clear.

So, though the seriousness of our situation may seem to call for the drastic, I personally am reluctant to embrace such measures. I'll place my faith in the compound interest of Continuous Improvement applied in every corner of our nation, every corner of our individual lives from how we birth our babies to how we mourn even our smallest disappointments and losses. *Feeling, recovery, integration, action in the world.* If we keep working this process, within a decade the gains will be exponential. Within thirty years, as we gaze back over the terrain we've covered, it'll seem as though we'd implemented a revolutionary master plan, but it'll be far more deeply rooted in the personal soil of masses of individuals across America and for that reason, it will be sustainable.

Chapter Twelve

Restoration

"The finest qualities of our nature, like the bloom on fruits, can be preserved only by the most delicate handling. Yet, we do not treat ourselves nor one another thus tenderly."

--Henry David Thoreau

The Superman tale is a myth of darkness. It speaks to us of Life's Raw Deals and the scintillating cape of denial with which we disguise them. Yet, in its starkly memorable metaphor of solitude, as well as in the glaring absences of its narrative, it shows us the way to healing, reconciliation and authentic community.

It's fair to generalize that as a culture we have become prisoners of our own red and blue costume, rushing at speeds that will never be fast enough, seeking gratifications that will never be sweet enough or come soon enough, amassing accomplishments and wealth that will never be great enough, and chasing an invulnerability that will never be enduring enough. In its attempt to outrun cataclysms that have already engulfed us, our national behavior comes dangerously close to embodying a kind of death wish. Our unique brand of affluence has yielded a stark spiritual impoverishment as well as a material threat to the physical world of which we are an integral part. In our pseudo-religion of responsibility, we have flagrantly avoided taking responsibility for our own wounds and for the wounds of neglect, abuse and manipulation we visit upon our children and the generations beyond them. Contemptuous towards a body and soul that can hurt so badly, we are indignant at the thought that we have no choice but to be human and do the inner work.

The brilliant physicist-philosopher, David Bohm, warned us of the folly of a society built on the endless urge for economic growth and consumption. In 1989, Bohm stated in an interview at the Neils Bohr Institute in Stockholm, "…people are committed now to the view of growth, economic growth, but that is just what will destroy the planet…(everyone) wanting to live at the present European-American standard of living…they will be like a swarm of locusts…so somehow there has to be a change where we say the desire for material goods has to be more limited which means people will have to find something else in life…if they want to survive. There won't even be material goods if we keep this up…"

Others have voiced the same concern but the colossal sticking point has always resided in that seven-letter word Bohm uses: "somehow." Somehow there has to be a change. How? By what process? Education is necessary but not sufficient. Social and political action are necessary but not sufficient. New business thinking is necessary but not sufficient. Like the leaders of Krypton, our brilliance in manipulating the visible, material world has actually blocked us from seeing into the core where the answer resides. But now, having unraveled the symbolic fabric of Kal-El's world, we have seen and felt the "somehow." The missing aspect of the exit strategy from *the superman syndrome* is grieving—the deep inner journey. *Grieving the tragedies of our existence constitutes an act of economic, social, political and historical importance.* Only through grieving can the unbridled "need" to consume-produce-consume-again be permanently released. When we move *through* the wound rather than over or away from it, healing comes. This includes an attenuation of compulsion, a re-balancing of our neurochemistry.

The movement from darkness to light will not be quick or easy and it will not happen at all without the courage of many individuals submitting themselves to the baptism of the water of life. Courage in the service of feeling. From inner work to outer work. Grieving, integration, recovery, action. Political, economic and social programs can and should support, facilitate and align with this process, but they will not assure it.

However, there will be enormous clout in masses of people recovering sufficient integrity to declare, "I don't need to fill my life with debt and more and more and more stuff. I don't need to be loved from afar as a superman or superwoman. I need time to be a person. I need genuine intimacy. I need to give my kids the real and present parents they deserve and need." Multiply this statement by even a third of America's working men and women and we'll begin to change the form and content of the nation's character.

Of course, unrepentant supermen will warn of dire consequences to such counsel. Techno-priests will preach about the abdication of creative power. Intellectual relativists will label my emphasis on grieving as "reductionist." Political paranoids will paint dark pictures of American decline. Materialist junkies will scream, "Without a constant growth in consumption, you'll bankrupt the country!" We'll have to remind ourselves that, for all their brainy brilliance, the leaders of Krypton couldn't see the most important truth of all. They were ultimately men without vision, possessed of a frigid arrogance. We'll have to remind ourselves that people who believe "only the paranoid survive" are not models of selfhood. We'll have to remember Deming's exhortation to drive out fear. We'll have to look somewhere other than boardrooms for examples of authentic heroism. We'll have to remind each other that our society and our race possess no more powerful leverage for positive change than to make the enormous and consistent investment in the quality of the parent-child relationship. None. Period.

A people that raises its children well flourishes.

We'll have to remember how frequently Deming spoke of

joy. Joy. Not fun. Not the adrenaline rushes that peak when we've worked a seventy-hour week and managed to finish the project "on time." Not the "thrill" of making the basket, goal, homer or touchdown in the final seconds of the game when victory was in doubt. Not that orgasmic relief we set up by acting out symbolic life and death situations. Joy is a sacred emotion. It goes far deeper than ego. It is the feeling that infuses us when our integrity is firm and our soul is in a conscious state of reverence for the blessing of life. How can souls be joyful when their children are hurting?

Yes, the economic statistics look very good right now. Yet, we are suffering a scarcity of intimacy amidst the abundance of productivity. We have survived tyranny and deprivation only to subjugate ourselves to a blind, unrelenting determination to escape the status of "Have-nots" and enter the firmament of "Have's." In the American psyche, quantity *is* quality. This is the mark of a fitful, arrested development.

Growing up in the Fifties, a lot of us thought our dads were already moving entirely too fast in the quest to provide and be somebody in the world's eyes. When we were toddlers, they left the house before we awoke in the morning and often came home after we were already asleep. The poverty of fathering is not new to this decade in America. But back then, our moms were home and generally functioned well as governors limiting the family's RPM's. There was talk back then about how technology and prosperity would shave the work week back to thirty, maybe even twenty hours. Three-day weekends would be common by 1960. That's what progress was thought to look like. The flourishing of the true blue nuclear family. The material American Dream was to own a home. The spiritual America Dream was *to be at home* with ourselves and each other, in every sense of the phrase...in the gracious embrace of a Higher Power. It all seems so quaint now.

And yet, many people across the spectrum of organizations throughout the country and around the world are awakening to the fact that the vaunted new Information Age has some definite downsides. It is also the Age of Distraction, the Age of Hyperactivity, the Age of Cynicism, the Age of Marketing and Advertising, the Age of Greed, the Age of Medication, the Age of Caffeine! They are feeling that we cannot live at depth when we live at speed. They are asking, "Why can't joyful family life and joyful work both thrive in this world and nourish each other?"

In fact, Yoneji Masuda, one of the pioneers of the Japanese computer industry, has actually rejuvenated the idea of the twenty-hour work week as a right and attainable goal. He believes the whole purpose of technology is to literally invert the relationship between work and free time because free time will do far more to support the flowering of personal freedom than material accumulation. Masuda may be a Utopian, or perhaps he's better at long-term thinking than many of us who would be thrilled to see credible progress toward a thirty-five hour work week. Still, we should take it as significant that one of the fathers of the Information Age is reminding us in strong terms that technology is a means and quality time, lots of quality time is the real end—speed at the service of depth.

Scientist Carl Sagan, author of the book, *Contact*, on which the film was based, pointed out before his unfortunate early death to cancer that we are merely in our technological adolescence. Personal computers and laptops with their primitive, incessant pointing and clicking, palmtops, email, the Internet, voice mail, cell phones, beepers, even 50-channel TV—these are all relatively new developments. Sagan's message is loud and clear: no matter where the most advanced technologies may take us, we will still crave close human contact—again, depth over speed.

Technological adolescence. Of course, we are a young species, mere infants on this planet. A consoling thought, an optimistic thought, for it clearly implies that maturity is a real possibility.

When will America reach its true maturity? When our men find the guts to grieve. When we are more in love with healing than with boasting of our scars. When we no longer need to admire or emulate superheroes. When we leave behind obsessive symbolic reenactments of survival. When we stop confusing getting with being. When we apply our genius every day to manifesting our integrity. When we discover how to support individuality with community and community with individuality. When we can provide for our families in a modest number of hours and go home unconflicted, ready to be deep in our kids' eyes, deep in our spouses' eyes, deep in our friends' eyes. When the minor and major movements of our lives are orchestrated by the savvy and strength of the father, the innocence, purity and imagination of the child, the constancy and wisdom of the mother.

Love is in the details.

Our children need us *now*. Our families need us *now*. Our communities need us *now*.

Love is in the details.

We must claim it now, for this extraordinarily vulnerable moment. We must stand up for it now, not put it off for later, after the numbers tell us it's safe, after work is done, after we get the degree, after this project is complete, after we get this new technology, after we move into this neighborhood, after we buy the right car, after our kids are in this private school, after we make our first million, after we get a corner office, after we're running the company, after we show everybody who doubted us, after we're wearing custom-tailored shirts and Italian shoes and they know our name in the best restaurants, after everyone in the industry knows us, after everyone in the world knows us, after God knows how great we are and gives us a free pass through the pearly gates...after, after, after! There is no after.

Love is in the details.

When we get this, really get it, there will be nothing more important than creating integrity and experiencing the delicate magic of our children. We will *make* each other lie down in green pastures. We will *lead* each other into the still waters and there, neck deep in the mythic truth of our species, cataclysm will gradually melt and wash away. What was sequestered in silence will arise into the full presence of a clear, sure, guiding voice. What was invisible will become obvious. Once divided selfhood will meld into wholeness. Fear will dissolve into purpose. Wild imaginings will fuse into reality. No longer will raging supermen put our children at risk. Our true nature as brilliant feelers will be restored. Fathers and sons, mothers and daughters longing for each other's arms will find them.

We can master this new world. You can master it. Deep in the eyes of your children and the children of your community you will find all the truth and inspiration you need. Go. Look there...and then begin the work.

End

FOOTNOTES

[1] Juliet Schor, *The Overworked American*, Basic Books, 1991, p.152.

[2] Jeremy Rifkin, *The End of Work*, Tarcher/Putnam, 1995, p.223. In its 1997 National Study of the Changing Workforce, the Families and Work Institute found that American working fathers spent an average of 50.9 hours of work a week on the job, including commutes and over-time. This is up from the 1977 figure of 47.8 hours. The same study found working mothers putting in 41.4 hours a week, a five hour increase over their 1977 figures. In the case of mothers, the number doesn't include housework and caring for the kids. Estimates of working moms' total hours factoring in all home activities run around 85 hours a week!

[3] Roach, *Harvard Business Review*, November-December 1996, p. 95

[4] By "small magnitude decision-making" I mean to draw attention to the fact that all of these various technological communication tools flood us with many little decisions in the course of the day. They're not generally on a "make or break" level of importance, but they matter, and we're highly engaged with them.

[5] 3 Lester C. Thurow, *High-tech boom or productivity bust? Who knows? USA TODAY,* March 9, 1998, p.19A

[6] The Wall Street Journal, April 30, 1998, front page article by Wysycoki.

[7] National Highway Traffic and Safety Administration, as cited on the NBC Nightly News, November 23, 1999.

[8] USAToday, November 18, 1999, front page.

[9] Newsweek, September 20, 1999, p. 55

[10] All four films starred Christopher Reeve. The first three were produced by Alexander and Ilya Salkind, the fourth by Menahem Golan and Yoram Globus. The first was directed by Richard Donner, the second and third by Richard Lester, the fourth by Sidney Furie.

[11] Psychologist Jean Liedloff, in *The Continuum Concept*, Addison Wesley, 1977,contends that from the earliest age we have an inherent ability to feel an inner sense of "rightness", which informs us, even as infants, when our needs are being met or transgressed in some way.

This serves our survival. We cry out to let our caretakers know when something is out of synch.

[12] The term "back pocket of the mind" is intended to be metaphoric but may have some actual correspondence in the brain. However, from what we know about the complexity of this organ at the time of this writing, it is not likely we will ever conclude there is a single specific location for the unconscious. It seems more likely there are major and minor "command centers or alternative processes" in the brain stem and central brain which have special electrochemical relationships with other "higher" areas of the brain. After all, in dreams, the full array of our five senses can be engaged. We also can think thoughts, feel feelings, move, speak and listen. This indicates that the process of the unconscious mind includes the ability to draw from the full encyclopedia of our life experience, pointing towards an elaborate communication network reaching throughout the various brain structures. By "alternative processes" I specifically mean those which underpin other than the so-called normal waking state. Those of us who are fascinated by the body/mind/emotions/soul connection can only hope that neurologists Antonio Damasio and Joseph LeDoux will continue to extend their work in this direction.

[13] If this law, as described here, is true and accurate, it can be used to explain a host of human experiences and behaviors across time and geography. This primary law is also likely to have ancillaries, although a fuller exploration will have to wait for another work. For now, I'm relying on the common sense and imagination of my reader to envision how it works…a risk I consider to be minor, given the fact that all humans operate within the bounds of this law, thereby providing each of us with the possibility of having immediate access to its truth. For those who would scoff and call this reductionism, I'd say that every law involves a kind of reductionism. The law of gravity explains why heavier-than-air objects all fall no matter from what hand or where on earth they might be released. The fact of that law does not diminish the mystery and joy of seeing a baseball player hit a home run. By the same token, the law of procreation tells us that, until the advent of test tube technology, every single hominid individual throughout the approximate four million years of evolution of our ancestral line, has been created as a direct result of sexual intercourse between two hominids. Does this incontrovertible "reductionist" fact deprive the

moment of conception, the process of gestation, birth itself and all of individual human development of their wonder?

[14] It should be noted that the early *DC Comics* had Krypton architectural style looking more like a cross between New York City and Constantinople. We can thank the 1978 filmmakers for a look that is not only more sophisticated but mythically more unique and powerful.

[15] Kryptonians are described in 1948 DC Comic Superman #53 as "humans of high intelligence and magnificent physical perfection".

[16] In fact, the original capital of the world government of Krypton was the city of Kandor, population one billion. The Greatest Superman Stories Ever Told, *DC Comics*, 1987, p 10.

[17] From the 1978 film, *Superman, The Movie,* starring Christopher Reeve, produced by Ilya Salkind, written by Mario Puzo, David Newman, Leslie Newman & Robert Benton, Directed by Richard Donner.

[18] Ralph Metzner, of *The Well of Remembrance,* Shambala, 1994, p 223

[19] David Whyte, *The Heart Aroused*, Doubleday, 1994, p.35.

[20] From the song, *The Phantom of the Opera*, music by Andrew Lloyd Webber, lyrics by Charles Hart.

[21] From the song, *The Music of the Night*, music by Andrew Lloyd Webber, lyrics by Charles Hart.

[22] In Maslow's hierarchy, our foundational need is physiological, followed by the need for safety, then the need for love, then the need for self-esteem in the social world and, finally the ultimate realization of personhood—self-actualization. In Maslow's model, each level of need must be reasonably satisfied as a precondition to our moving on to fully experience the next level. Consequently, we cannot rise to fulfill our complete destiny as individuals without the first four needs being reasonably satisfied. Otherwise, we are caught up in behavior motivated by the frustration of lower needs.

[23] Our workshop, LeaderOne, is based on a model initially developed by John Scherer and Menka MacLeod in 1994. I was licensed in 1995 to facilitate the process and was ultimately "liberated" from any legal or financial obligation at the end of 1998. The workshop has evolved substantially since we started, but I am forever grateful to John for his

talent, openness and generosity and to Mark Yeoell, who assisted me early on. Menka, having been my co-facilitator for more than two years, deserves special appreciation and gratitude for her extraordinary devotion to creating a safe environment in which my clients and I could discover a whole new realm of possibilities for business and personal relationships.

[24] Thanks to Dr. Barry Bernfeld of Los Angeles for this particular metaphor.

[25] Antonio Damasio, *The Feeling of What Happens*, Harcourt Brace, 1999, p. 78.

[26] Dr. Deepak Chopra, *Ageless Body, Timeless Mind*, Random House, 1993, New York, p.155. This entire discussion of the physiology of stress draws heavily on Dr. Chopra's writings, which include presentations of many of the most significant studies on the topic. Neurologist Antonion Damsio's discussion of stress supports these conclusions. See *Descarte's Error*, Grosset/Putnam, New York, 1994, p.120.

[27] Interestingly, a study began in 1965 by Lester Breslow, now the dean of public health at UCLA, of 7000 people revealed that longevity *has nothing to do with income,* apparent physical condition or even genetics. It is far more dependent on life style. You could rightfully point out that the average life span has increased by about thirty years since 1900. But you'd be hard-pressed to make the case that this is largely due to our having created a way of living that is kinder to body and soul. It is, in great part, due to the brilliance of relatively few individuals on whom we've become increasingly dependent— healthcare researchers who come up with more and more clever ways to save us when we're on the verge of breakdown. Raging Sympaths are nothing if not clever...because in the survival mode, one of the few choices we have is to be extraordinarily clever.

[28] Antonio R. Damasio, *Descarte's Error*, Grossett/Putnam, 1994.

[29] The appearance of Supergirl and Superboy later in the evolving serial rather than negating our point here only underscores the importance of the microscopic survival ratio.

[30] 1998 study by Families and Work Institute.

[31] Ibid, pgs. 12 and 13.

[32] As cited in U.S. News & World Report, December 20, 1999, p.20.

[33] USA Today, April 24, 1998.

[34] Statistical Abstract of The United States 1998, p.413.

[35] Schor, Ibid. p.29-30. Her assessment is confirmed by a careful examination of the most recent statistics available in the above-cited Statistical Abstract.

[36] Arlie Russell Hochschild, *The Second Shift*, p. 278

[37] Statistical Abstract of the United States 1999, p. 67.

[38] As cited in TIME, July 12, 1999.

[39] From a speech by President Clinton cited in the L.A Times 11/13/98.

[40] Annenberg Public Policy Center, University of Pennsylvania, as cited by Newsweek, August 2, 1999.

[41] USAToday, November 12, 1999, p. D1

[42] University of Michigan, Healthy Environments, Healthy Children: Children in Families report, November 1998.

[43] Psychology Today, November/December 1999, p.21.

[44] Journal of the American Medical Association, February 23, 2000.

[45] Federal Interagency Forum on Child and Family Statistics, as reported by TIME July 19, 1999.

[46] Bureau of the Census, March 1997 Current Population Survey.

[47] Los Angeles Times, 2/7/2000, p. A3

[48] Statistical Abstract p. 419.

[49] Children Defense Fund's Website, Helping parents work and children learn, updated 3/24/99.

[50] Ibid. Children Defense Fund's Website.

[51] U.S. News & World Report, May 12, 1997, p. 61.

[52] New York Times National edition, October 22, 1999, p. A16.

[53] Depression Study by Columbia University psychologist Suniya Luthar; connection with later drug or alcohol abuse problems, from a variety of studies cited by Yale Medical School epidemiologist Kathleen Merikangas, also increased suicide rates…all reported in USA Today August 13, 1998.

[54] Newsweek, June 14, 1999.

[55] U.S. Dept. of Health and Human Services, Child Maltreatment 1996: Reports from the States to the National Child Abuse and Neglect Data System, and Third National Incidence Study of Child Abuse and

Neglect (NIS-3) established that between 1986 and 1993 the number of seriously injured children rose from43,000 to nearly 570,000!

[56] I'm grateful to Professor Constance Hilliard of the University of North Texas in Denton, for citing in her USAToday, September 3, 1999 article, *Abuse at All Levels, Not Just Poor Youths*, the research done by Eli H. Newberger of Harvard Medical School and Robert L. Hampton of Connecticut College which indicated that hospitals tend to under-report both physical and emotional abuse by middle-class and upper-class whites. This leads us to yet another weakness in the measurement methodology in that statistics based on institutional reports give us no sense of how many incidents of both psychological and physical abuse *take place every day out of the view of professionals in the field.* I think we can legitimately push the discussion further yet by admitting that our very idea of what constitutes psychological abuse is still evolving as we become increasingly sensitive to the needs of children and, indeed, adults as well. We must remember that *syndrome* thinking emanates from a benumbed sensibility, which means any measurement process created out of it is likely to fall woefully short of the whole truth.

[57] The Center for Disease Control, 1998 reports.

[58] Los Angeles Times, September 27, 1998`

[59] 1998 National Household Survey on Drug Abuse, as cited in USAToday, August 19, 1999. It should also be noted that a recent study by the University of Kentucky pointed to the conclusion that the DARE anti-drug program which is taught at 75% of U.S. school districts has no lasting effect on kids' use of illegal drugs, in part because it doesn't identify and target high risk kids. Anecdotally, I watched the curve of reality with great interest as my son and his friends were treated to the DARE program in their pre-teens. At the time, most of them found it interesting and valuable. When my son was fifteen, in the full thrall of adolescence, the hair stood up on the back of my neck when my he told me he'd been to a party at which "everything" was available and being used by many of those same kids—LSD was back, cocaine, marijuana, magic mushrooms, even heroin. Raising kids who will not abuse alcohol, cigarettes or any of the illicit drugs is a daunting task in a world that glorifies so many forms of medication. The highest leverage prevention activity is great parenting, not well-meaning police visiting classrooms.

[60] The Tribune of San Luis Obispo County, August 21, 1999.

[61] Los Angeles Times, April 5, 1998.

[62] Dr. T. Berry Brazelton, *Working and Caring*, Addison-Wesley, 1987, p.xvi.

[63] As quoted in Discover magazine, June 1999, p. 74, my italics.

[64] National Center for Health Statistics, as cited by the 1998 Information Please Almanac, p. 366.

[65] Arlie Russell Hochschild, Ibid, p.278

[66] As quoted in TIME, August 11, 1997, pg 56

[67] U.S. News & World Report, May 12, 1997, article entitled "Lies Parents Tell Themselves About Why They Work," by Shannon Brownlee and Matthew Miller. The specific language of the unspoken message is my own, but it's dead on with the content of the article.

[68] Ronald Ruden, *The Craving Brain*, Harper Collins, 1997, p 105

[69] *The New York Times 1998 Almanac*, p. 394. For more on the connection between behavior and cancer, see the book, *The Type C Connection,* by Temoshok and Dreher.

[70] Christiane Northrup, M.D., *Women's Bodies, Women's Wisdom*, Bantam 1994, p 56.

[71] As a point of clarification, The Fortress of Solitude and other language referring to unprocessed or "stored" tears is used metaphorically. In all likelihood, researchers such as Damasio and LeDoux will confirm for us in the next ten years or so that our systems are shocked into an arresting of the conscious processing of painful emotions. A kind of electrochemical switch that allows such processing is turned off and stuck in that position. This doesn't have to entail the actual storage of tears—an idea that would be fatuous if taken literally. It does entail, however, the interruption of the necessary signals to the rest of our system that drive weeping. When that interruption is ended, the switch thrown back on, the signals sent and received, weeping can resume, even many years later. As living proof, a recent participant in our leadership workshop remembered the death of a dear friend when they were both 9 years old. By his own report, he had never wept about it, but was in shock and disbelief for decades. Now, in his late forties, in a safe and nurturing environment, the tears flowed. Such experience is common in our work and, we dare say,

fairly common (if not fully understood) among the general human population across time and cultures.

[72] William H. Frey, *Crying: The Mystery of Tears*, 1985 Winston Press, p 147. The Montagu referred to in the quote is Ashley Montagu, author of *Touching* and many other books.

[73] Antonio Damasio, *The Feeling of What Happens*, Harcourt Brace, p.61

[74] As reported by Dr. Barry Bernfeld in *The Primal Institute Newsletter*, December 1982. Dr. Bernfeld assisted Dr. Frey in this particular piece of the research.

[75] *Your Health*, October 8, 1991, accessed off the Web.

[76] Both quotes as cited in *About Mourning*, by Weizman and Kamm, 1985, Human Sciences Press, p. 83. My italics. The Kamm who co-authored this work is not the current author but his mother, Phyllis Kamm.

[77] Alice Miller, *Paths of Life*, Vintage Books, 1998, p. 186.

[78] Thomas Moore, *Care of the Soul*, Harper Perennial 1992, p.36.

[79] Ibid. P. 53.

[80] Ibid. Weizman and Kamm, pgs. 72 and 75.

[81] Joseph LeDoux, *The Emotional Brain*, Simon & Schuster, 1996, pgs. 205, 242.

[82] Joseph LeDoux, Ibid. p.303

[83] Re-decision Therapy championed by Bob and Mary Goulding in a book by the same title should not be confused with Re-evaluation Counseling, first articulated by Harvey Jackins in The Human Side of Human Beings, first published in 1965. Jackins' personal ethics and the structure of the Re-evaluation Counseling community, have been called into question by some former clients and workshop leaders, as evidenced by a Web article, *Excerpt from The Roots of Authoritarianism,* by Lundy Bancroft. This does not mean by any stretch of the imagination that all Re-evaluation Counselors are to be summarily dismissed through "guilt by association", but an extra measure of caution and diligence are only prudent when considering one.

[84] Peter R. Breggin, M.D*., Toxic Psychiatry*, St. Martin's Press, 1991, pgs. 375-379.

[85] Peter R. Breggin, M.D. & Ginger Ross Breggin, *Talking Back to Prozac*, St. Martin's Press, 1994, p.7

[86] Ibid. P.3

[87] Journal of Psychiatry Website.

[88] Ibid. Pgs. 3-9, 380-386, The author refers specifically to the Harvard-Radcliffe Mental Hospital Volunteer Program all the way back in 1954, as well as a federal government report from 1961and the work by Dr. Lorren Mosher with non-credentialed staff at Soteria House in the service of schizophrenics.

[89] Psychology Today, November/December 1999 as well as Journal of Psychiatry Website.

[89] Ibid. P386.

[90] Ibid, *Talking Back to Prozac*, p.249.

[91] Ibid, p. 9.

[92] The Type C Connection, The Behavioral Links to Cancer and Your Health, by Lydia Temosho, Ph.D and Henry Dreher, 1992 Random House, New York. See especially Chapters 13-15.

[93] Ibid, p. 358.

[94] Schor, *The Overworked American*, p 82.

[95] I make this statement from my own consulting experience, but the best formal inquiry into management and decision-making styles, in my opinion, is that of social psychologist and author Dr. Jay Hall, author *of Models for Management*, Woodstead Press, Second Edition, 1988 See his two books, *Models for Management* (1980) and *The Competence Connection* (1988), both by Woodstead Press, The Woodlands, Texas.

[96] Deming attributed the phrase to Lloyd S. Nelson of Nashua Corporation, one of the first American companies to seriously adopt his method of management. See *The Deming Management Method* by Mary Walton, Perigee Books, 1986, p. 93

[97] Morgan and Tucker, *Companies that Care,* Fireside, 1991.

[98] 5 *Lies Parents Tell Themselves About Why They Work*, by Shannon Brownlee and Matthew Miller, U.S. News & World Report, May 12, 1997.

Bibliography & Suggested Reading

This bibliography includes books cited as well as those which contributed to my thought but which, for one reason or another, were not explicitly used in the final version of this work.

Adizes, Ichak, *Mastering Change*, Santa Monica, Adizes Institute, 1982. *Corporate Lifecycles*, Englewood Cliffs, Prentice Hall, 1988.

Aguayo, Rafael, *Dr. Deming*, New York, Fireside, 1991.

Allen, Marvin, *Angry Men, Passive Men*, New York, Fawcett Columbine, 1993.

Autry, James, *Love and Profit*, New York, Avon Books, 1991. *Life & Work*, New York, Morrow, 1994.

Barker, Joel Arthur, *Paradigms*, New York, HarperPerennial, 1992.

Bauer, Gregory & Kobos, Joseph, *Brief Therapy*, Northvale, Jason Aronson, Inc. 1995.

Bennett, William, The Book of Virtues, New York, Touchstone, 1993.

Bennis, Warren, *On Becoming a Leader*, New York, Simon & Schuster, 1991.

Bing, Stanley, *Crazy Bosses*, New York, Morrow, 1992.

Bly, Robert, *Iron John*, New York, Addison-Wesley, 1990.

Bradshaw, John, *Home Coming*, New York, Bantam, 1990.

Brazelton, T. Berry, M.D., *Working and Caring*, New York, Addison-Wesley, 1985.

Breggin, Peter, *Toxic Psychiatry*, New York, St. Martin's Press, 1991. *Talking Back to Prozac*, New York, St. Martin's Press, 1994.

Buber, Martin, *I and Thou* (Kaufman translation), New York, Scribner's, 1970

Campbell, Joseph, *The Hero with a Thousand Faces*, Princeton, Bollingen Press, 1972. *The Mythic Image*, Princeton, Bollingen Press, 1974 *Myths to Live By*, New York, Bantam, 1972. *The Power of Myth*, with Bill Moyers, New York, Anchor, 1988. *Mythology and the Individual*, San Anselmo, Joseph Campbell Foundation, 1996.

Carter, Rita, *Mapping the Mind*, Berkeley, University of California Press, 1998.

Carter-Scott, Cherie, *The Corporate Negaholic*, New York, Villard Books, 1991.

Champy, James, *Reengineering Management*, New York, HarperBusiness, 1995.

Chopra, Deepak, *Ageless Body, Timeless Mind*, New York, Harmony Books, 1993.

Collins, James & Porras, Jerry, *Built to Last*, New York, HarperBusiness, 1994.

Cooper, Robert K. & Sawaf, Ayman, *Executive EQ*, New York, Grosset/Putnam 1997.

Covey, Stephen, *The Seven Habits of Highly Effective People*, New York, Fireside, 1990. *Principle-Centered Leadership*, New York, Fireside, 1992. *First Things First*, New York, Fireside, 1994.

Csikszentmihalyi, Mihaly, *Flow*, New York, Simon & Shcuster, 1994.

Damasio, Antonio, *Descartes' Error*, New York, Grosset/Putname, 1994. *The Feeling of What Happens*, New York, Harcourt Brace, 1999.

Deming, W. Edwards, *Out of the Crisis*, Cambridge, MIT, 1982.

DC Comics, *The Greatest Superman Stories Ever Told*, New York, DC Comics, 1987.

Drucker, Peter, *Managing for the Future*, New York, Truman Talley, 1992. *Managing In A Time Of Great Change*, New York, Truman Talley, 1995.

Eliot, Alexander, *The Global Myths*, New York, Meridian, 1993.

Elkington, John, *Cannibals With Forks*, Stony Creek, New Society Publishers, 1998.

Emerson, Gloria, *The Courage to Raise Good Men*, New York, Simon & Schuster, 1985.

Estes, Ralph, *Tyranny of the Bottom Line*, San Francisco, Berrett-Koehler, 1996.

Frankl, Viktor, *Man's Search for Meaning*, New York, Washington Square Press, 1952.

Frey, William II & Lngseth, Muriel, *Crying: The Myster of Tears*, New York, Harpery & Row, 1985.

Fromm, Erich, *Man for Himself*, New York, Henry Holt, 1947. *The Art of Loving*, New York, Harper & Row, 1956.

Fukuyama, Francis, *Trust*, New York, The Free Press, 1995.

Gabor, Andrea, *The Man Who Discovered Quality*, New York, Random House, 1990

Gardner, Howard, *The Shattered Mind*, New York, Vintage, 1974. *Multiple Intelligences*, New York, BasicBooks, 1993. *Leading Minds*, New York, BasicBooks, 1995.

Gates, Bill, *Business @ The Speed Of Thought*, Time Warner AudioBooks.

Goldberg, Herb, *The New Male*, New York, Signet, 1979.

Goldratt, Eliyahu, *The Goal*, Croton-on-Hudson, North River Press, 1984.

Goleman, Daniel, *Emotional Intelligence*, New York, Bantam, 1995. *Working with Emotional Intelligence*, New York, Bantam, 1998.

Gould, Stephen Jay, *The Mismeasure of Man*, New York, W.W. Norton, 1981.

Graves, Robert, *The Greek Myths: 1*, New York, Penguin, 1955.

Grove, Andrew, *Only the Paranoid Survive*, New York, Bantam, 1999.

Greenleaf, Robert, *Servant Leadership*, New York, Paulist Press, 1977.

Hall, Jay, *Models for Management*, The Woodlands, Texas, Woodstead Press, 1980.

Hammer, Michael, *Beyond Reengineering*, New York, HarperBusiness, 1996.

Handy, Charles, *The Age of Paradox*, Boston, Harvard Business School Press, 1994.

Herman, Judith, *Trauma and Recovery*, New York, Basic Books, 1992.

Hickman, Craig, *Mind of a Manager, Soul of a Leader*, New York, John Wiley & Sons, 1992.

Hochschild, Arlie Russell, *TheSecond Shift*, New York, Avon Books, 1989. *Time Bind*, New York, Metropolitan Books, 1997.

Jackins, Harvey, *The Human Side of Being Human*, Seattle, Rational Island, 1965.

Jackson, Phil, *Sacred Hoops*, New York, Hyperion, 1995.

Janov, Arthur, *The Primal Scream*, New York, Perigee, 1970. *Prisoners of Pain*, New York, Doubleday, 1980. *The New Primal Scream*, Wilmington, Enterprise, 1991.

Jaworski, Joseph, *Synchronicity*, San Francisco, Berrett-Koehler, 1996.

Katzenbach, Jon & Smith, Douglas, *The Wisdom of Teams*, New York, HarperBusiness, 1994.

Kohn, Alfie, *No Contest*, New York, Houghton Mifflin, 1986. *Punished By Rewards*, New York, Houghton Mifflin, 1993.

Kublerh-Ross, Elizabeth, *On Death and Dying*, New York, MacMillan, 1969. *Questions and Answers on Death and Dying*, MacMillan, 1974. *Death, The Final Stage of Growth*, New York, Prentice-Hall, 1975.

Kushner, Harold, *When Bad Things Happen to Good People*, New York, Schocken, 1981.

Leach, Penelope, *Children First*, New York, Vintage, 1994.

Leakey, Richard, *People of the Lake*, New York, Avon, 1978

LeBow, Rob, *A Journey into the Heroic Environment*, Rocklin, Prima, 1995.

LeBoyer, Frederic, *Birth Without Violence*, New York, Knopf, 1978.

276

LeDoux, Joseph, *The Emotional Brain*, New York, Touchstone, 1996

Lennox, Carolyn, *Redecision Therapy*, Northvale, Jason Aronson, Inc. 1997.

Levering, Robert, *A Great Place To Work*, New York, Avon Books, 1988.

Levine, Stephen, *Healing into Life and Death*, New York, Anchor Books, 1987.

LeShahn, Eda, *Learning to Say Good-By*, New York, MacMillan, 1976,

Liedloff, Jean, *The Continuum Concept*, New York, Addison-Wesley, 1975.

Mann, Nancy, *The Keys to Excellence*, Los Angeles, Prestwick, 1985.

McKenna, Elizabeth Perle, *When Work Doesn't Work Anymore*, New York, Delacorte Press, 1997.

Mead, Margaret, *Culture and Commitment*, New York, Natural History Press, 1970. *A Way of Seeing*, New York, McCall, 1970. *Letters from the Field 1925-1975*, New York, Harper & Row, 1977.

Metzner, Ralph, The Well of Remembrance, Boston, Shambhala, 1994.

Miller, Alice, *For Your Own Good*, New York, FSG, 1983 *Thou Shalt Not Be Aware*, Harrisonburg, VA, Meridian, 1986. *The Untouched Key*, New York, Anchor Books, 1988. *The Drama of the Gifted Child*, New York, HarperPerennial, 1997. *Paths of Life*, New York, Vintage, 1998.

Moore, Robert & Gillette, Douglas, *King, Warrior, Magician, Lover*, San Francisco, Harper, 1990.

Moore, Thomas, *Care of the Soul*, New York, HarperPerennial, 1992.

Morgan, Hal & Tucker, Kerry, *Companies That Care*, New York, Fireside, 1991.

Nance, John, *The Gentle Tasaday*, New York, Harcourt, Brace, Jovanovich, 1975.

Narby, Jeremy, *The Cosmic Serpent*, New York, Tarcher/Putnam, 1998.

Northrup, Christiane, *Women's Bodies, Women's Wisdom*, New York, Bantam, 1994.

Odent, Michel, *Birth Reborn*, New York, Pantheon, 1984.

O'Toole, James, *Leading Change*, New York, Ballantine, 1995.

Pearce, Jospeh Chilton, *Magical Child*, New York, Plume, 1992. Peters, Tom, *In Search of Excellence*, New York, Warner 1982. *Thriving on Chaos*, New York, HarperPerennial, 1987. *The Pursuit of Wow!*, New York, Vintage, 1992. *Liberation Management*, New York, Knopf, 1992.

Perls, Fritz, *The Gestalt Approach & Eye Witness to Therapy*, New York, Bantam, 1973.

Petit, George, *Prisoners of Culture*, New York, Charles Scribner's Sons, 1970.

Pfeiffer, John, *The Emergence of Man*, New York, Harpery & Row, 1969.

Pipher, Mary, *Reviving Ophelia*, New York, Ballantine, 1994.

Pollack, William, *Real Boys*, New York, Random House, 1998.

Reichheld, Frederick, *The Loyalty Effect*, Boston, Harvard Business School Press, 1996.

Rifkin, Jeremy, *The End of Work*, New York, Tarcher/Putnam, 1995.

May, Rollo, *The Courage to Create*, New York, Bantam, 1976.

Rosenbluth, Hall & McFerrin Peters, Diane, *The Customer Comes Second*, New York, Quill, 1992.

Ruden, Ronald, *The Craving Brain*, New York, Harper, 1997.

Sagan, Carl, *Contact,* New York, Pocket Books, 1985.

Schaef, Anne Wilson & Fassel, Diane, *The Addictive Organization*, San Francisco, Harper, 1988.

Scherer, John, *Work and the Human Spirit*, Spokane, JS&A, 1993.

Scherkenback, William, *Deming's Road to Continual Improvement*, Knoxville, SPC Press, 1991.

Schiff, Harriet Sarnoff, *The Bereaved Parent*, New York, Crown, 1977.

Scholtes. Peter, *The Team Handbook*, Madison, Joiner, 1988. *The Leader's Handbook*, New York, McGraw Hill, 1998.

Schor, Juliet B., *The Overworked American*, New York, Basic Books, 1991. *The Overspent American*, New York, Basic Books, 1998.

Semler, Ricardo, *Maverick,* New York, Warner Books, 1995.

Senge, Peter, *The Fifth Discipline*, New York, Doubleday Currency, 1990. *The Fifth Discipline Fieldbook*, New York, Doubleday Currency, 1994. *The Dance of Change*, New York, Doubleday Currency, 1999.

Siegel, Bernie, *Prescriptions for Living*, New York, Harper Audio, 1998.

Silverstein, Olga & Rashbaum, Beth, *The Courage to Raise Good Men*, New York, Viking, 1994.

Storr, Anthony, *The Essential Jung*, New York, MJF Books, 1983.

Suzuki, Daivd, *The Sacred Balance*, Toronto, Greystone, 1997.

Tannen, Deborah,*You Just Don't Understand*, New York, Ballantine, 1990.

Temoshok, Lydia & Dreher, Henry, *The Type C Connection*, New York, Random House, 1992.

Thoreau, Henry David, *Walden*, Boston, Shambhala audio edition, 1992.

Tucker, Robert, *Managing the Future*, New York, Berkley, 1991.

U.S. Department of Commerce, *Statistical Abstract of the United States*, 1998 & 1999.

Turnbull, Colin, *The Forest People*, New York, Simon & Shuster, 1961. *The Mountain People*, New York, Simon & Shuster, 1972

Walton, Mary, *The Deming Management Method*, New York, Perigee, 1986. *Deming Management at Work*, New York, Perigee, 1991.

Waterman, Robert, *What America Does Right*, New York, Plume, 1992.

Weizman, Savine & Kamm, Phyllis, *About Mourning*, New York, Human Sciences Press, 1987.

Wellington, Patricia, *Kaizen Strategies for Customer Care*, London, Pitman Publishing, 1995.

Wheeler, Donald, *Understanding Variation*, Knoxville, SPC Press, 1993.

Williams, Redfort & Williams, Virginia, *Anger Kills*, New York, Harper, 1998.

Whyte, David, *The Heart Aroused*, New York, Currency Doubleday, 1994.

World Publishing, New York, *The Holy Bible, King James Version*.

Videotapes:

An Interview with David Bohm, New York, Mystic Fire Video, 1992.

Superman The Movie, Warner Brothers, 1978.

Superman II, Warner Brothers, 1980.

Superman III, Warner Brothers, 1983.

Superman IV, Warner Brothers, 1987.

About the Author

Robert H. Kamm is a speaker, author, coach and consultant who inspires extraordinary devotion in his clients. Under his tutelage, they have achieved competitive advantage by creating great workplace communities. He was one of the pioneers of "Haggle-Free, Stress-Free Car Buying" in the early Nineties and gained national notoriety as the most outspoken advocate of ethical transformation in the automobile retail business.

After more than twenty years as an innovator in the trenches of retail, and thirteen years as a single father, Mr. Kamm created a unique consulting practice that spans the gaps between personal, professional and organizational development. His clients revere him as a Renaissance man of deep life experience and wisdom, someone with the rare ability to blend the pragmatic with the ideal. Corporate clients have included Ford Motor Company, General Motors, J.D. Power and Associates, Maritz Corporation, the Canadian Olympic Synchronized Swim Team, Mercedes-Benz of North American, Toyota of Canada and Honda American Finance. Individual clients attending his widely praised leadership workshop, *LeaderOne*, have come from fields as diverse as teaching, medicine, nursing, healthcare technology, the performing arts, real estate, public relations, engineering, consulting, counseling, psychology, a broad array of entrepreneurial endeavors and, most important of all, parenting. He lives with his wife, Della, in California.

The Superman Syndrome is the first work in a trilogy.

For further information concerning programs and practices, please call:

Kamm Consulting
(805) 544-9726

or write to:

Kamm Consulting
1282 W. Newport
San Luis Obispo, CA 93405

or

Visit our Website at
www.kammtown.com